3|19

BEYOND THE VERTICAL

BEYOND THE VERTICAL

LAYTON KOR

FOREWORDS BY
PAT AMENT AND **ROYAL ROBBINS**

FALCONGUIDES

GUILFORD, CONNECTICUT
HELENA, MONTANA

AN IMPRINT OF GLOBE PEQUOT PRESS

Copyright © 2013 Layton Kor

A previous edition of this book was published by Alpine House, Boulder, Colorado; ISBN 0-9611748-0-3; Library of Congress Card Number 83-071896

FalconGuides is an imprint of Globe Pequot Press.

Falcon, FalconGuides, and Outfit Your Mind are registered trademarks of Morris Book Publishing, LLC.

All interior photos by Layton Kor unless noted otherwise.

Text Design: Sheryl P. Kober
Project Editor: David Legere
Layout Artist: Melissa Evarts

Library of Congress Cataloging-in-Publication data is available on file.

ISBN 978-0-7627-8139-3

Printed in the United States of America

10 9 8 7 6 5 4 3 2 1

CONTENTS

CONTENTS

FOREWORD TO THIS EDITION

Beyond the Vertical is one of the most significant books in the rock climbing canon. This is not because it is a work of literary excellence, though the writing is as good as it needs to be; it is for the very reason of its rough edges, the plain, human accounts by each individual voice, around Layton's voice, that the book is so good. Most climbing magazines tend to edit the words of their writers into the magazine's own voice. Here we have a range of sounds that give us the sense of each different character. Most of the adventures described in Beyond the Vertical are from years ago, gathered for the book in the mid-seventies. Now, later in Layton's life, these writings mean just as much. This is not an autobiography, not even a fragmentary one. Layton's life is too large. Yet the many minds and memories that operate in these pages take the reader close to this unique personality and close to the earth. These pages get close to the heart of the man. Layton's journey has covered a good portion of the known rock climbing world. He is quintessentially a climber with the whole confused world to run in. The rock in Layton's day was a frontier and seemed to expand as he stretched his long arms toward and across it. Layton must surely have played some part in the actual expanse of the physical universe. That's how large he is, or how large we see him.

In Layton's prime, during the golden age of rock climbing in both America and Eldorado Canyon, I was one of his partners. A cadre of individuals formed a nuclear family that pursued our dream. Layton seemed to think we had a long way to go, and the faster we traveled, the faster the rock rolled past, under his big fingers, the further we got from the deprived, barren world we came from—barren in that on certain days we were no more than workers or students, and before we discovered such places as Eldorado we were not climbers. Layton knew how to take the shortest distance between two points. He lost the way at times but found it, lost it again, and found it. He brought some of the noblest climbs of the day, and some of them major undertakings, to a quick conclusion. The great Yosemite forebears, Royal Robbins, Chuck Pratt, and Tom Frost, were amazed at how readily Layton polished off their walls and in half their time. Layton's climbs lie as they fell, ultimately a kind of fabric woven carefully and at times wildly. Such is the fabric that weaves the spell of Beyond the Vertical.

There are many images of Layton: as he speeds in his car toward Eldorado, as he turns one of those comic glances your way and causes you to burst into laughter, or the terror certain situations on the rock with him inspired. This book gives a pictorial study and written reports of one of the most fully achieved human beings who ever lived. Layton Kor was the archetypal climber.

When Layton wrote letters to me from Yosemite of his adventures, he did not speak about the boulders. They were not central to his greater goals, the big walls that soared in his imagination. Yet one day (likely the fall of 1963, possibly spring of '64) he ambled over to a tall chunk of granite near the east end of Yosemite's Camp 4. On-sight, with his reach and long, spread-out body, Layton climbed the rock's smooth west face—what climbers, from this day, would call the "Kor Boulder." For the next several years, the Kor Boulder—as much as any other—would serve as a measure of a Yosemite boulderer's prowess or of whether or not a big wall climber was in shape. It became a ritual for many to work up to the Kor Boulder, as they readied themselves for the walls. The Kor Boulder would likely inspire more climbers than any big wall route Layton managed.

I feel I was witness to the ephemeral element of a man, his very soul expressed in the way he climbed, his body language, the posture of his tall body, the imagination of his face, the concentration in his eyes, his great arms and legs at times in almost whimsical motion, the way his eyes widened and closed, widened and closed. He was powerful, intense, yet with a childlike energy. To be with Layton seemed to awaken awareness. I understood, in some kind of mystic light, the spatial dimension, the wondrous exposure of Eldorado climbs. Comprehension was changed to vision, even for a young boy. For me it was a process, to become aware of life, and with Layton, combined with the spectacular atmosphere of Eldorado Canyon, I was hurled into so brilliant a revelation all the potential in me was activated. I had to fight with my tremendous fear, though. The danger all around seemed to be presented with equally rich clarity. Every unexpected turn upward through the dihedrals and off-balancing, steep faces was vivid.

Memory is like Da Vinci's *Last Supper*, made with oil and tempera on plaster and, thus, quick to decay. I'm not sure why I have such clear memories. I was told by a professor of biopsychology that memory is significantly solidified by the flow of adrenaline. That would explain much of my ability to remember. It was a very thrilling and miraculous time. On many climbs I watched my friend spin his fire, work with the immediate beauty and power of a rock's grandeur. To his pitonwork there could be a savagery or, at other times, an incidental fineness. You could know you existed in time, but also in a timelessness. You felt subservient to Layton's anarchy of imagination. I watched how he pressed forward and in completely defenseless simplicity pursued the life before his eyes.

I think for many people the memory of adventure is derivative, yet I think I can say adventure for me is firsthand and is involved to a notable degree with the name Layton Kor—as much so as anyone or anywhere. When I look back, Layton stands at imagination's first ecstatic stirrings. He was a big force alongside my delicate nature. Wild though he was, Layton was temperate—both in praising and in damning. He forgave me most of my sins, times I was too scared to reach back to remove a piton. Layton is too large to

The East Face of 14,259-foot-high Longs Peak, one of America's best alpine climbing areas, rears high above Chasm Lake in Rocky Mountain National Park.
Photograph Stewart M. Green

slight. He was a leader among fools and knaves, stupids and cupids, a champion among Gypsies, and an equal to the best souls of the day. I have always hoped I was somewhere relatively high on the spectrum. I will say we are great friends even today.

Having come down through a family of bricklayers, Layton was a natural and skilled artisan. He mused about his life, how he worked and saved sufficient money to take off to climb. Once near my school I ran into him at a nearby work site. Ever in his joking mood, he handled each brick. With his large hands he wielded a trowel expertly, judged the exact dollop of mortar, or chipped a brick's edges to a perfect fit. It was the same way he understood the rotten rock and the nature of holds. On a route he and I did on Eldorado's Rotwand Wall, a vertical line he named *Kinnder Rooten*, his Dutch for "kind of rotten," he seemed to hold the wall together as he climbed. He understood the loose blocks, the countless brick-sized chunks of sandstone that were not fastened well, many ready to pull out. He was a master at this sort of transcendence. Not only did Layton climb walls, he built them. A climb would go up before our eyes.

Layton was no ideal of artistic form. Sometimes it was a frantic groping for holds, a desperate act to understand their potential in the few seconds he knew he had. There were some very explicit situations he faced with gusto and determination. On a route in Eldorado he named *The Wisdom,* we surmounted a huge roof and stood together in slings, supported by a bad ring angle piton and a small bolt he managed to get halfway in. We were far above the ground in a place where there was no easy direction to proceed. A few inches from Layton, an acre of face before my eyes, I studied his smooth skin, its shadings, tone values, highlights, unlit, half-lit, beautiful happiness and despair, deep lines, the cornered mouth, the cynical smirk, fear, confidence, wide eyes that pierced whatever they opened toward. Somewhat frantic, Layton said, "This pin is shifting. I gotta get out of here, gotta get off of these anchors."

He threw the rope around my back. With my right hand I grabbed the rope at my hip and at the other hip with my left. I belayed, as he moved quickly to my right, across vertical rock. His shoes on small footholds not far above the lip of the huge overhang, there was a terrible sense of exposure. He tried to hammer a bugaboo into a horizontal crack. It didn't go, and he left it sticking out, in place. He did not clip his rope to it. Layton's eyes widened and jaw clinched. The muscles in his cheeks tightened. The handholds were small and bad. Layton was the most expressive climber I knew. He could succinctly tell you the horror-filled truth. Suddenly he said, "Ohhh, nyyyooo. My arms are giving out. I'm coming off."

There were other things I would have preferred to hear. In a type of agony, he now added the graphic and forthcoming, "We're both going to die." I stood in my slings quietly. There was nothing a person could add to these sensational, declarative statements.

I glanced around, began to familiarize myself with my last views of the world. If Layton came off he would drop straight into space below the big roof. His weight would come onto my body with explosive force, and onto the bad anchors. If I was able to hold him, his body then would make a big pendulum swing on the rope. I would have to keep the rope from sliding through my hands. Either I would have to lower him a long distance to the ground, provided the rope did not tangle or burn my hands, or I would have to hold him for some unbearable length of time until he could fasten prusik knots to the rope and foot-by-foot slide up the rope to me. What with the value he gave the anchors, it seemed there was no option but for him to succeed.

This cold, snowy Eldorado day all at once turned exquisite. At this critical moment, the clouds made the most brilliant move, opened, and the rock became sunlit, the rich Eldorado colors vivid and infinite, the rock's brown, red, orange, yellow, purple, and green fantastically enhanced. The snow seemed more like sable. I noticed the precise gray of Layton's lightweight parka, saw a hundred tales of adventure in those lines of his face. It is not possible to describe the glory of such a moment. Eldorado was never more resplendent. Life had never been and never will be more beautiful.

Layton made a couple moves to his right, and slightly downward. With all his strength he pulled his body to a poor, flat handhold at the bottom of a tiny inside corner. He grabbed the hold, pulled against the small inside corner above with his right-hand fingers in a lieback, and in a remarkable maneuver got a kneecap on the flat hold. He rocked up onto it. If he fell now, this far away from me, there would be nothing left of either of us, the situation so awe-inspiring and ultimate I felt no fear at all. Whatever should happen was going to happen. He stood up on the flat hold, took a great breath, looked back at me, and gave me one of his renowned mischievous grins. He chuckled, as though he had gotten away with a capital offense. In about another breath he gathered his wits about him, forgot that last stupendous stretch of rock, and returned to his normal fast pace. He sped above, out of view. I heard Layton yell down that he was on belay and I should not fall because he was only able to get a RURP in for an anchor. He added that it was only in halfway.

I made it across the traverse and rocked my knee up onto the small flat hold at the bottom of the little inside corner. I continued up and right, to a slippery slab. As I attempted to make the first step of this smooth, white, water-polished slab, my right foot slid down an inch. Unable to see Layton, I impulsively yelled up that my shoes didn't work very well. For Layton this could have been an opportunity to provide a measure of instruction, to offer a morsel of fatherly wisdom as to how a foot should be properly set, with heel lower than toe, so that the weight of the body might push the shoe and its rubber into the rock for greater adhesion. . . . He bellowed, "A good climber could climb in mukluks."

In a strange way his words jolted me to a higher reality. I knew what was expected of me. I no longer was the quivering sack of oatmeal and moved upward.

When he and I did the first ascent of *X-M*, the steep, dark north wall of the Bastille, he gave me the second pitch. I leaned out around that extremely airy corner into the shallow dihedral. Terrified by the heart-stopping exposure, I hammered in a RURP—that tiniest of pitons. I clipped my aid sling to it but was reluctant to trust my weight to it. If it pulled, I would go crashing down into a chimney below. Layton had me come back to him and tie in. I placed him on belay. He went out, clipped his aid sling to the miniature piece of steel, and, without testing it with his hammer, stood up on it. "See, it's good," he said. He returned and, again, gave me the lead.

On his twenty-fifth birthday, June 11, 1963, when I was sixteen, we drove to Eldorado in his blue Ford to celebrate with a climb. He thought we should solo the *Bastille Crack*, but at the last moment he grabbed his rope and a small rack of pitons and carabiners. I went up the first 75 feet and stopped on a stance outside the crack on the wall to the left. For a belay anchor I hammered in an angle piton halfway. Layton had just returned from Yosemite where he had made the first ascent of the *West Buttress* of El Capitan. He was not about to fall off the *Bastille Crack*.

I belayed him, his long legs and arms put to full length as he flowed easily up. My friend was in fantastic shape, possibly the best of his life. He arrived at my stance in what seemed a few seconds and instantly began to proceed past and above, in an undercling, where the crack makes a short jog to the right. With his left hand under the flake and his other hand on the flake's right side, he pulled backward and leaned against the flake. I suddenly heard a loud cracking sound. He dropped, back-first, with the flake in his lap. The flake quickly broke apart, and Layton turned head first. The full, downward-flying force of his weight came onto the rope. With the rope in my hands and wrapped around my back, I had only time to squeeze with both hands. I was jerked instantly outward from the wall into a straight-body, horizontal position. Stiff body, for an instant I jutted almost horizontally out from the wall, my feet on the stance. The halfway-in angle held the extreme weight of both our bodies. Both of us should have fallen to the road and died in a heap of blood and guts. That the piton only shifted downward in the crack a couple of inches remains one of the miracles of both Layton's and my life.

At the eternal moment, with my straight body in that horizontal pose, I gazed down the wall at Layton, as he came to a stop and swung in a pendulum to the right, across the wall directly below. As fast as possible, I bent my knees and turned my body inward to the wall to the right, in a kind of squatting position. Layton grabbed the rope and, with a few mighty pulls, hand-over-handed up the wall to me. He stood next to me on the stance, as I stood up. With the thumb and first finger of his right hand he pulled the piton out of the crack. He looked at the crack, looked at the piton, looked at me, and shuddered. He hammered the angle piton back in the crack and, with the moan of a madman, raced upward and disappeared above.

Layton had me skip school when we made the first ascent of Bear Mountain's *Rogue's Arête* in 1963. The final pitch is indelible in my mind. There were no cracks. The wall was so vertical it made a climber feel he was being pushed backward, off balance. The form of Layton Kor moved up into this kingdom of so few holds. He ascended unprotected, not a piton placement to be found, in the brilliant, blue, early afternoon sky. Layton was dazzling. As the wall tapered to a pyramid summit ridge, he crawled directly over its top. There was no fanfare. Only later would I realize, and time and experience confirm, that Layton had made one of the boldest leads not only in Colorado but in America, one of the early 5.10 routes in the Boulder region.

Even in recent years, plagued with dialysis and a kidney the size of a walnut, our dear Layton, the madcap Laytono Korino, fights on. He is the bravest person I know. He still has his sense of humor. He has his freshness. It's as though we yet are on some favorite climb with him. I think back to a night when he raced up snow- and ice-covered rock to rescue my friend Larry and me, in our early teens caught on the *Yellow Spur* in a storm. Call it a feeling of my heart. When I was with Layton, Eldorado was majestic. No eloquence can describe the rich yellows, reds, brown, and gray of the sandstone or the beauty of the canyon when we had it entirely to ourselves. I see the knee-length socks he wore, the sweater, or those beat-up gray knickers he often wore in earlier years, a rip in the crotch from wide stems. I have saved a ragged scrap of paper on which he scribbled a note he left on my car window one afternoon in Eldorado, addressed to my middle name: "Oliver, will see you later today and work on the walls tomorrow." No words, so many years later, are the measure of the sublime, larger-than-life celebrity of Layton Kor. What he said either filled us with horror or was excruciatingly funny. "Sandstone is very rotten, and one should never take it for granite." To bounce back and forth between the humor and the horror made us giddy. It was his wonderful, good being that seduced us. Indeed he was pure personage, with plenty of enrapturing imperfection thrown in. We followed Layton up into those rays of sun that angled down through the upper worlds. A quick look from him, and we knew we were in a special world. We knew we were in the presence of a magnificent spirit.

—Pat Ament, October 2012

Layton Kor passed away on April 21, 2013, in Kingman, Arizona, at age 74 just before this new edition of Beyond the Vertical *went to press.*

FOREWORD TO THE FIRST EDITION

When Layton Kor's name first reached our ears in the sixties, my generation of California climbers had been at it for some 10 years, and had put up the first big routes on Half Dome and El Capitan. It was the golden age of Yosemite rock climbing. Starting with John Salathé's multi-day climbs and his development of hard steel pitons, California climbers had invented new techniques and equipment which led them in a different direction from that pursued by Europeans, and by extension, different from other American climbers who were still looking for inspiration eastward toward the birthplace of alpinism. American climbers visiting Yosemite from the Rockies or eastern United States were nonplussed by the severe Valley granite, and the unusual techniques, both aid and free, required to deal with it. Hordes of Vulgarians (a New York climbing club) arrived from the East Coast and made a name for themselves, but not through their ability to scale Yosemite walls. Climbers arrived from the Rockies with respect, and departed with more.

This humbling of each and every visiting climber led to the conclusion that it was impossible to master Yosemite without, in effect, becoming a Californian—living and climbing in the sun, and spending months in Yosemite developing the special techniques and psychological attitudes necessary for success in the Valley.

When Layton Kor came to Yosemite he quickly gave the lie to that insular notion. We had heard rumors of a Colorado phenomenon who was setting new standards in that state, a climber whose "appetite for difficult climbs," in Jim McCarthy's words, "could only be termed voracious, and whose technical proficiency, tremendous reach, and energy combine to permit him to climb some of the most difficult routes in the country with incredible speed." When Kor actually arrived in the Valley, we were deceived by his appearance. Tall, gangly, pants too short for his legs and sleeves too short for his arms, he didn't fit the image we had conjured of a blond, muscular superman. When he walked on flat ground he seemed to be all knees and elbows. He had an aw-shucks, slightly goofy, country-boy air, and acted properly awed and respectful toward the Valley and its climbs. So, in spite of his reputation, we still expected that Kor, as all of his predecessors had, would have to face a period of humility and adjustment before he could get up a Yosemite climb worthy of the name. But Kor was different. He came, saw, and conquered. He went straight onto the hardest climbs, both free and aid, and did them in record times. That woke us up!

A relentless dynamo of energy, Layton had a passion for climbing as pure and intense as any I have ever seen. Beside his gargantuan appetite for climbs, he had a Rabelaisian gusto for life—loving wine, women, laughter, and food.

Layton Kor strikes a classic pose while rappelling down Standing Rock.

Photograph Huntley Ingalls/Layton Kor Collection

Kor's times on climbs were always very fast. He was, in fact, a sort of racehorse of the mountains, and woe to those (and there were many) who couldn't stay the pace. More than one story was heard of slow seconds being bodily hauled up pitches when they hesitated too long. Not that Layton climbed fast to set records—it was just totally natural to him. He drove cars and laid bricks at the same speed. He would have been at home in the pell-mell world of Jack Kerouac's *On the Road*.

Layton was quickly accepted into the Yosemite climbing community. Not only could he climb well and fast, but more important, he was a true climber: He climbed for love of climbing and he climbed to please no one but himself. In short, he was independent, self-reliant, and honorable. By "honorable" I mean he was the sort of climber who graded routes according to how hard he thought they were, rather than downgrading them to suggest how good he was. He was never one to sit around a campfire bragging of his accomplishments, or belittling the achievements of others. We needed more of his sort!

A typical example of Kor's indefatigability was his attack on the *Salathé Wall* of El Capitan when he himself was being attacked by a vicious virus. Few climbers would have considered going up in such weakened condition, but Kor was never looking for an excuse not to climb. He joined forces with Galen Rowell, and under tough, wet conditions, made the fourth ascent. And came down stronger and healthier than when he started.

When Layton became satisfied with his mastery of the Valley, following the first ascent of El Capitan's *West Buttress,* he wandered widely, climbing throughout the United States and in Canada, from California to the Shawangunks of New York, and from the great sandstone spires of the Southwest deserts to the crystalline granite of Canada's Logan Mountains, leaving a trail of firsts wherever he ventured. Then came his pilgrimage to the cradle of mountaineering, the French, Swiss, and Italian Alps, where he did some stiff routes, including big faces in the Dolomites and steep ice walls of the Mont Blanc Massif. This feverish activity was capped off with the *Eiger Directissima* in winter.

Sometime after the Eiger, Kor underwent a religious conversion. I can imagine that after the Eiger, after he had proven himself in so many facets of the climbing world; after he was, so to speak, at the top; he looked out and off into the distance, and as far as he could see stretched an endless range of mountains. I can imagine Layton eyeing those peaks receding into infinity and seeing in them insufficient food to satisfy deeper hungers.

Frankly, most of us were a little peeved when Layton chose God over Climbing. We were sorry to lose a climbing companion, and regarded such a defection as a sign of weakness. "Oh, no," we said, "Kor's got religion." And, "Poor fellow." Climbers are mostly not a holy lot. They tend to be egoistic, and egoism is not compatible with deference to the Prime Mover. So it was not surprising that climbers considered Kor as "lost." In fact, publishing this book would have been a slightly awkward affair had it been produced at the logical moment, which was shortly after Kor stopped serious climbing in the late sixties. 1983 is a more auspicious time for such a theme. It's in keeping with the times that serious artists are not ashamed to touch upon spiritual themes, as evidenced by the film *Chariots of Fire,* the songs of Dan Fogelberg, and the new Sierra Club novel, *The River Why.*

Speaking of why, we climbers are endlessly asked by nonclimbers, "Why do you climb?" The proper answer is, "If you have to ask, you'll never understand." But we usually give a variation of Mallory's classic "Because it is there." It never occurred to us that climbing could be a search for God. Yet the concept has a certain plausibility. Consider first the quasi-religious discipline needed to be mentally and physically fit to do hard climbs; next, the way one climbs toward Heaven; and finally, the willingness to give up luxuries and to endure hardship to get nearer . . . Truth (?). As for the endless queries "Why?" they are as likely to be satisfied with the response "Looking for God" as anything else.

Anyway, if Kor's climbing was a search, he has come full circle, and we can see in his intense and passionate climbing career a "fearful symmetry," in Blake's phrase, leading to a perfectly logical resolution.

I have long thought that one could measure a climber's love for climbing by how often he repeats climbs, having noted that some of the more famous climbers rarely did routes, even short ones, more than once. They made the newspapers occasionally, but as far as I could see, got no joy out of just climbing. If they did, I reasoned, they would repeat pleasurable routes. In fact, I can think of some big names in climbing who must have rather hated the sport. But Kor was not so neatly categorizable. He loved climbing, but he rarely did a route twice. Indeed, Kor, like Fred Beckey, was a sort of Don Juan of mountaineering, true to no climb, but endlessly seeking new ones. Or, to take the search analogy one step further, one can understand that when Kor had done a climb and not found what he was searching for, there was no use in looking there again!

Climbing with Layton was always an energizing experience. Vignettes of our experiences together pop into my mind: careening along mountain rocks in a jalopy with threadbare tires (it was typical of Kor that he would be blithely telling me how bad the tires were, but lessen the car's velocity not an iota); approaching climbs or descending from them, with me taking two strides to Layton's one; sitting in the infamous eating pit in Boulder, The Sink, guzzling beer and wolfing hamburgers; racing up routes in Eldorado Canyon, under skies as continuously blue as those in California. Those were the golden days, when we were the elite of a small group of practitioners of a rather esoteric discipline.

My favorite climb with Kor was the *Jack of Diamonds* on Longs Peak in Colorado. The year was 1963. Kor and I had just made the second ascent of the original route, and a day later climbed the "Jack." At that time, I had already made a name for myself as a climber of note, and Kor was, so to speak, an upstart, brilliant, but not sufficiently tested.

I was at the height of my climbing powers, and quite fit. I kept pace with Kor, but only by extending myself to the utmost, and I was keeping pace with him, rather than the other way around. The following notes sum up my recognition of Kor's stature as a climber: "Kor slept placidly, but next day his famous energy and drive became focused upon the problem of getting up this new route. The weather worsened as we climbed higher, and in the afternoon snow flurries swirled around us. Racing the setting sun to avoid a bad night in slings, Kor led the last pitch, a long, strenuous jam crack. On my last reserves I struggled up, topped The Diamond, and shook the hand of a great climber."

—Royal Robbins, February 1983

EDITOR'S NOTE TO THIS EDITION

Stewart M. Green

Beyond the Vertical came out in 1983 as a lavish four-color, coffee-table book published by the late Bob Godfrey and became a climbing world sensation almost overnight. All of my friends bought the book, despite its steep price, because it demystified the great one—Layton Kor, perhaps the greatest American rock climber of his generation.

Layton Kor is simply one of the legends in American climbing history. During a 10-year period from the late fifties through the late sixties, Layton did hundreds of first ascents on the crags around his home in Boulder, Colorado; the sandstone towers in the Utah and Arizona desert; the soaring granite walls in Yosemite Valley; the icy peaks and walls in the Alps; and on rock peaks in the Dolomites.

In 2012, almost 30 years later, I went climbing at the Garden of the Gods, my hometown crags near Colorado Springs, with Jimmie Dunn, another great American climber. Jimmie said, "If someone gave you a hundred thousand dollars and told you to go repeat all of Layton's great climbs, do you think you could do them in 5 years? In 10 years? I bet not. What Layton accomplished in the sixties was amazing!"

Layton Kor joins Ed Webster and Dennis Jump on the summit of Kor's Kastle in 2009.
Photograph Stewart M. Green

In some ways, *Beyond the Vertical* bolstered the myth of Layton Kor by giving direct details about the man and his motivations and recounting his amazing energy and uncanny ability to get up routes. When I read the essays about Layton's adventures written by his contemporaries, like Royal Robbins, Chuck Pratt, Steve Komito, and Pat Ament, I am reminded that he was a man driven to climb. Climbing was part of his life force, and Layton was happiest when he was leading a desperate pitch up an unclimbed tower or big wall. The book's beautiful photos, of course, depicted many of Layton's great ascents from Yosemite and the canyon country to the Eiger and the Dolomites.

Beyond the Vertical sold out by 1990 and over the last 20 years the price of a copy of the book slowly climbed to over $500. My own prized edition, which I bought in the early eighties after 4 months of scrimping, disappeared when someone borrowed the book and never returned it, but I was able to buy another one, almost new, for only $125 from a Florida book dealer a few years ago after a lengthy negotiation.

That negotiation and the general scarcity of *Beyond the Vertical* inspired me to ask Globe Pequot Press/FalconGuides to reprint the book. I told Layton, "We need to have the book republished. There's a whole new generation of climbers out there that would love to read about your great adventures." Layton agreed, and then FalconGuides agreed, that *Beyond the Vertical* needed to be back in print.

I talked with many of the contributors to the original edition, both writers and photographers, and all of them were happy to have their work reprinted in a reissue of *Beyond the Vertical*. I was able to track down many of the original photographs that appeared in the book as well as more images of Layton's adventures that have never been published. Deciding which photographs to leave in the book and which new ones to add was a difficult decision, but a balance was struck to tell the visual story of Layton Kor.

I offer special thanks to everyone involved in breathing new life into *Beyond the Vertical*. First, thanks to Layton Kor for having all those grand adventures and then sharing them in the first edition, and to Bob Godfrey, who passed away in 1988, for having the foresight to publish the book. Thanks to Dennis Jump in the United Kingdom who helped negotiate copyright details with Bob's late brother Peter Godfrey and his widow Gina, and Steve "Crusher" Bartlett provided many of the high-resolution digital scans of Layton's original 35mm photographs. Thanks also to FalconGuides' professional staff, including editors John Burbidge, David Legere, and Julie Marsh, and layout artist Melissa Evarts for creating this stunning new edition of *Beyond the Vertical*—an American climbing classic.

Sadly, Layton Kor passed just as this new edition of *Beyond the Vertical* went to the printer. I know that Layton would be happy to hold this marvelous book in his hands and know that his wonderful adventures, great climbs, and passionate spirit will continue to inspire future generations of climbers.

EDITOR'S NOTE TO THE FIRST EDITION

Bob Godfrey (1943–1988)

It was 1976. At the time I was working on *CLIMB!: Rock Climbing in Colorado,* with Dudley Chelton. During the sixties, the "Golden Age" of Colorado climbing, the central figure was Layton Kor. If *CLIMB!* was to be the authoritative work that we hoped, substantive coverage of Kor's climbing career was essential, and preferably firsthand. Kor, however, had dropped out of sight. Enquiries eventually produced an address in Golden where he was living at the time, working as a bricklayer for the Coors Brewery. Locating him solved the main problem (I thought), the rest should be straightforward. Two unanswered letters, and one politely but abruptly terminated phone call later, and I was back to square one. Layton had removed himself from mainstream climbing in the late sixties (he told me on the phone), and didn't care to waste time dredging up memories of a period of his life that to all intents and purposes was now behind him.

Commiserating with me on this frustrating turn of events, Bob Culp suggested that I try one final stratagem. "Layton might sound a bit gruff," Culp said, "but he does have a kind heart. If you just turn up and knock on his door, you'll probably find that he's actually much friendlier than he seems on the phone. If he likes you, he just might be willing to help."

So, armed with Culp's encouragement, one evening I drove to Golden and knocked on Layton's door. Culp's prediction was accurate. Kor was friendly and invited me back a few evenings later when he would be willing to sit down and answer a few questions about the sixties.

The appointed evening arrived and to my pleasant surprise I found Kor not in the least reticent. We sat until the late hours reminiscing about Colorado's Golden Age. I was impressed at his recall and surprised to find that he appeared to enjoy the process once we got going.

One outcome from the evening I was hoping for was to obtain from Layton certain photographs of important first ascents he had made: The Diamond in the winter, the Northwest Face of Chiefshead, and others. Partway through the evening, in response to my request, Layton went into a back room and returned with box after box of color slides. My eyes popped. There were some 5,000 to 6,000 color slides in all: a priceless repository of climbing history.

I felt like I had stumbled into Aladdin's Cave. Layton kindly provided the pictures I wanted, which were converted to black and white and subsequently published in *CLIMB!*

It struck me at the time that the photographs, together with Layton's personal story, could form the basis for a biography. I asked Layton to consider this possibility, and, displaying lukewarm interest at best, he agreed to think it over. We spoke on the phone a few days later and, despite my best persuasive efforts, Layton declined. He had been generously willing to spend an evening, but the large amount of time required for a biography was low on his scale of priorities in 1976.

In the years that followed, I occasionally thought about Layton, and the contribution that his biography would make to climbing literature. During the sixties, for a decade, he was at the forefront of American climbing, equaled perhaps only by Royal Robbins in terms of the quantity and quality of his first ascents. His energy and vitality were legendary, and wherever he went he had left an indelible mark on climbing history. More so than the bare statistics of the climbing record showed, Kor's was also the story of a spiritual evolution.

Together with the collection of photographs that Layton had showed me, I felt that his story was one that deserved to be told. Five years later, I approached him again, and this time, after much persuading (perhaps as much as anything to get me out of his hair), he agreed.

Layton's section of the following text is based on lengthy tape recorded interviews I conducted with him and wrote up in draft form. He then worked on the manuscript, adding and deleting as he saw fit.

In a career as long and varied as Kor's, a biography of this nature is necessarily selective. We have tried to present mainly climbs, which by Kor's standards, and by the criteria of climbing history, were significant. There are many, many climbs, and many, many climbing partners not mentioned, and we hope that those climbing companions who are not included will not feel slighted.

To round out the picture, we invited contributions from a broad spectrum of writers describing their climbing experiences with Kor and we thank all of them sincerely for their additions to this book.

Occasionally, Layton was unable to identify the person who took a certain photograph in his collection. We thank these uncredited individuals most sincerely.

A small amount of material has been reprinted from the previous book *CLIMB!*, to round out this picture of an American mountaineer whose journey from the work of climbing to a spiritual one has taken him beyond the vertical.

It has been my pleasure and privilege to work on this book with Layton. I trust that it will find a welcome place on the library shelves of climbing literature and that it will be found both entertaining and thought provoking.

INTRODUCTION

The late fifties and sixties were an exciting time for me as it was the beginning of my climbing career. I was beside myself for having found the key to the next 10 years of climbing pleasures. In those early days there were few climbers, yet endless new route possibilities. Another advantage afforded me was my parents' decision to settle in Boulder, Colorado. A short drive from our home were the beautiful multicolored cliffs of Eldorado Canyon. There were sizeable cliffs everywhere! My climbing friends and I feasted on the steep face climbs in the area, including routes on the Bastille, Redgarden Wall, and the amazing *Yellow Spur*. As our climbing appetites increased, it became obvious that our local crags were not enough, and we expanded our climbing interests and began travelling to other Colorado climbing areas. A 7-hour drive from Boulder was the mighty Black Canyon of the Gunnison—1,700- to 2,000-foot sheer black walls rose steeply above the Gunnison River. I would make many trips there over the years. When the weather grew too warm, we went to higher locations. The climbs around Estes Park were cooler and also lay in a gorgeous alpine setting. Hallett Peak, Chiefshead, and, of course, the magnificent East Face of Longs Peak provided many wonderful adventures.

Those Colorado climbs barely whetted my interest in climbing and travelling to new areas. My climbing friends and I were by no means immune to the distant yet powerful pull of the huge face climbs in Yosemite Valley in California. After several trips there through the years, I enjoyed the special privilege of climbing three of the great Yosemite classics—the North Face of Sentinel Rock, the Northwest Face of Half Dome, and the monolith itself: El Capitan. Also not far from Boulder was the Desert Southwest, virtually unexplored and unclimbed. Waiting for us were some very impressive freestanding sandstone spires. The Totem Pole, Spider Rock, Castleton Tower, and Standing Rock were but a few of the "never to be forgotten" climbs we enjoyed doing.

Part of my climbing involved doing research on climbing opportunities in other countries. Europe contained many countries with mountains filled with endless climbing possibilities. In addition, their trail system in the Alps was well-groomed and they had first-class huts that were placed in a great position for climbers. In all fairness to my climbing needs, I could not deny myself a trip to this climbing mecca.

When I finally arrived in Europe in the fall of 1965, I went directly to Leysin, Switzerland. John Harlin, Royal Robbins, and Mick Burke were among the instructors at the American school and college there. It was a great location, as it turned out, as I was badly in need of climbing partners. Using Leysin as a base, I made trips to the French and

Italian Alps, completed a couple of ice climbs near Chamonix, and then I was off to the Dolomites in Italy and then the Eiger.

The North Face of the Eiger in the Swiss Alps is far more than just a mountain wall. For the serious alpinist it truly is what dreams are made of. Beginning in 1935, bold mountaineers battled with their lives in pursuit of the first ascent of the 6,000-foot wall. Among alpine enthusiasts the Eiger shares honors with two other magnificent alpine walls: the North Face of the Grandes Jorasses in the French Alps and the North Face of the Matterhorn in Switzerland. Together they are known as the three great north face climbs in the Alps.

After reading several books and seeing actual photos of the Alps, I knew I had to be there. The tiny alpine village of Leysin, Switzerland, was home to the great American alpinist, John Harlin. He had already climbed the Heckmair route on the Eiger and was interested in doing a winter ascent by a new direct route. After introductions and a serious number of discussions, John invited me to join him on an attempt. I accepted even though there was a sensible amount of caution within.

At the time I wasn't sure if I had any business being up there; on the other hand I wasn't in Europe to pick flowers in the meadows . . . I accepted. A short time later John extended an invitation to the renowned Scottish climber, Dougal Haston. It would be three of us against one of the most notorious, dangerous rock and ice walls in the Alps. Excited about our upcoming venture, we began the rather lengthy process of sorting out the massive amount of equipment we would need for a winter ascent of the Eiger Direct. Suddenly—out of the blue—a phone call informed us that a team of eight German climbers were already up on the wall with the same intentions as ours. We were now confronted with high-level competition, a far more weighty situation than we were prepared for. Nevertheless, John Harlin was not going to give up a new route on the Eiger in winter without a fight. Three more contestants were brought into the equation and after packing our equipment into a van we made the short drive to Kleine Scheidegg, the hotel at the base of the Eiger.

Once on the wall proper we experienced storm after storm. The climb became for us a cold, feisty endurance test. Higher up on the face, a terrible tragedy unfolded: One of the fixed lines that John was prusiking broke, sending him 4,000 feet to the bottom of the wall. A wonderful friend was gone.

. . .

The German team also had bad rope problems—their main prusik line contained six bad cuts. In order to avoid another catastrophe, one of the German climbers, Karl Golikow, removed all of the fixed ropes between the Spider and the bottom of the wall. This ended

Layton Kor poses atop a small spire after making the first ascent at The Crags on the Twin Sisters in Rocky Mountain National Park.

the climb for me as I was in a small food store gathering supplies for the final push. Haston and a number of the German climbers went on to finish the ascent. I wasn't even able to watch the lads finish the climb due to a terrible storm that blew into the area. The final rope lengths were done in a blizzard. The entire summit team received serious frostbite and was hospitalized.

Thinking back after all these years the one thing I remember about the winter ascent of the Eiger was how incredibly cold it was. I eliminated that problem along with most of the white stuff when I moved to Arizona. Europe was an incredible experience—if I had a chance to do it over again I probably would have stayed there!

My travels, however, were not always climbing related. I spent 2 years in the Philippines, 4 years in Guam, and 1 year in Hawaii. For a while at least climbing had been replaced by fishing, swimming, and scuba diving. Island hopping too has its shares of worldly pleasures.

Nine years ago, in April of 2004, my wife, Karen, my son, Arlan, and I settled in Kingman, Arizona, directly under the watchful eye of the blazing Arizona sun. Our family became firmly planted into high desert living. Within the first month I made several trips into a wilderness area not far from Kingman. From those exploratory hikes I put together a list of ten climbs I hoped to do. Apart from a few climbs done with friends, the bulk of the climbs on my list were never done. Suddenly my climbing career ended as fast as it began—accumulated age along with health issues made continued climbing impossible.

Although I am physically unable to climb, I still feel very much a climber. Fortunately I have many climbing friends who never stop talking about climbing. Some of them come to visit, and many others call regularly. My friends, my library full of climbing books, the boxes full of climbing photos, and my long list of memories assure me that I won't be forgetting about climbing anytime soon.

—Layton Kor, November 2012

EARLY DAYS

In retrospect there are times, occasionally, when I look back on my climbing career and, in my most pessimistic moments, feel that they were just so many wasted years. For more than a decade I was obsessed by climbing, spending a sizeable portion of my existence involved in some activity directly or indirectly related to it.

In libraries I would pore through climbing books and magazines, some in languages that I could not understand, voraciously devouring every scrap of climbing information available. Images would flood my imagination to bursting point, of enticing summits and huge mountain walls. Spires and gargoyles beckoned from far horizons, cloaked in the romance of mountain mythology—El Cap, the Eiger, the Grandes Jorasses, the fabulous alpine routes of Buhl, Rebuffat, Cassin, and Comici, the readily accessible temptations of Eldorado Canyon and Longs Peak, the mysterious depths of the Black Canyon of the Gunnison, the many unclimbed possibilities of Yosemite, and the tantalizing desert canyons guarding who knew how many secret spires were in their labyrinths; and a thousand others. Scanning these myriad possibilities, with the appetite of a starving man perusing the pages of a gourmet magazine, I readily transformed the unknown to the known and I saw myself turning the hidden key that opened each new climb's secret and solved its mystery.

Caught up in a whirlwind of physical and psychological energy demanding release, I was driven by motives that at the time I cared neither to analyze nor dwell on. Not particularly introspective in these early days, I developed my abilities to the point where I became a driven climbing machine.

Today, when I think back, I am struck by the contrast between the person I was then and the person I am now. Could I really have been that driven, obsessed, single-minded individual that memory undeniably suggests? Could the ascent of rocks and spires and mountains really have been of such preeminent importance that other aspects of life receded into insignificance by comparison?

For a decade I was Layton Kor—"Climber," active in Colorado, in the desert in Utah and Arizona, in Yosemite, Canada, Alaska, and in the Alps. Most of this climbing took place during the sixties—that period of never-before-seen freedom, both social and geographical, in American history. The climbing "scene," finding quintessential expression in the then center of the climbing universe, Camp 4, Yosemite, populated as it was by various risk-takers, oddballs, misfits, and other escapees from social convention, did not lag behind the times. The interludes between climbs saw parties, drugs, and women, all

supplementing the escapism that propelled me and many of my contemporaries in our upward drive on the vertical walls.

Then, toward the end of the sixties, came a period of transition, of reflection, of re-ordering priorities. To a certain extent it was the natural end result of 10 years of hyperactive intensity, the burnout that anyone who puts too much energy into a single activity must inevitably experience. But it was more than tiredness, more than the ennui that comes from repetition. It was the gradually dawning awareness that whatever it was that I had been seeking in my headlong quest through the mountains, I had not been finding it. In 10 years of high-standard climbing I had done a good job of satisfying my earthly desires at the expense of denying spiritual needs. During this transitional period, I still did hard climbs—the North Face of the Eiger in winter, the first ascent of The Diamond in winter, and the *Salathé Wall.* It was a period of growing awareness that climbing of this standard could not go on forever. I had seen friends injured and killed over the years; most impactful among these was John Harlin's tragic death on the Eiger. Coming as it did at the time when I was beginning to reassess my own involvement, John's death made a strong impression. I had had more than my share of luck and after so many adventures was fortunate to have survived.

As I reassessed my needs and purpose in life my interest began to turn from climbing to spiritual matters. My quest for the summit transformed into a quest for a more fundamental sense of meaning, and it is from this perspective that I look back on my early, wilder years. But let me not get ahead of myself; the story that led me to this point began many years earlier.

My interest in climbing was first aroused when I was living in Colorado Springs with my parents in the mid-fifties. I was watching television one evening, and there was a movie showing called *High Conquest,* based on a James Ramsey Ullman book, that captured my imagination. The next day I went out with my dad's geologist's pick to a little canyon behind the trailer park where we were living. It was on the edge of the Manitou sandstone formations and there were a number of small rock outcroppings. I started chopping steps in the rock with the geologist's pick! I'd seen the climbers in the movies with ice axes and I thought that was the way it was done.

Shortly after that I acquired a few army pitons and a short hemp rope, and was ready for more ambitious challenges, when I received an unexpected setback. My parents announced that we were moving to Wichita Falls, Texas—the Land of the "Flat."

Apart from an occasional tree, and the bank of a creek behind our new home, there was absolutely nothing to climb in Wichita Falls. By this time I had developed a serious case of climbing fever and it demanded expression. I was desperate for anything vertical and on closer inspection thought maybe the creek's banks might work. I had seen a crude

Layton Kor did the first ascents of many classic routes, including *The Naked Edge, T2,* and *Ruper,* on the Redgarden Wall in Eldorado Canyon.
Photograph Stewart M. Green

drawing of rappelling in an army journal and decided here was my chance to learn how to do it. I pounded a cluster of pitons into the clay embankment above the creek and, aided by the memory of the drawing, wrapped the rope around myself, leaned back, and—the pitons immediately pulled out of the clay. I fell over backward, down the embankment and into the river!

Undaunted by the dunking, I next tried a tree. I found an overhanging one that was smooth and limbless on one side. With some crude stirrups that I had made out of rope, using the tree as a practice climb, I pounded the pitons in and went up and down, up and down. Words fail me in describing the astonished expressions I generated among the local Texans who thought outsiders were strange at best.

During study halls at school, when I should really have been working on my lessons, I would go into the library and research material on climbing. That year my parents moved a number of times, so I was in different schools (which didn't do a whole lot for my grades). By the time we eventually settled in Boulder, Colorado, the following spring, I had read everything I could find about climbing, and I had a reasonably good idea what it was all about. I was perfectly content to be living in Boulder, a major center of American rock climbing, surrounded by climbing opportunities. Once, I said to my parents, "If you leave Boulder, you go without me." I was more excited by climbing than anything I'd ever done before and there was no way I was going to go and live somewhere I couldn't do it.

Pat Ament (left) and Larry Dalke, two of Layton's young partners, pose in a Boulder neighborhood in the early sixties.

A childhood friend of mine from Minnesota, Paul Johnson, had come to Boulder to visit. Before he realized what I was up to, I grabbed him, the old hemp rope, and the army pitons, and we went out and climbed the Third Flatiron, the 1,000-foot slab nestled in the foothills above town. It was my first real climb and my technique was rudimentary, to say the least. I had read an article in a popular magazine about a mountain guide who was guiding a client who fell. The guide was holding the rope and did the only thing he could do in the situation, which was to jump over the other side of the ridge and counteract the

Layton Kor works up the initial slab on the *Northwest Corner* of the Bastille in Eldorado Canyon.
Photograph Huntley Ingalls/Layton Kor Collection

The Yellow Spur

David Dornan

After climbing the *Diagonal* with Ray Northcutt in the summer of 1959, Layton Kor became the central figure of the climbing renaissance that was taking place in the Boulder area. His impact was so complete that Colorado climbers thereafter referred to local climbing history as "before Kor." His energy, enthusiasm, and original approaches to climbing turned the climbing community in Boulder upside down. As an innovator, Kor was responsible for the following new ideas:

- It's possible to climb every day of the year.
- It's possible to climb with anyone you can talk into it.
- Every line in Eldorado Canyon is climbable whether it looks feasible or not.
- There's no excuse to slow down on a climb despite any obstacles.
- There's no excuse for not climbing, no matter how you feel.
- It's OK to drive pitons as hard as you can, despite what your second may say about tired arms.

One winter evening in December 1959, I remember Kor coming into the Student Union with a big grin on his face. Dean Moore, Peter Lev, some other friends, and I were drinking coffee and talking climbing. Kor sat down to tell us he had made a great discovery: The south-facing walls of Eldorado Canyon would clear up enough for climbing in just a couple of days after a snowstorm. At the time, this discovery was probably not as appealing to us as it was to Kor, but eventually, with some misgivings, I found myself swept away by Kor's enthusiasm. In fact, later, as he described to me this great climb that he wanted to do in Eldorado, I found that there was no way I could say no to him.

Kor arranged to pick me up early on the morning of February 21, 1960, and we drove to Eldorado Canyon in his Ford as the sun was rising. We drove up the canyon a bit, turned the car around, and as we drove back down the canyon road, Kor showed the route to me. The proposed route was a prominent, steep ridge on the west side of the Redgarden Wall. It really was a striking feature, and with the morning light on the yellowish rock, Kor told me he had come up with the name "Yellow Spur." Although it was a reasonably cloud-free day, there was a brisk, cold wind and I noticed lots of snow banks lying in the shade and on the ledges.

Kor parked his car and I followed him over the bridge and around the rocks to the west side of Redgarden Wall. Kor seemed to know where he was going, though I doubt that climbers had yet worked out the best approach to that side of the rocks. Without a trail it seemed a bit complicated; eventually we arrived at a little shelf with a conifer tree on the north end. Kor said that this was where the climb began; I don't recall doing much scouting around and I don't think Kor had previously checked it out. But if Kor said, "We start climbing here," it was fine with me. I never questioned his judgment about routefinding.

Another one of Kor's innovations was to take the business end of the rope and start climbing before anyone else could get organized. Ordinarily I would have wanted some discussion about leading, but this time I was happy to have him start off. The short wall in front of us had a single crumbling piton crack that overhung at the top. Kor quickly climbed up about 20 feet and placed a piton. He then tried out a combination of moves to advance a few more feet. He placed another piton, started out again and fell. I held him all right with the belay, but suddenly the nature of the climb was becoming a lot more serious.

Kor got back to his high point and decided that he had spent enough time free climbing, so he placed a couple of aid pitons and was soon over the lip of the overhang. He continued up another 20 feet and belayed me. I followed with some apprehension and, with weakened arms from pounding out his pitons, joined him on the ledge. Kor had decided that he should continue leading and headed up and to the left, climbing some steep inside corners. At the end of the lead Kor belayed me from a snow-covered ledge. The next lead had a short, steep step that was slightly bulging and it seemed to both of us that we had to use the adhesive properties of our clothing to help get over it. The climbing had been fairly strenuous to this point but we were now able to follow some easy ledges to the right where we could enter the huge dihedral that we had noticed earlier from the road.

We were in high spirits as we started up the easy part of the dihedral. We knew that this section would be the key to the climb. If the dihedral panned out we would make the top. I remember Kor saying as he started off on a hand traverse around the first roof in the dihedral, "Just stick with the Old Trooper and you'll get up!"

The dihedral soon ended, however, and we still weren't up. Kor had set up a belay on a small, exposed ledge in the full force of the cold wind, so I was feeling very much alone as he took off around the corner not knowing if it would go or not. Kor was climbing slower than usual and then after 40 or 50 feet he came to a stop altogether. From his shouts I eventually understood that the situation was desperate. Finally, I heard Kor place a bolt, which I must admit made me feel better since it improved my chances of holding him if he fell. Still, I numbly waited a long time before the signal to climb came. When I was able to

The *Yellow Spur*, first climbed by Layton Kor and Dave Dornan in 1959, climbs to the sharp summit of Tower 1 on the Redgarden Wall.
Photograph Stewart M. Green

see around the corner myself, I could fully appreciate the lead that Kor had done. He had climbed a very steep wall without an obvious exit, and he was full of glee as he shouted down from the belay stance, "How do you like this? Isn't it great?" Looking up I could see his etriers swinging in the wind from the top of the bolt ladder, and I yelled back to him to keep a tight rope on me.

There was one more lead to the top of a perfectly shaped summit. We were tired, cold, hungry, but also very happy. We had just finished a great climb and were the first people ever on this fantastic summit. It was a grand way to end a fine adventure.

Since the climb had taken about 8 hours, we had to hurry in order to get off while there was still light. Kor knew the way down some horrendous third-class chimney on the west side that he told me he had once climbed with Ben Chidlaw. It was an enormous relief to be on the scree slope, pick up our pack and run directly down the slope to the stream, the road, and Kor's car. Layton later told me that he thought this was the hardest climb he had yet done in Eldorado, but with Kor glory was very transitory since it seemed he was doing a hard new route every week.

In any area that has been carefully worked over by determined climbers, the easier and more natural lines are the first to go. What remains are the obscure, unreasonably steep, or serious and unfriendly possibilities. As my learned climbing companion Huntley Ingalls and I were to find out, *Psycho* would fall into the latter category. From beneath the long overhang that guards the lower section of Redgarden Wall, the view upward was not encouraging. We studied the earth-colored flaky rock that led to a horizontal ceiling some 70 feet above the ground. As our view of the wall above was blocked by the overhang, we backed away from the cliff, revealing something we really didn't want to see: a high-angle slab, polished and apparently without cracks.

Carefully placed pitons took us up the wall to below the roof. From there, three expansion bolts were necessary to surmount the overhang, and the rope cut sharply into my waist as I hung there for some considerable time drilling.

Above the roof we reached a point where we were in a sling belay in a little corner just above the lip. Huntley protected me while I leaned sideways and peeked around the corner. "Looks like there's a

Layton Kor takes a lunch break in Eldorado Canyon in May 1960.

blank spot about 20 feet away," I told him, and gingerly balanced my way around the corner. I was surprised to find a series of large holds. Things were going better than I expected and I confidently told Huntley that I didn't think the pitch would be too bad at all.

I spoke too soon. Fifteen feet higher the holds disappeared, leaving me contemplating a distressingly smooth section of rock. Balancing there, I was about 20 feet out from Huntley, with no protection. I experimented for a while, trying different holds, looking for protection. Directly above me there appeared to be a decent handhold. The trouble was that it was out of reach. If I was going to use it, the preferred practice of keeping three points of contact on the rock was out of the question. I called to Huntley. "Be careful, I'm going to have to try lunging for a hold up here," all the time wondering to myself, if I fell with this much rope out, would I hit the ground?

Studying the hold carefully, I said to myself, "Well, Layton, this is it. Just try your best and hope. If it doesn't work you can try to drop back down and grab the holds you're on

Layton makes a swinging rappel off the Redgarden Wall in Eldorado Canyon.

now." My arm strength was going quickly, so without wasting any more time I lunged up. It was an unnerving, frantic leap for the handhold, which turned out to be just large enough and solid enough to take the shock of all my weight. For a moment I struggled, then found my balance. I could only imagine what had been going through Huntley's mind during the last few minutes, but it was probably better that he had not observed my ordeal.

The smooth slabs above were difficult but not too bad. Before long we ambled up onto the grassy meadow and the end of a great climb.

Psycho presented aid climbing up to and over the roof, and then difficult and unprotected free climbing above the overhangs. Clearly, if the route was to go, then high-standard free climbing was demanded. But generally, I wasn't interested in investing large amounts of time working out complex free moves on short training climbs. The long alpine climbs that I was primarily interested in demanded the ability to do hard free climbing and difficult direct aid fast.

The main literature that was available when I started climbing was from the Alps. Like most climbers of the day, I grew up on a diet of Buhl, Comici, and Cassin. These were the philosophies we adopted, and the techniques we employed. Even in those early days I dreamed about someday going to the Alps and trying the great climbs. I considered Eldorado a training ground for bigger climbs where speed was at a premium. There was no stigma attached to direct aid in those days; in fact, just the opposite. Climbers knew how strenuous and complex hard direct aid was, and respected it, and certainly aid climbing could have its exciting moments.

Virtually all the top climbers in the Boulder region in the early sixties climbed using a combination of free climbing and direct aid technique, but there were a few individuals who stood out in terms of their free climbing ability. Larry Dalke was a naturally brilliant free climber, able to float up hard rock fast and seemingly effortlessly. Royal Robbins would pay his periodic lightning visits to Colorado, bringing with him a Californian free climbing mentality. Pat Ament climbed with Robbins and became interested in pushing the Colorado free climbing standards. This proved to be Ament's forte, and coupled with his natural gymnastic ability enabled him to leave his mark on the Colorado free climbing scene.

In England during the sixties, climbers like Joe Brown and Don Whillans would do on-sight, very bold, unprotected leads of extreme climbs. But, generally, if anything I was overprotective in my climbing. There were, of course, times when I wouldn't be able to get anything solid in. We had located an area some distance above the railroad tracks, not far to the south of Eldorado Springs, called Mickey Maus, almost a miniature of Redgarden Wall. On a route we called the *Red Dihedral,* the first section was straightforward, up the main dihedral to a sling belay under a big roof. Then the climb traversed left under the roof for some way. It was very hard direct aid. I had knifeblades behind tiny flakes, and

Layton Kor leads below a big roof on the *Red Dihedral,* a massive left-facing dihedral that splits the Mickey Maus Wall, in 1964.

Layton leads the roof pitch on the first ascent of *The Wisdom* on Redgarden Wall in 1961.
Photograph Pat Ament/Layton Kor Collection

RURPs, all tied off. I had a vision of everything pulling and me tumbling down to the bottom of the cliff.

In situations such as these I had various techniques that I would use to minimize the risk. On the *Red Dihedral* traverse I found a small hold, not great, but enough that I could use it as a fingerhold to take some of my weight. I had placed a knifeblade that I didn't trust, so I took as much of my weight as I could on the handhold, and very, very gently eased some of my weight onto the knifeblade, making sure that the rope was running through a short sling from the previous pin to hold me in case it came out. Hardly daring to breathe, keeping as much weight on the handhold as I could, I gradually transferred my weight to the knifeblade, watching it like a hawk for any sign of movement. It held, fortunately, and I kept going across the traverse. The difficulty was sustained and I placed one expansion bolt partway across to give a measure of security. I heard later that subsequent ascent parties placed two more bolts, for a total of three, making the traverse a lot easier.

During my early years I climbed with many different people. One of these, with whom I was later to make the first winter ascent of The Diamond, was an enthusiastic young fellow named Wayne Goss. He had energy to spare, was always ready to go on a new project, and was a person with whom, as his following account tells, I shared a number of interesting experiences.

Early Experiences

Wayne Goss

Before I knew Layton, I had climbed, but had never been a climber. I had never crossed that line where people on one side were crawling grubs wallowing in shallows and in miseries, and those on the other were doers of visions—fire in their eyes, questing after the mystical crystal, or whatever might be their personal ideal.

One of the joys of being a climber is that one must embody the coexistence of contrary qualities. A climber must be a visionary, but that vision is underpinned by what must be a deadly accurate appreciation of the realities of tooth and claw survival on a wall. If one is not driven to schizophrenia by a deep involvement in climbing, a dynamic tension results. There was no shortage of this quality in Kor when I climbed with him in the sixties. To the question, "What matters most in life?" he paused a second, then quickly looked around the room, which was the back room of the infamous Sink. He was not thinking about what the answer was going to be. He knew it cold. Rather he was scanning the images running across his mind: a catalogue of heroic ventures. Of firsts to be: El Cap, The Diamond, the Eiger, and others. Layton leaned forward across the table, his elbows sliding over the many names, oaths, and fantasies carved into it, looked me square in the eyes, and said, "The big walls, man, the big walls." And he meant it.

I met Layton by accident, before I had climbed seriously. His girlfriend—that's what we called them in the mid-sixties—was sunbathing in Eldorado and I tried to pick her up. When I explained what a hotshot climber I was—being able to follow 5.7 and owning a $\frac{9}{16}$-inch goldline rope—she suggested I talk to her boyfriend, who was a pretty good climber. Even then Kor had a formidable reputation.

On the strength of her introduction I ventured to call Layton. At that time he lived with his parents in a small, and as I recall it, pink trailer. The sight I got upon opening the door was not what I expected. Layton was sitting down and was clearly too tall to spend much time standing up. He was dressed in black from head to toe. His grip was firm, and his bricklayer's hand wrapped around my small and nervous one as we shook. He quickly put me at ease and we zeroed in on a climb he wanted to do in Colorado Springs. I had something I could contribute to the trip: a working car.

Layton lived up to his reputation of being something special on that very first venture. On the way down he had me apprehensive about the climb, describing it as a horrifying, rotten, overhanging cliff. This, as I grew to know him, was typical pre-climb talk. Also, as things turned out, the climb was a horrifying, rotten, overhanging cliff.

On one pitch, due to a shortage of Bong-Bongs, Layton was leapfrogging an A3/A4 crack a good way out from the belay, when both of his pins shifted. The rotten sandstone was pouring out under the pins as they creaked and groaned. Layton, terrified I'm sure, rammed a fist in the crack in the headwall. It was at least a 110-degree overhang. He hung there on one arm and beat the pitons until they finally sank in deep enough to hold his weight. So much for delicate nailing. That he had the guts and skill to do the pitch was truly amazing.

What I remember most from the trip though, which, when I think about it, brings a smile that can't be held back, was what happened in a pizza joint at which we stopped. We sat at a table adjacent to that of a stuffy couple with a young daughter, perhaps 3 years old. Layton looked at the little girl, put a finger in each corner of his mouth, drew it out as wide as possible, stuck out his tongue, and made as terrifying a face as he could muster. I choked on my pizza. The little girl's eyes grew wide. She screamed and pointed accusingly at our table. Naturally, when the concerned parents turned around we pretended nothing had happened and quietly continued our meal. As soon as their backs were turned, Layton repeated his performance. The little girl got the giggles this time and pointed again. When the parents looked, we, of course, played dumb again.

Perhaps because of his level of dynamic tension, climbing adventures with Kor were frequently characterized by a sense of imminent disaster. It spiced up the experience and gave all of us the feeling we wanted, perhaps needed: that of living on the edge. This, coupled with his convincing characterization of the cord of a tire on his old Ford bursting apart going through a corner on the way to Eldorado Canyon, was unnerving.

I recall gripping the door handle of his black Sunbeam Alpine once while in the middle of a "controlled" four-wheel drift on the North Rim of the Black Canyon. All the while Kor was talking about the seriousness of the upcoming climb. I was always relieved to get on the rock and quit thinking about it in the abstract. It was there that Kor could unleash all the drive and energy for which he was justly famous.

Layton seemed to enjoy everything about climbing, but I never saw him more gleeful than once in the Black Canyon. He, Dalke, Covington, and I were doing the left arête of the Painted Wall. We had started before dawn and soloed half of the climb, maybe 600 feet (across a few too many hard pitches for my taste—especially with a pack full of hardware, bivy gear, and food). Layton was enthralled with the climbing. I recall him saying, "Boy, if this group can't climb this route, no one can." Finally we bunched up below a hard pitch and broke out the ropes. In the moonlight near the end of the climb, even the darkness didn't slow him down. He was a climbing machine working perfectly. He ran the rope out, a 165-foot lead up a lovely slab, and yelled down, "Tie on another rope. I think I can make it!" We did, and he did. Just ran it out up to the rim. It was dream climbing. Layton, as well as the rest of us, reveled in the joy of climbing.

Layton Kor regularly climbed at the Garden of the Gods in the sixties, doing several first ascents including *Kor's Korner* on South Gateway Rock.
Photograph Stewart M. Green

As in my early climbing days, during later times I would periodically have difficulty finding partners and occasionally I would climb solo—on easy rock unroped, and on hard climbs using a self-protection system. I had a ⁵⁄₁₆-inch-diameter rope, which, when doubled, was 17 feet long. One end of this I would thread directly through the head of a piton. Ring pins were best because the ring was bigger and the rope would slide out more easily. As I climbed I would slide a prusik up the rope, the other end of which was tied to my waist in case the prusik failed. I deliberately kept the rope to 17 feet to limit any fall I might take. If I got more than 17 feet away from the piton, I would either have to unrope, or place another pin. When I reached a secure place, I would untie and pull the rope up and get ready to go again. I just wasn't prepared to take long falls soloing, for one would be the last.

At one time or another I returned and soloed most of the routes that I put up in Eldorado—*T2, The Naked Edge,* and others. I had very few problems with this system. Once, however, I was soloing the Third Buttress on Hallett Peak and the rope hung up. For most of the climb I wasn't tying in at all, only when I came to a hard spot. When the rope hung up I was high on the face. My 17-foot rope was threaded through a pin and I was struggling with a sequence of difficult moves. Then the rope snagged. With a struggle I untied one end of the loop from my waist, pulled some slack through, and, feeling desperate, somehow managed to make the remaining hard moves onto a ledge unprotected. I was very scared. It was an exposed position and I hadn't done a great deal of soloing at the time. So, the system had some limitations but generally it worked fine.

It was important in my early, more risky climbing years that I stay fit. Bouldering and weight lifting on alternate days gave me the needed strength to deal with the climbing lifestyle that I was becoming more and more involved in. Bouldering also helped me find an excellent climbing companion. On Flagstaff Mountain above Boulder is a popular practice climb called Cookie Jar Rock. One afternoon a climber who I had never met arrived. We sized each other up, started chatting, and eventually started climbing together. This was Bob Culp with whom I later went on to do new routes in Eldorado, the Black Canyon of the Gunnison, and the Northwest Face of Chiefshead. One climb that I did with Bob Culp, as he describes here, became first a popular direct aid classic, and then a popular free climb.

Layton Kor free climbs up a steep wall on the Redgarden Wall in the early sixties.
Photograph Layton Kor Collection

The Naked Edge

Bob Culp

In the summer of '62 the big plum in Eldorado was *The Naked Edge*. Following the knife-edged corner of Tower Two, the line dominated the canyon and promised to be the hardest route yet done there.

At that time there were enough possibilities for first ascents so that competition for new routes was not very intense. My eye had been on the climb, however, and when I heard others talking about it I quickly made plans.

On a sunny September afternoon, Jack Turner and I went up for a look. The first pitch went smoothly as expected to what we figured would be the crux pitch, the slab to the right of the sharpest part of the edge. It looked like hard free climbing without protection. To complicate matters, it seemed possible that a fall could drag the rope along the edge with disastrous results. After taking turns climbing up and down a few times, Jack and I retreated.

I was surprised the next day to see Layton Kor and Steve Komito rappelling from the same spot. Kor had climbed almost to the top of the slab and, not seeing any cracks above for protection, had downclimbed with great difficulty.

The following day, Stan Shepard was seen working on a variation to the slab which looked promising. He too backed off.

Layton called me and suggested that the two of us get together on the route before someone else climbed it. Next morning at dawn, laden with all the climbing gear we owned, we began third-classing *Redguard* to the base of the *Edge*.

Although we had the first pitch wired by then, it still demanded a few points of aid. On the second pitch we followed Stan's variation and Kor led a hard traverse across the top of the slab on RURPs driven into an incipient crack.

Modern day climbers might not fully appreciate Kor's ability as an aid climber. In the early sixties most of the big walls had yet to be climbed and they were widely regarded as the last great challenges. We felt that for big wall climbing, especially if it was to be done in remote settings, the emphasis had to be on speed. Direct aid accomplished this. Spending excessive amounts of time working out a few free moves was considered, in that context, bad style.

Kor stood out among fast climbers, not only at direct aid. His ability to do hard free climbing was legendary and all the more significant when one realized that he seldom paused while doing it. He also managed to climb the hardest aid pitches on the most marginal placements with the same emphasis on speed. Thanks mainly to his efforts, aid climbing in Eldorado in the sixties was developed to a level that has seldom been matched anywhere.

The thing that set Kor apart from other good climbers was his drive. He had a single-minded determination to get up a climb that rarely failed him. This inflexible will to succeed would have made him a standard setter in any generation.

We who knew Layton well at that time fully expected him to become one of the all-time greats of climbing along with our other storybook heroes. He was already one of America's most accomplished rock climbers, so we waited expectantly to hear of further Kor exploits as he moved into extreme alpine climbing—and we were not to be disappointed.

On the second pitch of *The Naked Edge* the traverse passed quickly but not before I had time to wonder how those absurd little RURPs driven straight up into a rotten seam of rock managed to hold our weight.

It was on that same traverse that a spectacular and unnerving incident happened several years later. Jim Logan and Wayne Goss, brilliant but inexperienced young climbers, were repeating the climb. Jim was leading and had moved out onto his second RURP, when his rope came untied and dropped from his swami. He was compelled to stand there for some minutes contemplating that solitary minuscule piton on which his life depended until Goss managed to third-class up to him and hand him back his rope.

The third pitch was a surprise—relatively easy free climbing. Partway up the fourth pitch we were forced back onto aid, and followed the left side of the *Edge*. Kor would later return to climb the overhanging crack just right of the edge, which would become the standard last pitch.

Kor's style of climbing seldom failed to evoke strong feelings from his partners. Almost always they were of respect, even awe. Occasionally they were of amusement. I have a very clear picture in my mind to this day of Kor aid climbing. Savagely rooting through his rack of gear (organized in ways apparent only to him), he seizes a piton, glares at it as if he has never seen it before, jams it into a crack, yanks his hammer up by its cord, catches it one-handed in mid-flight, beats the offending piton into submission with rapid jack-hammer blows, drops the hammer like a hot potato, clips in his etriers, threshes into the uppermost loop, and while teetering there in the most precarious and (one would think) tiring position, repeats the same process again and again without pausing.

Layton Kor aid climbs on one of the Roof routes on the Redgarden Wall.
Photograph Pat Ament/Layton Kor Collection

Kor was especially good at moving from aid to difficult free climbing. Seconding one of his mixed pitches could be a nightmare, hanging by fingernails trying to remove one of his "well-placed" pins. When Bonington followed Kor on a mixed free and aid pitch on the Harlin route on the Eiger, he frankly admitted later that he had never seen anyone climb at that level before.

Kor also had the ability to place his pitons further apart than any other living climber. Many a second found a Kor pitch virtually unclimbable without jumars because he couldn't begin to reach the placements.

The last pitch of the *Edge* passed uneventfully. Pleasant free climbing soon led to the summit with most of the day left.

We had expected the climb to be impressive. It had been. The exposure and beauty were greater than anything we had previously experienced in the canyon. Surprisingly, though, it had not been as hard as other routes we had already done in Eldorado.

Layton Kor and Charlie Roskoz made the second ascent of the 900-foot-high Diamond on Longs Peak in 1962 by climbing the first ascent of the *Yellow Wall*.
Photograph Stewart M. Green

2

HIGH MOUNTAINS

When faced with the question, "Where shall we go climbing today?" on those days when Eldorado was too hot, we would frequently head up to Rocky Mountain National Park. But that was only part of the decision, for this magnificent high mountain area offers endless possibilities. Longs Peak alone is an amphitheater of lovely granite offering a hundred lines. Then there are the buttresses of Hallett Peak, the Crags above Twin Sisters, the Twin Owls above Estes Park, Sundance Buttress, and countless other unnamed slabs and walls tucked into high mountain valleys. They were all readily accessible, waiting, and frequently unclimbed.

One thing was certain, the best experiences were usually first ascents, the feeling of heading up into unknown territory. More than anything else in my life up to that time, climbing, particularly first ascents, made me feel truly alive and it was always a letdown to descend and return to mundane day-to-day affairs.

In 1958 I met Ray Northcutt, who was certainly the most capable climber in the Boulder region at the time. Climbing with him in Eldorado Canyon that year, I accompanied him on an early attempt to free climb the direct start to the Bastille. Ray tried, and tried, but he just couldn't do the traverse at the top of the pitch free. Some time later, I heard that Stan Shepard fooled Northcutt by telling him that I had led it free a few days earlier, which wasn't true. It was just Shepard's way of getting Ray going. It worked apparently. Climbing at his limit, Ray led the pitch free, saying to himself, "If Kor can do it, so can I." This ascent was generally regarded as the first 5.10 free lead in the Boulder region, and gives a good indication of what a capable climber Northcutt was.

Ray worked hard at being physically fit. He'd run and do pull-ups every day reaching a point where he could do a hundred pull-ups in three sets of thirty-three. I didn't know anybody else at the time who worked out as intensely.

Northcutt's big dream was the *Diagonal* route on the lower East Face of Longs Peak. In those days the Park Service had put The Diamond off limits, but the *Diagonal* was allowed. Ray had been working with George Lamb on the route before I met him. Lamb dropped out and I became Northcutt's partner. We made one attempt in October 1958, but then it became too cold, and we ended up leaving fixed ropes on the wall though the winter. When we returned in 1959, the fixed ropes had been abraded by the wind. Northcutt hiked up to Broadway, rappelled down, and replaced them prior to our next attempt. To do this he had to place a rappel bolt in the middle of the wall, which is going to mystify some future climber.

Ray Northcutt leads a pitch on the first ascent of the *Diagonal* on the lower East Face of Longs Peak.

As soon as the weather improved in the spring we began work on the climb again.

Northcutt was a fast hiker, and would just kill me on the way up to the bottom of the wall. I'd pant after him, up the Longs Peak trail, past Chasm Lake, and arrive at the bottom of the *Diagonal* exhausted.

Previously Ray had fixed ropes up to a large narrow ledge called Gillette Ledge and they hung straight down from it. The weather that spring was terrible. We made three or four attempts. Each time we'd get partway up the wall, and each time a storm would come in and blast us off. It rained a lot that summer and the water would wash rocks down from

Broadway. We'd rappel down in high winds and snow and head back to Boulder to wait for the storm to clear. None of this deterred Northcutt in the least. He was totally committed to the climb and wanted it badly.

Generally the aid climbing on the *Diagonal* was not terribly hard. We swung leads, though Northcutt ended up leading more pitches than me. He was by far the more experienced climber at the time and I always felt comfortable when he was leading. He would never do anything foolish. Even though he wasn't the fastest climber in the world, he knew exactly what he was doing and was very sound. He'd get the job done safely, and wasn't about to fall off.

Ray had certain interesting ways of doing things. For example, he would rappel off only two wraps of thin alpine cord. He claimed they were strong enough to rappel from but I didn't trust them. Not wanting to start an argument, every time he would rappel down ahead of me I'd wait until he was off the ropes and then quickly put on three or four more wraps.

On the final day of the climb we cleared the overhangs about halfway up the wall and then we took off going as fast as we could for the top. About halfway up the face the nature of the rock changed. The cracks above looked foreboding. We reached a point where Northcutt spotted a line of holds and small ledges traversing right across the face. We discussed the two options and decided that the traverse looked more promising. We were partway across when another of the afternoon storms that had been plaguing us hit. Immediately the rock was awash with water and stones came bouncing down from Broadway. It was no place to be and we rappelled down and off the face just as fast as we could, leaving our ropes in place.

A couple of days later we returned and prusiked back up the ropes. Ray went first. However, rather than prusiking all the way back up to the high point he got off the fixed ropes about 40 feet lower down, on a small ledge, and placed two bolts for belay anchors. I prusiked up to join him on the ledge and we started climbing from there. [Editor's Note: This sequence of events was to confuse later parties. By rappelling the 40 feet between the retreat point and this belay ledge, Northcutt and Kor had missed out on a smooth holdless slab in the middle of the crucial traverse. Later parties, including Kamps and Rearick as well as Ament and Dalke had been unable to figure out how Northcutt and Kor had free climbed the smooth section.]

Ray climbed out across the traverse. I looked up and I could clearly see the soles of his feet edging on tiny flakes. In those days he wore tight klettershoes, so tight you could see his toes bulging out at the front. Looking up, all I could see were his soles. They'd scurry for a couple of moves. Stop. Scurry again. Just like a little mouse zipping across the wall. Then he shouted down, "I got it! I got it!" and he was across. This traverse was the key

The Northwest Face of Chiefshead.

part of the climb. It took us into the bottom of a big blocky corner, which led all the way up to Broadway. In the corner we used direct aid in places including some bolts and some wooden wedges. There was a good deal of bad rock and we pulled a fair amount down as we climbed. We reached Broadway by late afternoon without further trouble and then made good time descending.

The *Diagonal* was the most difficult and most serious high-mountain climb in Colorado at the time, and I counted myself fortunate to have been able to accompany Northcutt. I learned a great deal from him about technical rock climbing that was to stand me in good stead in the future. Had The Diamond not been off limits at that time, there is a good chance that Northcutt would have made the first ascent of it also. This was not to be and the *Diagonal* in 1959 was to be Northcutt's last major climb.

Northcutt, myself, and Dale Johnson actually had a long-standing arrangement that we would try for the first ascent of The Diamond if the Park Service ever opened it to climbers. In 1960, the rangers announced at short notice that qualified climbers could make application for The Diamond, and it transpired that Kamps and Rearick were in Colorado at the time ready to go. The announcement took me, Northcutt, and Johnson by surprise and we were not prepared. The first ascent permission was given to the Californians.

In 1961 the experience I had gained with Northcutt on the *Diagonal* was to be put to good use on the first ascent of two new routes on the North Face of Chiefshead: the Northwest Face with Bob Culp, and the Northeast Face with Bob Bradley. Prior to the Northwest Face ascent, I had been ill for some time with a respiratory infection. I had seen a number of doctors in Colorado and had already had one operation, which had not cured the problem. The doctors felt that the condition was serious and after the first unsuccessful operation wanted to perform a second one. The proposed second operation was to be exploratory surgery, rather than an operation aimed at curing the problem. After months of diagnostic attempts they seemed no closer to pinpointing what was wrong with me than they were at the start. At this point I decided to follow a different course. I knew of a health clinic in San Antonio, Texas, checked into it, and embarked on a long fast. The fast worked and I left the clinic skinny, but healthy again. The only long-term residual effect was a certain amount of scar tissue in my lungs.

Because of my respiratory problem, I was never interested in high altitude mountaineering in the Himalayas. It would have been foolish to think that I could have functioned in the rarified atmosphere of the big Himalayan peaks.

Shortly after I returned from the clinic in Texas, a great adventure was soon in the making. Some time earlier, from the vicinity of Hallett Peak, I had noticed far off in the distance a huge concave slab to the west of Longs Peak—the Northwest Face of Chiefshead. From such a long way away its steep, polished appearance raised the question, could it be climbed? It was a long hike into the face and I was still in weak condition from my fast, but Chiefshead beckoned and, as Bob Culp describes, the climb demanded a maximum effort.

NW Face of Chiefshead

Bob Culp

The Northwest Face of Chiefshead was one of the biggest unclimbed walls in Rocky Mountain National Park when Layton Kor pointed it out to me in the winter of 1960. Its remote location and forbidding appearance had discouraged attempts to climb it.

Kor was excited. "The best thing left in Colorado," he boasted. "It'll take everything we've got to get up it! It's got to be climbed!"

We prepared for the climb with uncharacteristic care. During the cold, snowy months, I sent away to the Dolt Hut for a collection of CCB pitons, which we thought might work better than the Simonds and Army angles we normally used. We made sporadic attempts to get into shape by climbing ropes in the CU field house and traversing the university buildings to strengthen our fingers. These sessions usually ended up with our searching the library for climbing books or photographs we might have missed.

One day at the gym we watched the wrestling team working out and Layton suggested we give it a try. After a few minutes of threshing about I was ready to call it quits but Kor was still raring to go. We were approached by the wrestlers, who seemed to be fascinated by the commotion we had caused. I waved them on to Kor. What followed was an incredible melee that left everyone rolling on the mats—those not actually wrestling were convulsed with laughter. They could do nothing with him! He had no wrestling experience but possessed an abundance of energy. I remember him frantically leaping about trying to dislodge a young man with a death grip on one of his long legs who gasped, "Just like trying to pin a giraffe!"

My first close-up view of the climb was not very encouraging. It was early June and the face was running with water. The wall loomed dark and ominous with smooth rock that seemed crackless. Kor had stayed behind at Black Lake to shake the last lingering effects of an illness and had sent me ahead with all the gear and instructions to take advantage of the light and pick out a good line. It was impossible to pick out a real line so I invented an imaginary one right up the center.

Next morning as we surveyed the climb, Kor's only comment was, "Looks good as any."

With some uncertainty I began climbing. Although there were seldom any cracks, the rock was fantastic and little holds seemed to sprout under my fingertips. The rope reached to a convenient ledge. The route above was uncertain, but that was Kor's problem for the moment.

Pausing just long enough to grab the hardware, he was off. He had completely shaken the previous day's lethargy and was impatient to get on with it. "Move your belay down to the end of the ledge," he shouted. "I'm gonna need all the rope I can get."

Somewhat reluctantly I untied from my anchor. By the time I had re-established the belay most of the rope had been taken up. "Good flake up here," I could hear him shouting as he banged in a pin. Clipping in a stirrup he leaned back for a view of the route above. "It's gonna go—it's gonna go!" I could hear him humming happily as he moved out of sight.

Seconding the pitch gave me a preview of what was in store above: consistently difficult climbing on good but small holds with little protection. One piton driven upside down under a flake had protected the lead.

As I approached him Kor began getting me ready for the next pitch. He always preferred to lead and had been known to psyche out his partners so he could get all the pitches. "You're gonna love the next

Bob Culp sits at a belay stance high on the Northwest Face of Chiefshead.

part." I could hear him gloating. "Perfectly smooth." "No holds at all." "You might get in some protection about 50 feet up." On and on.

As I started off it dawned upon me that his predictions were absolutely accurate. Reaching up at arm's length I was barely able to get fingertips on a small edge. Working my feet up on friction I pulled up. Above, about 6 inches farther than I could reach was another tiny nubbin. Maybe with a lunge? I decided against it and stepped back to consider other alternatives. There seemed to be none. Kor was getting restless. After all, we were wasting time with most of the wall above us. "OK, Layton, you give it a try," I relented.

Bob Culp seconds one of the long face climbing pitches on the Northwest Face of Chiefshead.

Moments later I was trying to get tied onto the belay anchor with Kor already halfway to my high point and climbing rapidly. Without hesitation he pulled up on the small edge, shot up an incredibly long arm to the high nubbin, and stepped neatly up. "Good holds up here," he remarked, as he began an upward traverse to the left that ran out the rope without a single piton.

Groaning inwardly, I cursed myself for not leading the pitch. At worst I would have faced a relatively short fall. Now if I came off I was in for a pendulum halfway across the wall. With clenched teeth and pounding heart I pulled up. The nubbin looked impossibly high, but from the extreme of a thumbtip mantle I was just able to reach it. It was good. I gradually calmed down before rejoining Kor.

"You're gonna love this next one," I could hear him beginning.

The climb progressed. Kor was a genius at routefinding. Or maybe he was uncommonly lucky. Perhaps it was just that he had the commitment to climb through whatever he encountered. Probably it was all three. At any rate, although the difficulties and uncertainties persisted, we were soon halfway up the wall. It was here that we encountered the crux.

It was Kor's lead. The rock above looked blank. Nothing new. He moved up a few feet and placed a shaky pin behind a small flake. "Probably ought to put in a bolt," he fretted, but decided against it when he thought he could see a small crack above. A few minutes later he had half the rope out and the crack was nonexistent. "This is serious up here," he shouted, "get ready. Get ready!" Standing on a ledge barely big enough for both feet and tied to a questionable anchor, I was in no mood to think of catching a 150-foot fall.

Layton Kor was a unique phenomenon. It has been my pleasure to climb with many superbly talented rock climbers but never, I think, with any who possessed the qualities of Kor. To be sure, some may have been technically better but none had the animal energy that would come bursting out to see him through the worst situations.

From my ledge I could see him spread-eagled above, finger and toe tips touching the rock. He rarely paused; just long enough to scan the rock above and then he was moving on. Such was his commitment that he was able to bring to bear the full focus of his immense drive without even entertaining the idea of retreating.

Eventually, came the dreaded words. "Sorry about this but the rope won't reach. You're gonna have to come up a ways."

It wasn't so bad on my end. The climbing was reasonable, but I knew Kor was in a difficult spot. If he came off while I was climbing? . . . "Oh, well," I tried to convince myself. "It's Layton. You're probably safer here than on the drive up."

Kor made it safely to a ledge. I followed what had been for him a totally unprotected and even unbelayed lead that may have been hard 5.9. "I really feel good today!" Kor chortled.

There was a lot more to come but nothing desperate. One false start high on the wall required Layton to climb down with me directing his feet to tiny holds. An apparently blank area that had us worried suddenly developed a perfect piton crack that ran to the end of the difficulties. By that time we hardly needed it.

We used three pitons for aid and placed three bolts for belay anchors in crackless rock. The famous CCB pitons had been of no use whatsoever.

We were met by our friend Huntley Ingalls, who had soloed the north ridge to take pictures. At the summit, in the fading light, we had one final surprise. Kor was hopping up and down in excitement. "Roberto, get up here! You've got to see this." There to the south was a great wall that neither of us had known about: the East Face of Mt. Alice. Kor lingered for the better part of a minute to enjoy the view. "Now that has got to be climbed," was his parting comment.

Layton Kor and Charlie Roskoz sort gear in the bivouac cave on Broadway below The Diamond in 1962.
Photograph Huntley Ingalls

In contrast to the Northwest Face, the Northeast Face of Chiefshead was an entirely different proposition: much easier. Bob Bradley and I hiked in to the face one morning, started climbing at one o'clock in the afternoon, bivouacked, and reached the top after only about 2 hours more climbing the next morning. The rock was excellent and the route was one of those nice, enjoyable climbs that I just loved to do.

By 1962 I had done a number of climbs in Rocky Mountain National Park, including new routes on Longs Peak. After Kamps and Rearick's first ascent of The Diamond in 1960, the wall awaited a second ascent. I examined the face, and worked out a new route possibility just to the left of the Kamps-Rearick route.

In those days the Park Service had a rigorous checkout system and permitting procedure before climbers were allowed to attempt The Diamond. Climbing gear had to be presented for inspection, and the climbing records of each member of the party had to be submitted to the rangers for approval. Additionally, we had to arrange for a support party, which also had to be approved by the rangers, in case anything went wrong.

The East Face of Longs Peak, scene of many Layton Kor first ascents, looms over Chasm Lake in Rocky Mountain National Park.
Photograph Stewart M. Green

Layton Kor leads up the *Yellow Wall* on The Diamond.
Photograph Charlie Roskoz/ Layton Kor Collection

We went through all the necessary steps and finally myself, Bob Culp, and Jim McCarthy were given a permit. The day finally arrived for the attempt—Saturday, August 11. Unfortunately Culp went down with a virus a couple of days prior, and on the day itself, McCarthy was sick too. It was frustrating. The weather was good, all the preparations were made, and my two partners were sick. So, I asked Charles Roskoz, a member of the support party, whom I had previously climbed with in Eldorado, if he was interested in trying The Diamond with me. I didn't have to talk him into it. With a big smile on his face he agreed without hesitation. His wife at home didn't even know he was climbing until she read it in the paper the next day.

The new route I had picked out started about 150 feet to the left of the Kamps-Rearick route, and followed a smoother buttress of yellow rock, suggesting the name the *Yellow Wall*. The rock was excellent but the crack system was not continuous, necessitating a number of traverses, and we pushed our way slowly upward to a point midway up the face. Unexpectedly, a piton on which I was standing gave way and instantly I started to drop. The next pin held and the expert hands of Charlie Roskoz held the fall.

"Gotcha, old man," said Roskoz, seemingly unperturbed.

Charlie Roskoz on
Broadway below
The Diamond.

A delicate traverse in the middle of the face requiring knifeblades and RURPs, warranting an A4 rating, led to a comfortable flat bivouac ledge. We relaxed for the night, roped in, gazing down at Chasm Lake from our airy perch.

The first rays of sun rising in the east hit The Diamond next morning and warmed us up. We welcomed it and soon felt ready to go, eager to be active and climbing again.

The next two pitches went smoothly. By eleven o'clock the sun left The Diamond and it became cold in the shade at that altitude.

Unexpectedly, a thunderstorm burst on the mountain and sent cold rivulets splashing down over us. Clipping into our anchors, we waited it out. After a few minutes it stopped, leaving the rocks wet and slippery.

It was one o'clock by the time we topped out on the summit of Longs. We had been on the wall for 28 hours, 19 of them spent climbing. We had carried expansion bolts but had not had to use them.

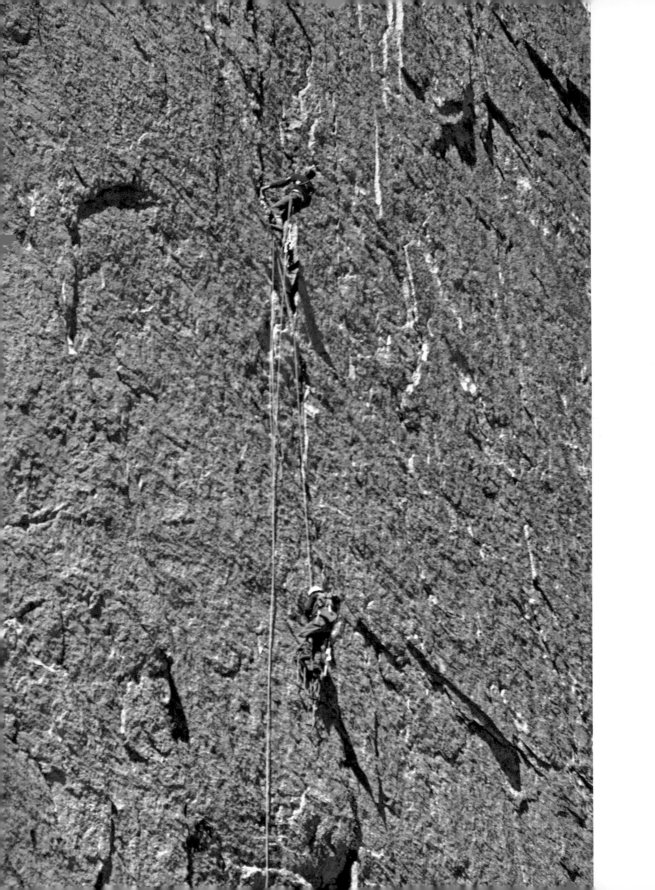

After the climb, Charlie was summoned to appear before the local US commissioner, accused of having climbed The Diamond without permission. He pleaded guilty and was assessed a small fine.

All in all the *Yellow Wall* was a fine climb in a wonderful location, on excellent rock. It was relatively straightforward and in retrospect was the most enjoyable climb I did on the East Face of Longs Peak.

The following year, 1963, I climbed The Diamond again twice, both times with Royal Robbins. I had made my first trip to Yosemite the previous fall, and had climbed the *Lost Arrow Chimney,* the *Steck-Salathé* on Sentinel, and the *Northwest Face* of Half Dome. In the process I had learned a lot about direct aid climbing, and had met Royal. His reputation preceded him and I knew of the many Yosemite Grade VI climbs that bore his name. Here was truly a master climber.

Royal had not climbed The Diamond before so now I was to have the opportunity of climbing with him on my home ground. Our goal was to climb The Diamond in a single day, repeating the Kamps-Rearick route, *D1.*

After bivouacking on Broadway, we were up at first light the next morning, working tremendously hard, climbing as fast as we could. Watching Royal leading direct aid, I was impressed by his speed. His piton hammer was a blur. Swinging leads, we gave it all we had and arrived at the top tired after a grueling 16-hour day.

Two days later we returned to The Diamond intent on a new route. We selected a crack system that started close to the start of *D1,* just left of the top of the North Chimney. Mainly the climb was a long, straightforward nail-up.

Partway up the wall I was leading an aid pitch when, without warning, a pin pulled. As I went flying backward in midair down the wall, a turn of the rope somehow wrapped itself around my thumb and went tight as my weight came on the rope. My thumb was painfully sore for the remainder of the climb.

Midway we encountered a 5.9 crack which was too shallow for pitons. It was Royal's lead and he jammed it. I watched him carefully and he was doing fine until close to the top. He reached a precarious position in a shallow trough, and I could see him struggling to place aid pitons to finish the pitch. When my turn came, I decided to lieback the crack, and it turned out that this was the easier way to do it for the second man. It was the hardest pitch I'd come across on The Diamond up to that time, and I was full of admiration for Royal's skill. As with our ascent of *D1,* we climbed this new route, which we called *Jack of Diamonds,* in a single day.

Climbing with Royal was inspirational. As his account of the climb tells, it seemed to bring out the best in both of us.

Charlie Roskoz belays Layton Kor high on the *Yellow Wall.*
Photograph Huntley Ingalls/Layton Kor Collection

Jack of Diamonds

Royal Robbins

Dear Bob, you asked me to reminisce a bit about the first ascent of *Jack of Diamonds,* which Layton Kor and I did in the summer of 1963. I remember that summer fondly. I was doing lots of climbing, was fit, and Liz and I had saved enough money to travel and climb as we pleased. I spent a lot of time around Boulder that year, making the most of the rich lode of climbing opportunities offered by the eastern Rockies. I climbed in Eldorado and Boulder Canyons, fell off Ament Routes on Flagstaff, couldn't get high enough to fall off Gill Routes in the marvelous Split Rocks, scraped skin on the Owls and Sundance, and came to grips with the prince of Colorado walls, The Diamond of Longs Peak.

It's a long but lovely walk up to Chasm Lake. I remember more the loveliness, at this distance, than the length. Embedded in my memory are pictures of the pines and twisted aspen, the fresh stream bubbling downward, the wildflowers, and, up high, the meadows and lakes. It has always been a wonder to me that the Colorado Rockies, which appear desolate, barren, and dry from a distance, can present to the visitor such an abundance of alps, wildflowers, lakes, and streams.

There were a number of parties camping in and about the stone shelter at Chasm Lake when Liz, Layton, and I arrived. We were ambitious to make the second ascent of *D1,* because of its reputation as a Yosemite wall in an alpine setting, and also simply because the Kamps-Rearick route was an elegant line up a stunning face. We were doubly ambitious, for we hoped to get up in a day.

I knew there was no one in the country, perhaps in the world, at that moment, with whom I stood a better chance of climbing The Diamond in one day than with Layton Kor. He was fast. Kor, in fact, had never developed the knack of climbing at any speed other than flat out. He was always in a hurry, and climbed every route, even the most trivial, as if he were racing a storm to the summit.

Climbing with Kor, one could not remain unaffected by his tumultuous energy. It was stressful, because to climb with him as an equal required that one function at the limit of one's abilities. Layton was ever alert to a weak moment, and perceiving one, would pounce with the ever-ready phrase, "Maybe I should take this lead?"

Layton was certainly highly competitive, and inwardly driven to make an impact upon climbing history. His list of first ascents of technically difficult rock climbs, both free and old, is perhaps unmatched by any American climber. But Kor was one of the very few highly competitive climbers who never criticized the efforts and achievements of others. He was interested in action, life, joking conversation, and plans for the next climb. In fact, although he never talked about religion, Kor was a sort of natural Christian, generous when others were wrong, and not in the habit of finding fault with his neighbor. There was one exception to this. I once heard Layton express scorn for a Coloradoan who had made a tasteless bolt route up one of Kor's favorite sandstone spires in the Utah desert.

During the afternoon of July 12, Layton and I left the shelter cabin and trod the fine brown granite along the south shore of Chasm Lake. We were soon on Mills Glacier and then followed Lambs Slide to Kieners Traverse, which brought us to North Broadway, and a several hundred foot descent to our bivouac at the base of The Diamond. It was comfortable, and our sleeping bags assured a good night's sleep.

Our ascent went smoothly, except for a 10-foot fall when Kor pulled an aid pin. The icy chute at the top of the wall provided interesting variety to what was otherwise a straightforward, if difficult, technical rock climb. That Rearick and Kamps had climbed this route with only four bolts was evidence not just of their technical competence, but even more of a stern, anti-bolt discipline, which had its roots in Yosemite climbing at that time; a discipline that, though occasionally violated, would later prevail in American mountaineering.

According to Bob Culp's prodigious memory, we did *D1* in 16 hours. Sounds about right. At any rate, we reached the refuge before dark.

After 2 days' rest, we were back on Broadway, this time by way of the 500-foot North Chimney. This approach was shorter, but not without its dangers. We climbed unroped with packs, and at times I felt we were engaged in a daring enterprise. There were several unpleasant passages, and at the top a steep section of loose rock. Layton swarmed up it, but I was thwarted by a hold out of reach. Kor, seeing my distress, lowered a vast paw which I gratefully clutched and used to reach safe ground. I excused myself with thoughts of a heavy pack and lack of reach, conveniently forgetting how often shorter climbers than I had managed stretches where I deemed a long arm essential. Hoping to avoid a bivouac, we started even earlier than we had on *D1*. I remember Kor swarming up the first pitch, pulling off a great block of loose rock, which crashed down the North Chimney.

One of the lovely things about an east face in the high mountains is that the morning sun so quickly takes the night chill from the air. For a while, everything seems warm, secure, and safe. Hard to imagine suffering from cold in such a place. Quite different from Yosemite, where the breezeless morning sun is an enemy. But mountain weather is ever fickle, partly because we are ever foolish, wanting to believe it is being nice just for us, when it is just one of her inconstant moods.

By noon, the winds were being rude and clouds swirled overhead. Now, to lead was a pleasure and to belay a cold hell. Not that either of us fiddled about on the leads. We were competing against each other, yes. After all, each of our lives was given to climbing, and we both wished to excel. In this sense each of us was an obstacle in the other's path, or so it seemed. In this sense we were competing—but our cooperation was far more important. Thus, it is off the mark to say we climbed The Diamond rapidly because we were competing. It is more accurate to say we climbed fast in spite of the running dog of competition that raced us to the summit.

The East Face of Longs Peak loses its benign aspect when the sun disappears westward. The wind brings numbing cold to fingers and cheeks, and snow whirls about. Discomfort is intensified when one is in a hanging belay, becoming impatient even with the speed of Layton Kor.

I quote from a note about the ascent that appeared in the 1964 *American Alpine Journal:* "Racing against the setting sun to avoid a bad night in slings, Kor led the last pitch, a long strenuous jam crack. On my last reserves I struggled up this final pitch, topped The Diamond, and shook the hand of a great climber."

It was a long walk down. Mile after mile through the night I paced steadily behind Kor, through the Boulder Field—which seemed an enormous area. Kor showed no signs of weakening, and I forced myself to thrust my legs forward, long strides trying to match his. I wouldn't weaken. I would keep up behind this natural force that wouldn't slow down. Aching feet, legs, back. Mind numbed, but there was the light of the shelter; crowded, sordid, smelly, but warm and welcoming. I well remember Liz, but, oddly, I can't recall booze. Ah, I have grown so sophisticated that I can't imagine a climb like that with a walk like that, not being followed by wine, as well as love.

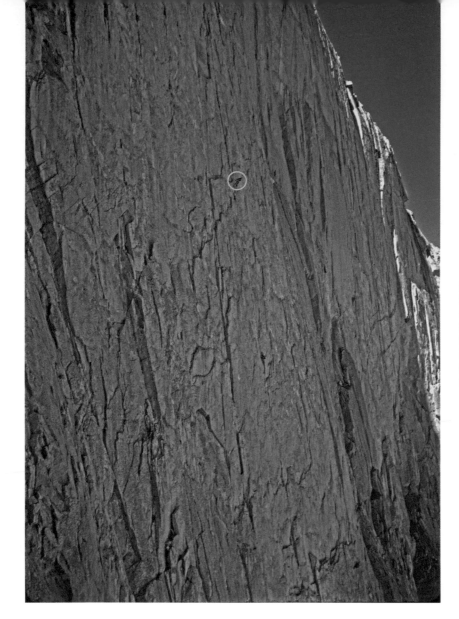

  In 1963 I returned to the East Face of Longs Peak with Tex Bossier. I felt dissatisfied that Northcutt and I had traversed out of the main crack line two-thirds of the way up the *Diagonal*. The direct continuation of the crack intrigued me and by 1963 I had a great deal more experience than when I climbed it with Northcutt. Just above the point where we had traversed, the crack narrows, and the wall banks up and gets steeper. I placed one bolt in a blank section, but the main problem was the weather. It was sleeting and snowing extremely hard. The snow would build up higher on the wall. Eventually, big sheets would slough off and smash into us. It was an adventure for both of us, and, as Tex Bossier tells, it turned into a fierce fight for survival.

Diagonal Direct

Tex Bossier

I had dropped out of school and had a job as a hod carrier working for Kor. He just loved to shout, "Hey, Mud." (I was supposed to bring the mortar, so my name was Mud.) We decided we were going to try the direct finish on the *Diagonal*. I had expected the thing to be tremendously difficult from its reputation, and we treated it as such. I was very apprehensive. We were using direct aid where we didn't need to in the lower sections, but there wasn't any really extreme climbing. We were climbing very fast.

Going over the overhang wasn't anything as bad as I had expected. I had all these horror visions in my mind. . . . It was a little bit messy because there was water coming down and we had to climb through it. One thing that slowed us down was bolt chopping. When Northcutt first climbed the *Diagonal,* the only pitons around were ex-army, and he placed a lot of bolts to make things secure. A lot of them were belay bolts. I was kind of irritated at Kor doing this. I just wanted to say, "Forget about the bolts, let's go!" He had "style" in his mind in those days. If a bolt was there and it wasn't supposed to be there, then you were supposed to get rid of it.

We got to where the traverse started. Didn't take us too long to get there. About 4 hours. We could have done it in 3 hours, had we been less cautious and not spent time bolt chopping. Right there, a storm came in. It started to rain. We talked about it, and under the circumstances it looked harder to do the traverse than to go straight up. We also thought it wasn't going to be that bad, and we didn't want to go down, but the nature of the climbing changed dramatically. The face became scooped out with boiler plate slabs, and the cracks were very shallow.

The storm was really getting bad. Rain was severe. We still thought we were better going up. We had a feeling about the difficulties of retreat and thought it was safer to continue. Water from the upper part of the wall was channeled down the crack system. It was coming down the rope and ending up in my swami belt, just like a water spout. I was freaked out. Then it started getting cold, but we were committed. It was getting later and later and we were making extremely slow progress. It started to turn into snow, and ice, and the wall started to freeze up. Fog also was coming down. Kor was off somewhere above, and we couldn't see each other. It was extremely cold by this time. I would go into uncontrollable shivering and cramps on the belays. I had the feeling that if we didn't get off the climb that day, I'd never be able to live through it.

It turned into a full-fledged, full-blown storm. There was a ranger with a telescope on Mt. Lady Washington, and he said it was a terrible storm. We just weren't prepared for the conditions. We didn't have any bivouac gear. We had down jackets, but they were completely soaked before the temperature dropped. We had no idea where we were in the fog. I have no idea how difficult the climbing really was. We were really scared. The conditions were so bad. In the guidebook they mention Kor getting knocked out of his stirrups by an avalanche. That's true. He was leading one of the scooped-out sections. I heard this hollering, and screaming, and cursing. "What's going on!" I shouted. We were enshrouded in fog and I couldn't see him. It just knocked him straight out of his stirrups, backward.

We started leaving pitons in place. We didn't even clean the last pitch of the climb. We just left everything. I kept thinking, "What's gonna happen if we get stuck? Who is there to come and rescue us?" We just had to keep going. I thought, "There's only one person in the whole of the United States who can get me off this climb, and I'm with him! If I get stuck, that's it."

Kor belayed me to Broadway. We got the pack up and were going to coil the haul rope. Part of it was over the edge, down the face, and it got stuck! Kor said, "To hell with it!" That was unprecedented. Never in my whole climbing career had I ever considered abandoning a rope . . . and all the pitons? I wasn't arguing though.

We started to traverse Broadway. There are some hairy spots on Broadway. I knew Kor was pressed. He led off on a traverse. There was freshly fallen snow over previous icy snow. He sank in up to his knee in the new snow. There was one steep place, fifty to sixty degrees. The ledge was very narrow, with The Diamond above you and that whole lower wall below. Kor nailed in a piton for a belay and said, "On belay." Crossing in his footsteps, I got about halfway across when some of the snow gave way and I half fell over backward. One leg stayed in the step. I was on my back with my head looking down the lower wall. The whole panorama of the face went by as I fell backward. I expected to go shooting off into space and take a horrible pendulum across to Kor. It was in slow motion. Everything was on film through my eyeballs. But one of my legs stayed. I got straight up and went over to Kor.

He's got one knifeblade in, that you could take out with your fingers! I was about 80 feet horizontal to him when I slipped. I said, "Oh, no, Layton. This thing would just never have held." "I know, I know," he said. He said that when he saw me fall over backward, his heart just went into his throat and he knew we were both dead. It wasn't as though he'd looked for the best belay. He just found the first place and stuck in a knifeblade. He knew it was inadequate, but that was the situation. I said, "Look, if the belays are going to be like this, should we stay roped?" "Yes," he said, "we stay roped."

"OK," I said, and we took off again, making our way over to Alexander's and Mills Glacier.

Obviously, we were in an emergency pressure situation, and we were not performing according to the accepted rules of climbing. This wasn't the "adrenaline rush" that people talk about in climbing. This was the constant pumping of adrenaline the whole time. "You gotta go, you gotta move. Time's running out." The feeling was that if you let down your guard in any way you just wouldn't make it. It was a momentous thing for me. I've never in my whole life had anything like that happen to me, before or since.

We got down to the shelter and the storm lasted for days. Next day we looked up and could see the wall. It was encased in ice. It was completely frozen over. If we'd been up there, we'd just have been frozen icicles along with everything else. I said to Kor afterwards, "I don't think I would have made it if we'd had to stay the night up there." Kor replied, "Yes, you would. You'd have made it if I had to stay up all night and beat on you with my hammer." But the way he said that, I also had the feeling that he didn't know for sure whether he would have made it or not.

Climbing wasn't always epics like the *Diagonal Direct* by any means. The majority of the time I climbed in good conditions, on sunny days. Two favorite places were Lumpy Ridge above Estes Park, and the Crags area on the Twin Sisters, also above Estes Park. The Crags in particular was such a pleasant place to climb. No pressure. It reminded me somewhat of the Dolomites, both the nature of the rock and the atmosphere.

During the early part of the sixties, I did a number of first ascents with Pat Ament: *The Wisdom, Canary Pass, Grandmother's Challenge, The Grand Course,* and *Exhibit A* in Eldorado Canyon. We also climbed together in the high mountains, and as Pat describes in the following account, made the first ascent of *Overhang Dihedral* on the lower East Face of Longs Peak together.

Pat Ament, one of Layton's regular climbing partners, holds a photograph of another rock idol, Bob Dylan.
Photograph Pat Ament Collection

41

Overhang Dihedral

Pat Ament

Layton was 8 years older than I and 8 inches taller. For every four steps he took, I took eight. In the sixties, Kor was looking for new climbs. He was a little bit like Mark Twain's "mysterious stranger," come to show a young soul certain mysteries of the world.

The dream was, for me at that time, delicately lifelike. Rock climbing was fresh and beautiful. It was dauntless confidence over a concealed crevasse, but there is something to be said for the wonder and impetuosity of those times.

There were many adventures with Layton. I could write about one as easily as another because the harsh stone was not the life. Rather it was Kor, molding a personal and living experience from solitary places. He ascended with strength and drive, with an alpine instinct for speed. Some climbs with Layton felt serious, threatening even. Occasionally he fell, but fate seemed always on his side.

Overhang Dihedral on Longs Peak was an unclimbed route Kor was keen on. We approached the face together, up the tiresome 5-mile trail and past Chasm Lake. The proposed route was a 600- or 700-foot straight line up a distinct left-facing dihedral. It was positioned directly beneath the magnificent wall of The Diamond. The dihedral formed a clear, aesthetically pleasing line. I think we envisioned free climbing the entire route, but clouds moved in and created a stir. A moderate but continuous rain fell. So we used whatever means—artificial or otherwise—to just get the route done.

There remain certain visual pictures . . . of the storm, the rock, the pitons, the diffused light. A dihedral is a very natural thing to climb in. Two planes of rock converge to form a protective inside corner. A crack can usually be found in the back of the corner for fingers, toes, or pitons. The exposure is less grim, and the elements don't seem to reach you as easily. We did, however, encounter several small rain waterfalls that found their course exactly in the dihedral. I recall an icy stream running into the sleeve of my shirt, through my pants, ending up in my shoe. Even Layton couldn't cope with the slippery rock. Therefore we began nailing—the happy out which enabled us to go almost anywhere when things began looking mildly desperate.

A few of Layton's pitons had that hollow dead sound as he hammered them into places that weren't really cracks. At one point, the dihedral presented a large overhang that extracted from us great struggles, while our climbing shoes slid around on the wet lichen. Higher, a severe roof taxed our creativities and shorted a few neurons. Kor applied his full weight to a meager RURP. I remember removing that same small piton with the most quiet tap of my hammer.

My thinking was, "It's looking a little bit thin in here." I also thought, as always, that Kor was eluding the probable and defying the fragile. His dimensions and magnitude as a physical being seemed in certain upward perspectives to dwarf the wall itself.

We inhabited that dihedral for only a few short hours. Apparently, we were the only climbers in the entire cirque of the East Face of Longs Peak. Our voices floated outward, gently ricocheting off small gendarmes of rock in the distance. The slightest pebble knocked loose went skipping and glancing downward, striking the snowfield below with a thump. There seemed a peculiar absence of incident, and the immense void aroused tranquility. Even the rain had a friendliness to it, sweeping in such a long, slow fall across and down the great rock face. The mountain was peaceful that day, through mist and gray. I saw Kor's jaw tighten and a stark intensity veil his stare. At the end of the dihedral, and after a handshake, we kicked steps across a steep, narrow snow chute. The smallest slip meant a fall over the wall we had climbed.

Overhang Dihedral **climbs the obvious large left-facing dihedral with double roofs directly below the sheer vertical face of The Diamond.**
Photograph Stewart M. Green

Kor had his madness in the sixties, but also serenity. I characterize him then as a bright and searching spirit, a sort of wild form, excited and unrestrained, usually moving, usually climbing, on rock or in life, but occasionally stopping to reflect. He had to make allowance for one such as I who occasionally crashed through into personal disorientation. We had a strong connection, companions on a rope in rain and emptiness.

The East Face of Longs Peak was a wonderful high-mountain climbing area, but I liked climbing on the North Face of Hallett Peak as much as anywhere else in the high mountains. Both the *Northcutt-Carter* and the *Jackson-Johnson* were very fine routes and I was to repeat them many times over the years, in fact so often that it seemed only natural to go there in the winter.

One clear winter morning saw Rick Tidrick and me heading up to the North Face of Hallett Peak. Above us was a beautiful sight, the buttresses of Hallett, 1,100 feet high. All three of the buttresses had been climbed—in summer.

Rick and I were planning to try the first winter ascent of the Second Buttress. From Bear Lake we hiked steadily for 2½ hours, the last half hour consisting of kicking steps in the hard snow directly below the face.

Under normal conditions the first two rope lengths are pure fun. In winter we were faced with severe climbing because of the snow-covered ledges and low temperatures.

About a hundred feet up, a narrow sliver of a ledge crossed the face to the right, and an 8-inch covering of snow made the going tricky. Time had to be devoted every few feet to warming our hands. Overhead, a 120-foot moss-covered crack pointed the way.

We both climbed as fast as our cold hands allowed and gained height rapidly. Three rope lengths more put us at the base of a yellow buttress, a tremendous 300-foot flake leaning against the main wall. A combination of good holds and steep rock made this section very enjoyable.

The last 15 feet of the next lead were overhanging and called for everything I had, taking us to a large platform. Two hundred feet above us was the summit; in between, the hardest lead of the climb.

The next overhang stopped me cold just a few feet from the belay ledge. Hammering a piton in under the overhang, I clipped several carabiners in and leaned back almost horizontally.

Stretching upward to my limit, just a few inches more were needed. Abruptly, the piton detached from the rock and I found myself 15 feet lower, upside down and speechless. The overhanging rock and a perfect belay from Rick had saved me from injury. Without hesitation, I placed an expansion bolt where the piton had failed and was soon on the stance.

Two small overhangs, the final chimney, and we stood on the snow-covered rocks of the summit. The ascent, though very cold, had taken us only 5½ hours. Food and water, a little rest, and the fact that we had done the first winter ascent made it a perfect day.

During the early and mid-sixties I made trips to various mountain areas outside Colorado. One of these trips was to the Wind Rivers with Fred Beckey, one of the most knowledgeable and experienced climbers I was to spend time in the mountains with. Beckey's climbing was prolific. He seemed to have an inexhaustible supply of energy, constantly

Many of Layton Kor's climbing adventures were up the Second and Third Buttresses of Hallett Peak.

Photograph Stewart M. Green

travelling from Alaska to the Desert Southwest, relieving the different climbing areas of their first ascents. I think that there must secretly have been at least two or three Fred Beckeys circulating in the mountains for surely no one person could accomplish so much? As Beckey describes in the following account, our climbing trip into the Wind Rivers was to result in a close call.

Musembeah

Fred Beckey

Layton and I were involved in a number of climbing exploits in the sixties. We not only had common zealous climbing ambitions, but we were prone to a distaste for a life filled with hollow ennui. The vicissitudes of nature compelled us not only to seek rocks and mountains in varying seasons, but also in varying ranges.

Layton had a host of secrets in the mountains—most of them only of interest to the climber afflicted with the odd desire to be the first human atop an eroded chunk of landscape, sculpted by wind and water into slender shape.

Layton and I sometimes competed in minor ways, but we struck it off in companionship and our zeal for climbing problems. I sensed him to be a bit eccentric and peripatetic (not the type of individual who would be prone to conform to the tight office procedures and rules of labor in an insurance company), but so was I.

The Wind River Range provided gripping realities on sight during a visit in 1962. Many peaks with names on the map—Bonneville, Raid, Hooker—caught our attention, but one that was not on the map stuck in our minds. It reared just east of Baptiste Lake, and, according to the book, its name was Musembeah—a Shoshone term for mountain sheep. Unlike Hooker, with its sheer north wall and flat summit, Musembeah was craggy and distinct among the important peaks in sight. It had a marvelous west buttress that climbers would have to call a classic in any land. That buttress began to take importance in our minds but was not to be ours that year.

Layton and I returned to the range in September of 1963, with the wall of Hooker and the buttress of Musembeah in mind. Finding a schoolteacher who moonlighted in pack trips, we hiked rapidly up the rough trail from Dickinson Park, whenever possible hanging onto the tail of a horse. The pace was fast and the air cold. It was nice not to carry a heavy pack laden with pitons and rope.

Next day clouds threatened snow and we wondered if we had enough pitons and bolts for the great wall of Hooker. Touching its north-facing rock we found it cold and unfriendly and thin cracks suggested slow progress, not an inviting prospect under the rapidly blowing clouds. Our attention moved to Musembeah's great west buttress. It was an alpine marvel, cast into prominence by frost shattering and erosion of weaker rock on its flanks. The buttress faced the afternoon sun, an advantage over Hooker, and it seemed sufficiently broken to perhaps be climbed in one long day. Routefinding was no problem; what way there was lay along the crest, for the flanks fell away sheer. Layton and I agreed that this challenge would be our goal, but that we would spend a day or so on warm-up climbs (hoping it would warm up). We scrambled and climbed the west face of Musembeah's lesser north peak, an ascent that gave us the opportunity to study our nearby goal, soaring on our right.

It seemed that Layton and I became closer friends as we enthused passionately about the beauty of the buttress, its elegance of formation, and its prize from the climbing standpoint. There would be no gallery to watch, as perhaps in Eldorado Canyon, but the presence of others was not desired. We wanted the solitude of the high mountains, a quiet contest between the two of us working as a team and one of nature's loveliest alpine sculptures. I felt the power of Layton's mind and I think he understood my determination.

Early in the morning we stood at the base of our coveted objective wearing rock shoes, carrying a rack of some twenty-five pitons and two ropes. Our pack was small, for we wanted to move fast (Layton's usual style) and did not think we would have much time to relax, or eat a heavy lunch.

The buttress rose into the sky above us, its features becoming flawless with height. As a climbing problem it seemed baffling, yet broken spots and disconnected cracks suggested that a route might be found. At first the pitches went well, being, perhaps, of middle fifth-class rating. We shared leads, the leader carrying the rock and the second, the pack. The sun was behind the mountain but the wind was not. I remember wearing finger gloves during the belays and putting in or letting out the rope with gusto to stimulate the circulation.

The buttress was often devoid of cracks near its crest, but sufficient holds appeared in the gneiss. The climbing was magical: tiny holds for fingertips and shoe edges, occasional finger cracks, and belay ledges when needed. The climbing became more difficult and exposed, but the route continued. Sometimes we pondered taking to the flanks, but this would take us off an elegant line, and regaining the crest higher up might be impossible.

Swirls of migmatitic rock faded far above into a steep crown seemingly overhead. The buttress had been steep to this point but above the angle reached the vertical. There was hope, for cracks could be detected with the eye. Meanwhile, the wind had increased and the expected sun had not materialized because of rapidly thickening clouds. The white layers thickened and darkened as I completed what seemed a particularly difficult lead. Layton continued from a hanging belay, groping his way up the steepening route, alternately cursing the individual difficulties and exclaiming delight at the individual problems. At times I could not hear him over the wind's shriek, but could always see his progress. Then came my turn. Another relentless pitch, with still no end in sight. It began to rain and tension built. Quickly the rock became slimy and colder than ever.

At the belay point we discussed the need for urgent conclusion of the climb, for it was late in the afternoon and we had no bivouac gear. It was apparent that soon we would be soaked. We were beyond the point of no return for that ebbing day and did not even discuss the possibility of rappelling off.

The holds were soaked and Layton was getting wetter as he struggled with a crack that would have been continuous 5.8 when dry. Exhibiting marvelous control and stamina he kept moving, using finger and toe jams with finesse to gain height. For some distance he could not rest to place a piton. By the time Layton completed the lead and anchored safely the situation was as miserable as any I have seen on a rock wall. We were both doused and the rain was turning to sleet. Fortunately, the sheer buttress broke into steps at this point.

The route led into a depression on the left, and, after more belaying, we carried coils and third-classed through broken rocks toward the summit crest. Musembeah was no tabletop, but a complicated crown of angular ridges and parapets converging at the highest point. Clouds engulfed us and the rain-sleet pelted hard. Fortunately our earlier climb of the north summit clarified the descent. We spent only seconds on the summit and beat a hasty retreat.

The rock was dangerous in its soaked condition, but we were confident and elated at success in the face of a serious situation.

That evening at dark, so wet we could barely move, we collapsed at our campsite, found some kindling still dry under the green pine needles, and managed to get some external heat. The rewards of companionship shone through our shivering talk as we huddled over the friendly flames. We needed to dry out—not readily possible until the next day—then escape from the Wind River country, for winter was arriving early.

The sheer Southeast Face of Mount Proboscis, in far northern Canada, was climbed in 1963 by a strong American party that included Layton Kor.

In 1963 Yvon Chouinard published his now-classic article in the *American Alpine Journal*, which concluded, "The future of Yosemite climbing lies not in Yosemite, but in using the new techniques in the great granite ranges of the world." That same year the American Alpine Club began a program of "vigorous encouragement of modern technical climbing in North America." Jim McCarthy was asked by the AAC "to pick an objective that you feel will contribute something to the development of American climbing, gather the strongest group of technical climbers available to do the job, and the AAC will back the venture." McCarthy selected the Southeast Face of Mount Proboscis in the Cirque of the Unclimbables in the Logan Mountains of the Northwest Territories of Canada—an enormous face in a remote location. The team comprised McCarthy, Royal Robbins, Dick McCracken, and myself, and, as McCarthy's account tells, was to result in the first Yosemite-style Grade VI on such a remote mountain face.

Proboscis

Jim McCarthy

It's hard to believe that it was almost 20 years ago. Some of the memories are vivid, even now. I had dreamed up an ambitious project and had obtained the backing of the American Alpine Club. Carl Fuller, then president of the club, had inquired as to how the AAC could support mainstream climbing and I had suggested that it might be interesting for the club to back a venture into some remote area that would involve highly technical climbing. Such ventures were practically unknown in those days. At that time the best American climbers were busily exploring the big walls of Yosemite. Chouinard had suggested, in a prophetic article in the *American Alpine Journal,* that the next logical step was to employ the techniques of Yosemite climbing in the far mountain ranges. I agreed and went about assembling the strongest group I could. The most obvious person to choose for such a venture was the leading American climber of that era, Royal Robbins. Royal asked if he could be accompanied by his friend Richard McCracken, another outstanding climber. I chose Layton Kor.

I remember my first meeting with Layton as clearly as if it were yesterday. It happened a couple of years before Proboscis in the Shawangunks. It was in the fall and I had enjoyed a good day of climbing in the Gunks on a Saturday. That evening I retired, as was my custom in those days, to one of the local pubs. The place was crowded and one of the locals approached me and told me that there was a visitor. I was introduced to a most unusual fellow. Tall, gangling, seemingly awkward, Layton interrupted a massive dinner to say hello. It appeared that he had just returned from a brief trip to Europe.

When he returned to New York City from Europe, Layton located the Shawangunks on a map and proceeded to hitchhike to the area. Having no place to sleep, he promptly passed the night in a friendly ditch. When I first met him, Layton was working on his second plate of roast chicken accompanied by as many bowls of ice cream as were obtainable and occasionally slaking his thirst with a pitcher or two of beer.

All of this was impressive, but not nearly as impressive as the next day when I actually saw him climb.

In the spirit of friendly camaraderie I immediately took Layton off onto the hardest climbs that I was capable of doing at the time in the Gunks. Not only did he not fall off, he flew up everything with amazing speed. None of us had ever seen a person climb as fast as Layton did. To this day I have seen few to equal his speed. It wasn't just the technical climbing. It was the sheer energy, the joy and the fun he had. We had a great time for several weekends; then Layton found his way back west to his home in Boulder. We kept in touch and I heard some of his adventures in the Valley. Layton was the first outsider to make a big impression on the Valley climbers, just as he had with us.

I knew I was going to have a lot of trouble with Proboscis. I had just finished taking the bar exam. I had figuratively dropped the pencil and climbed straight into my old Volkswagen. When I left, my preparation for such a climb was practically nonexistent. As I drove out to Colorado to meet the others in Boulder, Layton and Royal had done the first ascent of the *Jack of Diamonds* on the Longs Peak Diamond in a single day. McCracken and Robbins had recently completed two major new routes in the Valley. All three were certainly fit.

Arriving in Boulder I checked in with Steve Komito, who then as now, ran the local climbing hostel. The next few days were spent merrily assembling and sorting the gear that we would be taking as well as buying the food. Kor was short on patience for such details and spent a considerable amount

of the time in one of his favorite places, The Sink. Layton, in those days, was pretty fast company in a bar. A person could do himself physiological damage by staying with Kor in a bar for any extended period of time.

We had originally planned on using Layton's car along with my own. One look at the proposed vehicle convinced all of us that that was only asking for trouble. Therefore, we were forced to crowd into my aged Bug. I can visualize the scene now. A roof rack with some 700 pounds of gear. The interior with the back-seat removed. Layton, all 6'5" of him curled up in the back. Royal, about 5'11", squashed in. Dick McCracken, about 6', also squashed in. In addition to the writer we also took along Liz, Royal's wife, who was headed for the Tetons. Most of the local climbing establishment gathered to watch us depart. It must have been a comical sight. The Bug was so flattened that the wheels were almost sticking out sideways. Nonetheless, we managed to make it to the Tetons.

While resting in the Tetons for a day or so, Layton literally dragged me up to Disappointment, where he flashed *Satisfaction Buttress*. The crux pitch was rotten and involved a difficult traverse beneath a ceiling. Above was a comfortable belay ledge and the day was warm. Layton placed the anchors and settled in to bring me up. There was considerable rope drag and he drew the conclusion that I was resting or something, and proceeded to fall asleep! Eventually, after much screaming and cursing on my part, I managed to force him into consciousness and complete the pitch.

The rest of the trip to Watson Lake was a nightmare of constriction and flat tires. Fortunately, no major mechanical difficulties occurred and we reached our destination some 3 days later. We were able to load up and start for Glacier Lake the next day. In those days the Cirque of the Unclimbables was the essence of remoteness in the mountains. No one was there and we expected no one. A couple of days of thrashing found us in a meadow at the base of Mount Sir Harrison Smith in deteriorating weather. Dick and Royal had one tent and Layton and I shared another.

As we waited out several days of rain we discussed all sorts of things. Royal loved to tease Layton about his musical tastes. Layton loved rock 'n' roll. Royal loved Beethoven. After supper one evening in the rain, we returned to our tent and Layton turned to me and said, very seriously, that he didn't really mind being teased by Royal about his lack of musical taste. He felt it was okay because Royal and he were just the same—climbing dominated their lives.

Layton could also tease and had been unmerciful since we had left Boulder. He had purchased the latest in climbing technology from Sporthaus-Schuster in Munich, a small nylon net hammock. The three of us were constantly regaled by Layton on the terrors we would face standing up in a bivouac on a vertical wall, while he reclined in comfort. This ragging continued as we waited below the face of Proboscis.

Proboscis has a huge face that looks as if it were an ordinary mountain split in half. Due to the bad weather we waited several days scoping out the route and waiting for a clear spell. To me the route we chose looked awesome. It was a beautiful line, practically straight up, and it looked terribly difficult. Nonetheless, I had deferred to the vastly greater experience of my companions. Layton and Royal gazed at the route for hours. The more they looked, the easier it got. Midway up the wall there was an obvious break and we realized there would be ledges somewhere in the break. Above that the wall steepened. As Layton and Royal studied the route they decided that we would reach a bivouac ledge the first day.

The storm broke at mid-morning, so we started late. Royal and Dick took the first lead since we had agreed that they would lead until the midpoint of the climb. Layton and I had the job of hauling. This was before Royal invented the present hauling system. Layton had brought two pieces of leather about 12 inches wide and about 2 feet long. Nylon straps were grommetted to this and, presto chango, we had something that looked like a modern belay seat. However, he intended to use it somewhat differently. As we were jumaring, we placed the leather patch over our stomachs and hips and hung the huge hauling bags behind us.

Layton leads a traversing pitch into a big dihedral high on the Southeast Face of Mount Proboscis.

A perfect day on the summit of Proboscis after the successful ascent—Dick McCracken on the left, Layton Kor in the middle, and Jim McCarthy on the right.
Photograph Royal Robbins/Layton Kor Collection

Jumars were new in those days and I had the unpleasant experience of discovering that they had to be reversed on diagonal pitches. I discovered this on the very first hauling pitch as the second jumar popped off and all my weight, plus the bag, came on the first jumar, all to the accompaniment of high-pitched giggles from Layton.

Eventually Layton and I caught up with the lead pair. The obvious crack systems had dwindled and progress was slow, as the nailing became extremely difficult. As the subarctic evening came upon us we were only a few pitches off the ground and we were hung up, one above the other, in a vertical crack faced with a bivouac. Layton was just above me. Throughout the night his boots beat a constant tattoo on the rock just in front of my face, since he feared that his feet would freeze. The only thing that made the night tolerable was the thought that Layton had left his vaunted hammock at the base of the climb, and his moans echoed in our ears the whole, if short, night.

The next day Dick and Royal completed one beautiful pitch after another with skyhooks, RURPs, and very sophisticated nailing. That evening we reached the break that we had seen from below and located a decent bivouac ledge just below the next steep part of the wall. It snowed that night, but the wall was so steep it wasn't really a problem.

The next day it was our turn and the flame of Layton's energy burned bright. On our second pitch I was standing in etriers in a small alcove. As it happened, I was wearing a helmet. Layton moved around the corner, placed a couple of pitons, pulled a pin and came rocketing down. The force of the fall dragged my left hand through the carabiners and drove my head into the alcove with shattering force. Somehow I held on to stop the fall. Unfazed, Layton moved up as fast as he had come down. Somewhat the worse for wear, as I was, Layton and Royal teamed up, making short work of the rest of the climb. McCracken and I hauled all day. This time we bivouacked at the summit.

At dawn we started down. I still have a memory of Layton on the way down the ridge of Proboscis, almost dancing, his exuberance was so great.

3

SANDSTONE THRILLS

The crowds that inhabit Yosemite, Eldorado Canyon, and the Shawangunks are notice-able by their absence in the Four Corners canyon country of Utah, Colorado, Arizona, and New Mexico. As far as the eye can see—wind-lashed plains, huge mesas, and slen-der red pinnacles, nature's masterpieces in erosion, tantalize the climber. It is the massive

Layton Kor monkeys up the original pipes placed in 1911 by John Otto on the final pitch of Independence Monument in western Colorado.
Photograph Harvey T. Carter/Layton Kor Collection

detached spires—Totem Pole, Spider Rock, Cleopatra's Needle, the Standing Rock, and a host of other equally slender obelisks—that give desert climbing its unique character.

In the desert, seemingly barren expanses of sand are broken up by steep cliffs, narrow spectacular canyons, and eroded geologic relics, reminiscent of vistas we have come to associate with the Moon and Mars. Everything seems a little on the wild side at first. Strange initially, eerie even, it is an environment that grows on you. Its stillness, spaciousness, and fragile beauty eventually seem friendly. What at first seems like a dead environment is actually profusely alive—peopled with small animals, reptiles, and fragile desert flowers.

Desert rock assumes abstract geometric designs and the sandstone has its own special beauty. Its color ranges from white to red, to browns, purples, and burnished gold. Spires and grotesque formations cast harsh black shadows across the desert, the playground of such idiosyncratic pioneers as Mark Powell, Don Wilson, Jerry Gallwas, and other connoisseurs of the obscure.

Climbers anywhere have to be, by definition, a bit more masochistic than most; perhaps nowhere more so than in the desert. In his classic article "The View From Deadhorse Point," Chuck Pratt gives an eloquent description of the singular attractions of desert climbing.

"Why the desert should exert such a fascination on a handful of climbers is a mystery to those who are not attracted to it, for the climbs in the Four Corners, with a few remarkable exceptions, have little to recommend them. They are generally short—often requiring less time than the approaches. The rock at its best is brittle and rotten and at its worst is the consistency of wet sugar."

In Yosemite and Colorado in the sixties, first ascent plums hung ripe on the trees in well-tended and easily accessible orchards. In the desert labyrinths no such ease of access existed. The few individuals who roamed the region did so with all the zeal and optimism of miners seeking the Lost Dutchman.

The earliest explorations in the desert focused on Shiprock, the noted great volcanic plug of New Mexico. Attempted by the Colorado climbers Robert Ormes and Mel Griffiths four times, unsuccessfully, between 1936 and 1938, it was finally climbed by a party from California in 1939 consisting of Dave Brower, Bestor Robinson, Raffi Bedayn, and Johnny Dyer. Situated in a no man's land between the major climbing centers of California and Colorado, desert climbing in following years was to be characterized by the gentlemanly interstate rivalry that was a feature of the first ascent of Shiprock.

After Shiprock's first ascent, a lull of almost 20 years elapsed before the desert was to again see first ascents of major significance. While I was climbing in the Boulder region in the late fifties, rumors trickled in of daring and mysterious desert ascents by

Kor aids up the tricky second pitch of the *Long Dong* route on the Bell Tower in Colorado National Monument.

Photograph Harvey T. Carter/Layton Kor Collection

the California climbers Powell, Wilson, Gallwas, and Feuerer. They had carefully picked three outstanding pinnacles, Spider Rock, the Totem Pole, and Cleopatra's Needle. Spider Rock, they felt, was the longest, Cleopatra's the most dangerous, and the Totem Pole the most difficult. Their ascents of these pinnacles had laid the groundwork for others to follow and they had done an excellent job into the bargain. My interest was aroused and in 1960 I made my first tentative exploratory visit to the Four Corners area.

My first trip to the desert was in part due to the urging of the Colorado Springs climber Harvey T. Carter. He suggested that we spend the entire month of April climbing as many spires as time allowed. In those days quantity was certainly available.

Harvey had the most desert climbing experiences at the time. To add to that, he was a very strong individual, with a bulldog determination, coupled with a unique ability to handle soft sandstone in a gentle manner.

John Auld, the third member of our expedition, was also from Colorado Springs. Like Harvey, he too had been well trained on the soft sandstone pinnacles of the Garden of the Gods.

Harvey had done his homework well. He knew the desert and had carefully planned the hop, skip, and jump from one area to another.

Colorado National Monument near Grand Junction was our starting point and the first area to feel the wrath of our steel pitons.

Things went well for our little group and three first ascents followed. One of these, the Bell Tower (park name, Kissing Couple), was an excellent climb about 350 feet high, one of the few desert first ascents that I later repeated. We located the correct starting place and went to work.

We were immediately faced by a 120-foot artificial pitch close to the ground. In a very short time I was initiated into the mysteries of sandstone climbing, and gained knowledge that was to be useful on the many trips that were to follow.

On that first pitch a thin crack, ⅜ of an inch wide, split rock so soft that our ¾-inch angle pitons could be hammered into place with very little effort. Unfortunately, after the piton had been extracted a visible keyhole was left in the rock.

More so than anywhere else I have climbed, climbing on the desert spires has a particular nerve-racking fascination to it. In other areas I might do one climb after another on the same trip. Frequently, in the desert, nerves on edge, I would do one climb and then go home to recover. The rock is breathtakingly steep and rarely solid enough to allow one to feel secure. On any climb at any time a piton might shift, leaving you feeling jittery. It was correctly named, this rock of the desert, this "sand" stone—the soft stuff that our feet had walked on earlier but which we were now climbing on in its vertical solidified form. Unfortunately, the solidification process left something to be desired.

On the first ascent of the Bell Tower, these intricacies of the desert sandstone were new and strange to me. The best way to learn is by experience, however, and we persevered upward. The last pitch included a bottomless chimney, which we nicknamed "The Belfry," and soon we were gathered on the spacious summit platform—a happy threesome indeed.

A rappel and a long car ride took us to the Land of Our Dreams, Monument Valley, Utah, with its ocean of intriguing formations. What secrets would be revealed to us in its many hidden recesses and unexplored canyons?

Our first prize was a huge tower shaped like a slightly compressed beer barrel, which Harvey named "Shangri La." Strenuous free climbing via a series of cracks and dihedrals carried us upward to where the top was split by an enormous rotten cleft. We broke through to the summit saturated with dust, befitting three sandstone chimney sweeps with yet another first ascent in their pockets.

Pride invariably comes before the crash, and any delusions of grandeur we had been laboring under were soon shattered. A day or two later, after an ascent of the East Dike of the "Agathlan," we were back at the car, a short distance from the main highway, and noticed a vehicle approaching at high speed. Sand flew in all directions as it slid to a stop in front of us.

It was a Navajo patrol. It didn't take them very long to make an accurate assessment of our purpose in the area. Even though we were still miles away from our ultimate destination, they adroitly forestalled us and informed us that there was to be no climbing on the Totem Pole or Spider Rock. We had been slapped hard by the glove of Navajo authority. Spider Rock and the Totem Pole were the top climbs on our agenda, and for some time we had been keenly anticipating the prospect of attempting these classic routes. We were saddened and our plans were devastated.

Leaving Monument Valley, we headed in the direction of Gallup, New Mexico, in the hope of bagging Cleopatra's Needle, but that too eluded us. Deciding that there would be another day and another chance, we decided to temporarily desert the Desert. However, the sandstone had me under its spell and in the following decade I was to return time and time again to these strange formations.

In 1961, the year following my first explorations in Monument Valley, Huntley Ingalls persuaded me to go with him to check out some towers he had found near Moab, Utah, while working for the Geological Survey in Canyonlands. In a small, concentrated area Huntley proudly showed me the Fisher Towers, a conglomeration of gargoyle-like spires, and not far away an isolated pinnacle named Castleton Tower. We decided to attempt Castleton, a polished red marble pinnacle, and it is appropriate that as Huntley discovered it, he tell the story of the first ascent.

Castleton Tower

Huntley Ingalls

In the early sixties speed limits were high and gasoline cheap. We thought nothing of running over to Moab, or the San Juans, for a weekend where there were superb first ascents for the taking. The anticipation, excitement, and carefree nature of these adventures seemed the cutting edge of life.

The long rides with Kor were memorable and sometimes as wild as the climbs themselves. His noted energies were commonly taken out on the driving while holding forth at great length and in great detail about the climb ahead. His riotous driving style could be hard on his passengers, constantly pitching and lurching, rocking and rolling in their seats. Miraculously, there was never any worse damage on these epic drives than frayed nerves.

At calmer moments we would exchange adventure stories and discuss esoteric topics. Do animals have minds? What would it be like to land on the Moon? Climb the Eiger?

It was late afternoon when we arrived at Castleton Valley. Above us the 400-foot prism of Castleton Tower, topping a 1,000-foot-high ridge, dominated the valley. Dark, red, old, weathered, it looked eerie in the last rays of sunlight.

Next morning the desert was still and bright in the clear air. We had the valley, sparsely inhabited at the time, to ourselves. Late in the morning, trudging up the steep, loose slope, our excitement grew. This was not only an unclimbed tower, but a new area; nothing quite like the mystique of being the first to reach an untouched summit.

The base of the Tower was a surreal jumble of great red blocks and ledges. There was only one obvious route, a system of dihedrals on the south face. The first pitch was easy and we rapidly gained 100 feet. Excellent by desert standards, the rock was hard and reliable with sharp, clean edges. Then followed three taxing leads up cracks, chimneys, and dihedrals, which Layton led mainly free with a few points of aid, taking us to a point more than halfway up the Tower. It was mid-afternoon, the weather was unsettled, and it was already raining toward the La Sals. It looked as though the hardest part of the climb was just above us so we decided to rappel off, leaving the ropes in place, and finish the climb in better conditions next day.

Layton Kor used a bolt for aid on the off-width crack on the third pitch of his route up Castleton Tower.
Photograph Huntley Ingalls/Layton Kor Collection

Next morning we prusiked up the fixed lines to our high point and we were faced by the crux pitch: a foot-wide chimney about 70 feet high blocked by a large chockstone in a bulging section, which Kor bypassed on direct aid. Another 40 feet of chimneying led to a good ledge, from which moderate climbing led to the summit. The climb had been a marvelous combination of enjoyability and difficulty.

The summit view was magnificent, larger than life, immersing us in a spectacular landscape: the green and red Colorado River Valley to the north, the blue La Sal Mountains to the south, the nightmarish Fisher Towers to the east, the tranquil Castleton Valley and looming Porcupine Rim to the west, and nearby the uncanny Priest, Nuns, and Chapel. The first to stand on this summit, we were elated.

The *Kor-Ingalls Route*, first climbed in 1962 by Layton Kor and Huntley Ingalls, follows obvious cracks and corners up the south face of Castleton Tower.
Photograph Stewart M. Green

The first ascent of Castleton Tower was but one of many ascents that I did with Huntley Ingalls. The word which best describes Huntley in those days was "intrepid." The nature of his work prevented him from taking time off to climb regularly and condition himself. Yet, despite this, he was always willing at short notice to tie on the rope and involve himself in extreme climbing. On a number of occasions we were to team up and make the long trip following the sun to the Desert Southwest, one of our favorite climbing areas. Having left school with only an eleventh grade education, I appreciated Huntley's scholarly knowledge and the amount he knew about the environments in which we climbed. We were to spend a great deal of time together throughout the years and he came to be a special friend whom I could always rely on.

A few days after climbing Castleton Tower I met up with Fred Beckey to climb an interesting-looking pinnacle, named the Priest, close to Castleton. Beckey and I had planned to try it together, and when we arrived, Harvey and Ann Carter were already up to the chimney at the end of the first pitch on the west side of the spire. Renailing the first pitch, we started climbing after them, and caught up with them at the first belay, where we talked and eventually joined together as a team of four.

The Priest, a freestanding tower at the north end of The Rectory, is usually climbed up a wide chimney to airy crack climbing.
Photograph Stewart M. Green

The next pitch was a beautiful chimney giving 80 feet of consistent back and knee jamming. Sunlight filtered through, giving the chimney a burnished copper appearance. It took us to a small ledge at the base of a smooth, crackless wall requiring four bolts. Then, after a slab, a difficult overhang followed by a vertical wall for 35 feet led to the summit. Other parties who made a subsequent ascent said that the overhang was A4. Due to a lack of anything solid on top, to descend we had to wrap slings around blocks on the summit for anchors.

After the first ascents of Castleton Tower and the Priest, my liking for desert climbing was solidified, but rather than heading for further new ascents immediately, I was interested in repeating some of the classic Californian desert ascents. Located in Monument Valley, the Totem Pole is one of the great classic climbs of the desert. A 400-foot-high unbelievably slender pinnacle, steep on all sides, it prompted Steve Roper to describe it as

Layton Kor leads a thin aid crack on the
first pitch of the Priest.

Layton works up the wide chimney on the
second pitch of the Priest.

"a fearsome red shaft, so thin and precariously built that the thought of climbing it sends shudders through my body." From certain angles the top of the Totem Pole is thicker than the lower sections, giving it a dauntingly overhanging appearance.

The first ascent of the Totem Pole was made by the Californians Mark Powell, Don Wilson, Bill Feuerer, and Jerry Gallwas. The climbing was almost exclusively artificial and wide aluminum channel pitons (the forerunner of the Bong-Bong), made by Feuerer, were used extensively. They used fixed ropes most of the way up and on the final day the winds were so strong that they blew the prusikers halfway round the 40-foot-thick pinnacle. The final pitch was a blank headwall, requiring bolts. Powell and his party made the ascent in excellent style, resorting to bolts only when absolutely necessary.

At the time of my visit in November of 1962 with Rick Horn and John Auld, the Totem Pole had received a second ascent by Dave Rearick, TM Herbert, and Tom Condon. We hoped to make the third ascent.

Layton Kor nails out a roof on the Totem Pole, a sheer and slender spire in Monument Valley, a Navajo Tribal Park.

At the time of Powell's first ascent the Totem Pole was open to climbers, but by the time of our visit in 1961 a climbing ban had been imposed by the Navajos, and rangers patrolled the area to keep climbers out. I wanted to climb it very badly and, less concerned about matters of conscience in those days than I am today, we decided to ignore the ban and sneak in to do the climb.

We carefully parked Rick's Volkswagen around the back of the Totem Pole and started climbing very early the next morning.

The first day we fixed the first two pitches and descended. It was extremely cold and we stopped climbing mid-afternoon as the climb fell into shadow.

The next day we headed back up the fixed ropes and toward the summit. Partway up we reached a cave, which necessitated nailing out past the overhanging section. Rick said to me, "Kor, you're not going to hog all the leads on this climb." I said, "That's fine by me. It's nerve-racking. If you want to lead—great." Rick began leading. He placed the first piton, clipped his stirrup into it, stepped up, and the pin shifted, almost coming out. He let out a blood-curdling scream that echoed out until it was swallowed up by the desert silence. Rick climbed back down and I took over the lead.

Rick was a fine climbing companion, very dependable and trustworthy. He had a poetic side to his nature and was sensitive to the moods and subtleties of the climbing and our desert surroundings. Tremendously alive, he had that capacity to infuse the climbing endeavor with excitement and genuine enthusiasm.

A little way higher I looked out across the desert and saw a Navajo patrol heading toward the Totem Pole. The patrol came to a turnaround not far away, on the main road, certainly close enough to see us. I froze in a spread-eagled position. Fortunately I was wearing a red parka that blended with the color of the rock, and I just stayed as still as I could. There we were, playing Cops and Robbers in the middle of nowhere. Eventually, the patrol turned around and drove out without seeing us.

I had carried a big red apple in my pocket all the way up the climb. About three-quarters of the way up my parka snagged on a piton. The pocket tore, and the apple went sailing downward, smashing to pieces on a boulder at the base of the spire. The Totem Pole had eaten my lunch.

On the second to last pitch Powell had placed four bolts about 20 feet apart to the side of a crack, supplementing a number of poor piton placements. I was glad they were there. About 30 feet from the top this rotten crack system petered out. A short, scary traverse to the right led to a sling belay at the bottom of the summit block. Ten bolts in a row carried us to

Layton Kor and Rick Horn pose atop the Totem Pole in waning afternoon light.
Photograph John Auld/Layton Kor Collection

the tiny tower top, where John Auld surprised us by pulling a small bottle of wine out of his parka pocket. The Totem Pole was one of the most difficult and exciting things we had ever done, and in the fading desert light we drank a toast to a climb we would never forget.

The following year, 1962, was to be one of my best years in the desert. I was devoting more and more time to climbing, working only the minimum amount required to stay out of trouble financially. A major first ascent was the Titan in the Fisher Towers. This impressive tower, one of the largest of the desert spires, was also brought to my attention by Huntley Ingalls. Originally, Huntley had shown some of his spelunking slides to the National Geographic Society. He also showed them some desert slides and asked them if they would be interested in covering a first ascent. They looked at slides of Castleton Tower, and weren't interested, but they were interested in the Titan. With backing from *National Geographic,* we embarked for the first time on a climb with a profit motive as part of the agenda.

The Titan looked foreboding and we decided that a third climber would strengthen our chances. After some discussion we selected George Hurley, an easygoing, solid, and experienced climbing companion from Boulder with whom I had made the first ascent of the *Grand Giraffe* in Eldorado Canyon 2 years previously. The Titan was George's first taste of the delights of desert climbing, as described in his account of the ascent.

The Titan

George Hurley

Thinking back 21 years is not easy. Layton, Huntley Ingalls, and I climbed the Titan in the spring of 1962. I climbed it again 4 years later with TM Herbert and Tom Condon. The two ascents blur together even though Layton led all of the first ascent while we shared leads on the second.

But certain things remain distinct. For one thing, I, and probably all of Layton's partners, will always remember the drives to the distant climbs. Layton was as fast a driver as he was a climber and he was able to stay behind the wheel for long stretches. I was a wet blanket on these drives, pointing out speed limit signs, children or dogs near the road, anything to slow the pace.

Another sort of speed record was set in a bar when Layton, the Great American Don Juan, met and romanced a young woman on one of these whirlwind climbing trips.

Arriving at the Titan, we started the route with Layton standing on my shoulders to gain a ledge. From there he started aiding up the only crack in the north face. The crack was full of mud (solid, dried mud), but most of Layton's pin placements were firm. After 2 days of fixing ropes we had to stop because we had to wait for a *National Geographic* photographer, Barry Bishop, to be at the site for the final push. The high point after 2 days was at a step on the ridge, a level step blocked by a duck-shaped small gendarme, which we had to creep around on a downsloping ledge. Those gritty downsloping ledges scared me.

Layton Kor uses a hand drill to excavate a bolt hole high on the Titan in the Fisher Towers.
Photograph Huntley Ingalls/Layton Kor Collection

Layton Kor proudly holds a rack of homemade bolt hangers to use on the first ascent of the Titan in 1962.
Photograph Huntley Ingalls/Layton Kor Collection

George Hurley smears across the aptly named Duckwalk, while Layton keeps a watchful belay halfway up the Titan.
Photograph Huntley Ingalls/Layton Kor Collection

Four days later we again drove west from Boulder, this time to meet Barry Bishop at the airport in Grand Junction, Colorado. Once we had climbed past our high point we found a small bivouac ledge one short lead above the Duck Tower. Bishop had been photographing us on the lower leads and now he was off to Moab to rent a plane for use the following day.

Our bivouac was a bad one as desert bivouacs go. The wind was very strong. On the ground, my wife, Jean, had to use large stones to weigh down all the equipment. Huntley paced about on our tiny ledge looking distracted. When he finally went to sleep he unfortunately practiced his nighttime avocation of speechmaking. At one point in that long night he shouted: "Gentlemen, gentlemen, I must have your attention." He certainly had mine, but he was sound asleep.

On the final section of the summit tower, Layton had to drive bolts to get up approximately 100 feet of crackless rock. He was fast, and he spread out the bolts almost as far as he had the pitons. After the bolt ladder he nailed up a large crack in the overhanging summit layers of harder sandstone.

While Layton was getting up to the overhanging summit, Barry Bishop was flying around the tower taking photographs from a plane piloted by George Huber from Moab. The plane left before Layton gained the top. We knew they were going back to the airport to refuel.

We got to the summit and Layton quickly drilled the final bolt, this one to hold down a round screw-top metal fishing line box, which was to be the summit register. Then we waited. Barry had emphasized that it was important that he take an aerial photograph of us on the summit. That was to be the final picture in a planned *National Geographic* article (Nov 1962). So we waited . . . and grew nervous. We started talking about the difficulty and folly of mixing climbing and show business, about the possibility of another bivouac, about trying to descend in the dark, about an accident late in the day. We scared ourselves right off that tower without waiting for our glory picture.

Down one long rappel (ropes still in place), Barry Bishop and George Huber came flying back past the Titan in their Piper Cub. Barry leaned out of the plane and motioned that we should return to the top. We consulted quickly and decided we were downward bound. Glory is nice but we had been on the Titan too long. We made negative signals at Barry and disobeyed his emphatic upward-inspiring sign language.

Once down to our bivouac ledge we packed most of our hardware, our extra food and gear, into the shoddier packs and Layton threw them (with glee) off the ledge. Each pack exploded when it hit; pitons and prunes, slings and granola were instantly mixed and scattered over the desert floor. We later felt that this unseemly haste was probably not in good style, but by that time we were in full retreat.

In spite of the lack of a proper summit picture, *National Geographic* did publish the article, which Huntley wrote, paying him handsomely for it and his pictures. Huntley generously shared equally with Layton and me. We talked a bit about the ethics of being paid for climbing the Titan, and even in that golden age we thought it was a great idea.

Layton Kor, anchored below the Titan's summit caprock, belays George Hurley as he cleans pitons on the upper ridge.
Photograph Huntley Ingalls/Layton Kor Collection

Layton Kor and George Hurley relax on the sunny summit of the Titan.
Photograph Huntley Ingalls/ Layton Kor Collection

In 1962 I made a number of other serious first ascents in the desert, including the Mitten Thumb with Steve Komito. This spectacular pinnacle, located in Monument Val-

ley, presents a thin blade of rock some 400 feet high. The upper part of the wall becomes very flat and overhanging, and gives difficult climbing.

On the way down Steve's brand-new rope hung up in a crack. It was getting late and we didn't want to risk being benighted, so we had to cut it in half to get it down. Later I cut it up into short lengths to use for slings.

A particularly interesting experience in 1962 was the first ascent of the Standing Rock. One of the most remote of the desert spires, Standing Rock is reached by following an interminable dirt road that winds through the northern part of Canyonlands National Park. In his account of desert climbing in *Ascent* magazine, Steve Roper was to later describe the Standing Rock as one of the "most difficult and dangerous routes in the desert." Huntley Ingalls and Steve Komito accompanied me on this adventure. Komito was one of the noted figures in the Boulder climbing scene in those days. His big old house on University Avenue was temporary home and meeting place for both local climbers and those passing through from other areas. Steve's easygoing nature made him a fine climbing companion, and, as his following account of the first ascent of Standing Rock tells, he could be relied on for high spirits and a sense of humor in the face of adversity.

Steve Komito belays Layton Kor during the first ascent of Standing Rock in remote Monument Basin.
Photograph Huntley Ingalls/Layton Kor Collection

Standing Rock

Steve Komito

I met a traveler from an antique land
Who said: Two vast and trunkless legs of stone
Stand in the desert. Near them, on the sand, Half sunk, a shattered visage lies . . .

"Ozymandias"
Percy Bysshe Shelley

Even now I can still hear it, however muffled by the mists of time. That pitiless grinding of sandstone on steel causes an involuntary contraction of my abdomen.

It's the underside of my recently purchased station wagon dragging itself across a rut of slickrock on a meaningless joke of a road far from the comfortable haunts of men who know better than to drive a car like mine out into this unplayful sand pile high on the Colorado River Plateau.

I relinquished the helm of my little car to Layton when my will to go forward had faltered at the second incidence of high-centering, only a few miles off the paved highway from Moab. Kor had ended my whining protests by growling, "You don't think we're gonna turn back now that we're this close, do you?" I hoped weakly that we would, but resigned myself to sitting in back, gripping the seat as if I could somehow lift the rear wheels gently over the rows of ruts arrayed ahead of us like the sabers of an enemy host.

I sit thinking of how explorers since the dawn of humanity have ventured out into the unseen backsides of the earth with less information and more risk than we have, but how probably none of them was riding on such low clearance or such high monthly installments.

CRRUNCH!!

Layton's immense form is hunched over in the front seat holding the steering wheel like a wind-up toy. "Don't worry, Comici, we'll chip in and get your little car fixed after we get up Standing Rock and sell an article about it."

Oh, miserable wretch that I am! Not only do I have to endure this abrasive wandering in the wilderness, but I am committed to following Layton up a giant stack of sandstone plates in the event that we are unlucky enough to find what we are out here looking for.

The car wheezes up over yet another ridge that lies between the dry washes where the worst of the oil pan scraping has taken place. Was that the fiftieth dry wash since the end of the highway, or maybe was it the hundredth? I'm too numbed with grief to keep count any longer.

"COMICI!! THERE IT IS—STANDING ROCK!"

Could there ever have been such a wild surmise, even among the Spanish conquistadors who first sighted the Pacific from the coast of Panama? Just look at it! A chasm measureless to man cut through the high desert, and on its floor a pile of fantastic, crumbling, goblet-shaped spires. One tower stands apart from the rest and is truly awesome in its fragile, graceful proportions. The Standing Rock!

Layton is bubbling with joy at having beaten Harvey Carter to this hidden treasure house. Huntley Ingalls is raving about the "significant summit unique on the planet," and I'm wishing that it would maybe fall over now, so we wouldn't have to climb on it tomorrow.

This had seemed to promise such a fine, wild adventure when it was conceived in the safe womb of Boulder. There in an old *National Geographic* was the photo of an amazing sandstone tower somewhere in the Utah desert near Grandview Point. My youthful desires for conquest and glory had been kindled by Layton's enthusiasm for the project, so I readily volunteered myself, my car, and my all for Kor and country. Now, in the hushed presence of this somber monument I feel inadequate to the task and unworthy to put my hands upon it.

At that moment our reverie is broken by the sight of a dust trail coming up the frightful road we have just travelled. Layton is at once alarmed. "That's probably Carter coming to beat us to the climb. We'd better get our rope fixed on it first." He seizes the climbing gear from the car and with Huntley hurls himself down the gully that leads to the basin floor. I watch from the rim as he sprints across to the base and is several feet up the rock before Huntley arrives to take hold of his belay rope. For half an hour or so this lonely land echoes with the ringing of furiously hammered pitons. A rope hangs from the side of Standing Rock. Our claim has been filed.

The dust trail arrives in the form of a jeepload of tourists who seem as lost in this vastness as I. Did I know if this was the road to Grandview Point? I reply that I don't think this is the road to anywhere on earth where people ought to be going. The dust trail heads back out of the wilderness, I sit looking into the basin, feeling very small. A long shadow and a long Kor stretch across the sand by the now silent tower.

Next morning, the blinding dawn refuses to hold back any longer. Today Huntley gets to take photos, and I get to take out pitons. What is there in our cult of manhood that makes it so awful to admit to fear? As I shuffle in leaden klettershoes toward the start of the climb, I catch sight of a gigantic boulder leaning against the far side of the tower. Oh God, spare me! That's the summit block that has toppled off this rotten stack in some dreadful cataclysm of the past. I start thinking about how much more debris will lie half-buried in the sand at the base after our game has been played. In a moment of despair I wonder if we too might become part of that shattered litter.

A hail of stones signals the beginning of my tour of duty. Layton can't help knocking down pieces of this primordial smokestack in the process of getting on top of it. I take cover under one hand while the other holds obediently on to the belay rope. They told me that it would be too hot to wear a hard hat here. Right now I would accept even the shelter of a spittoon over my head.

Our leader is a man of intense emotional swings on a climb such as this. In addition to stones this morning, I am alternately bombarded by shrieks of despair and cries of relief as the rope winds slowly out of my sweaty, clenched palm and up into the still, dry air.

After hours of gloomy contemplation, I am summoned into the Great Beyond. "OK, Comici, c'mon up, and don't trust the pitons!"

Can any person of sound mind and body really believe that this thing is climbable? The bottom of Standing Rock appears to be composed of layers of Rye Krisp held in place by bands of moistened kitty litter. I leave the good, flat earth behind and mount to the sky on stirrups clipped into pitons, most of which I can remove behind me without the aid of my hammer.

Past the first bulge I can see the rope trailing up to Layton, who is pasted to the wall above me. Nothing that I can grasp is sound, including my reasons for being here. Maybe this antique land is better to look at than it is to touch.

Higher up, the rock becomes better, to the extent that the pitons now require one or two hammer blows for removal. As I draw closer to his stance, I am filled with admiration for Layton. There he is, as calmly at home on this vertical, crumbling nightmare as an old salt on the deck of a wildly pitching sailing ship. A mischievous colossus, he bestrides the arc of sky on a narrow shelf above my head and grins down between his legs. "Don't hang on the rope so much, Comici. These belay pins shift every time you do." A howl of delight rolls among the silent pillars as my face blanches white with fear beneath its red dust coating. My displays of terror are a never-ending source of amusement to this climbing jester.

Huntley Ingalls and Layton Kor stand on the small summit of Standing Rock.
Photograph Steve Komito/Layton Kor Collection

In the hazy peace of evening we rappel. The desert floor comes spinning up toward my out-stretched feet. Our ropes now hang about two-thirds of the way up Standing Rock, and tomorrow will surely bring an end to the campaign. As I try to gag down dinner I feel as though I have been overcoming this tower by absorbing it. There is red sand packed into every pore and orifice of my body. The thought of having to go back to play on that vertical sandbox tomorrow makes me nauseous. Fortunately it's Huntley's turn to clean the pitons. All I have to do is prusik up on their shaky anchors and dodge the rocks that bound downward in their wake!

Sleep begins to knit my raveled skein of cares and a gentle breeze blows through my matted hair, wafting my troubled thoughts high out over canyons and spires and dry washes and ruts where almost nothing lives, but where everything is alive.

The gentle breeze becomes a dust storm, and the dawn is filtered through a bank of clouds. It does not augur well for today's battle. Huntley is having difficulty ascending the fixed lines with the primitive prusik slings and stirrups that we employed on those early climbs. He too must endure the torrent of stones and shouts that whistle down from our tireless leader, already swinging high above our heads in his eagerness to finish it off.

Huntley, scholarly and withdrawn, provides a sharp contrast to the roguish bricklayer with whom he has shared a number of desert derring-dos. They are both single-minded about knocking off these towers, in Kor's words, " . . . not so much because they're there, but rather because they may not be there much longer."

"Start up the ropes, Comici! Let's get on top of this thing before the rain comes and washes it all away!" A peal of laughter cascades down from the two gargoyles peering down at me from high up on

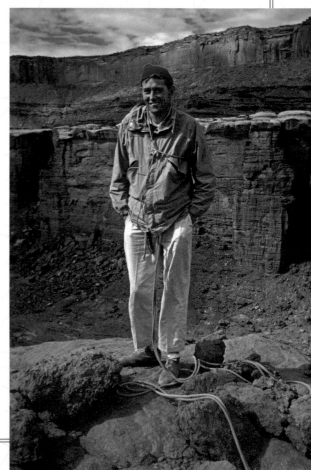

the tower. Deep inside me a solenoid is stuck and I can't get my engine started. "Uh . . . I'll wait 'til you guys get a little farther round, so I won't be under your rockfall." Besides, I need to get back from the tower a bit to get some photos of the lads way up there.

The wind is picking up and billowing the ropes and stirrups out from the wall. Huntley and Layton are shrieking at each other over the dusty blasts. The drama has taken on a surrealistic tone that makes me uncomfortable. I turn my back on Standing Rock and shuffle off across the shifting sands. After a bit I stop and look up again at the Spider and the Fly in their webs. They finally reach the top. I gaze downward to that massive shattered boulder (which used to be the top!) lying at the base. From a long hidden recess of my mind I hear the lines of a poem by Shelley that I was once compelled to memorize for a high school English class:

"My name is Ozymandias, king of kings: Look on my works, ye Mighty, and despair!" Nothing beside remains. Round the Decay

Of that colossal wreck, boundless and bare

The lone and level sands stretch far away.

A happy Layton Kor on Standing Rock's summit.
Photograph Huntley Ingalls/Layton Kor Collection

Another of Mark Powell's classic first ascents in the late fifties was a spectacular slender pinnacle south of Shiprock in northeastern New Mexico, named Cleopatra's Needle, about 200 feet high, which had repulsed myself, Harvey Carter, and John Auld on my first trip to the desert 2 years previously. Though relatively small, this spire had developed a terrifying reputation due to an expanding flake that didn't like pitons, and was composed of rock that was even softer than other desert rock—if this could be possible.

Three weeks after climbing Standing Rock I found myself heading south again in the company of Frank Magary, a university student from Boulder, intent on trying Cleo again. If successful it would be the third ascent. We were also keen to try the first ascent of Venus Needle, another improbable spire located in the same vicinity. It was to be Frank's first taste of desert climbing, and an exhilarating experience for him, as his account tells.

Layton Kor and Harvey Carter take stock while on a ledge at the end of the first pitch on a failed attempt to climb Cleopatra's Needle in 1961.
Photograph John Auld/ Layton Kor Collection

73

Cleopatra's Needle

Frank Magary

In the early sixties Chouinard published his famous tract announcing the imminent swarming forth of Yosemite's climbers to scale the great faces of the world. Only in Yosemite, it was judged, could an alpinist hone his perseverance, technique, and ethics to a sufficient gloss. In 1962 Kor was not yet one of the elect. He was still combing the ranks of middling climbers to find partners. Eventually he got to me and I was asked to join him that November to climb Venus Needle and Cleopatra's Needle.

At the time I had little notion of what it would be like to be involved in the kind of enterprise that resulted in Significant Ascents. Behind me lay several years of jolly, sociable ascents of mossy New England crags, a few mixed snow-and-rock climbs, and endless warm, amiable afternoons in Eldorado Canyon climbing 5.6 with girlfriends. It was unseemly, I thought, to be obsessive about the business of climbing.

Kor's version was another kind of alpinism. As I sat low in the well-decayed upholstery of his old Ford, watching the phone poles flit by in the Utah night, Kor kept up an unnerving monologue on the sufferings entailed in the early Californian ascents of Totem Pole and Spider Rock; the treachery of sandstone in general; the unknown intentions of Indians who might be lurking nearby; and, of course, Pratt's famous story of how the wind, rattling the fixed ropes on Cleopatra's Needle, had actually shaken the pitons out of the rock. Kor's mastery of detail was absolute. He was a scholar of adversity, of hunger, danger, and thirst.

Hunched over the wheel, Layton told me about his preparations. He had brought along several bags of apples, our main diet for the climbs. We had to hurry; unspecified persons, perhaps from Yosemite, would flap in on leathery wings to steal the ascent away. Venus Needle was unclimbed, one of the few "significant" technical-on-all-sides summits left. Cleo had already fallen to the Californians, but it was a classic, an obligatory stop for anyone intent on mastering the worst of the Desert.

A webwork of roads made by Navajo pickups threaded among the spectral, tottering forms of pinnacles, mysterious by moonlight. The way was obscure but Kor seemed to have done his homework: He went directly to the base of Cleopatra's. We juddered to a stop, confronting the column. The moon was down, and, seen edge on, Cleo's was so narrow it eclipsed very few stars. Kor finished his monologue. Cleopatra's was the most dangerous spire in the desert. We would climb it in the morning and then on to Venus Needle to find out which superlative characterized it.

By morning light Cleo looked barely more probable than it had the night before. Kor sorted hardware, I ate apples, the pieces sticking in my throat. Cleo rose clean from the ground as though it had grown there; no talus, no pedestal, only one faint crack system: the perfect technical rock problem stripped of all other considerations. If Kor fell and I did not hold him he would land, free of the rock, right on the sleeping bag on which I now lay eating apples.

I received a short homily on the need for good rope work. He would climb and I would follow and pull hardware. The style of following was irrelevant. Flakes the size of grand pianos might part company with the rock. Sand and small rocks were sure to sift down blinding the belayer. He, Kor, could easily zipper out the best-placed pins. The cracks were full of ill-assorted sediments and most parts of the rock had the texture of rotten sugar. In short, we faced the whole panoply of horrors as recounted in the ravings of the pioneer Californians, Powell, Feuerer, and Pratt. No elegantly simplified Yosemite rope work for us either; two-rope tension was the method. Kor's fate as he hung in his etriers was to depend on my ability to apply, in turn, slack or tension to two identical dirty ropes.

Kor started up. He climbed the first 50 feet or so free and set up a belay. With a few impatient pulls he had me up beside him—a disconcerting experience for one who was used to climbing with equals rather than as token second man.

The second lead began vertically, then inclined inexorably well beyond that. Kor's minute-by-minute predictions of destruction sifted down with the sand as he carried on a desperate, Sisyphean struggle with sugary rock, with expanding flakes, with pitons tight at one blow, loose with the next. Occasionally came a scream of despair when one rope (or was it the other?) was not stacked off or tightened at the apposite moment. Finally, Kor gained a belay ledge on the summit block. More bellows and lusty tugs on the rope as I came up trying to dislodge the hardware that squirmed under my hammer blows, deeply recessed in cracks. We would need every pin for the deadly struggle with Venus in the morning. I reached the summit block and there was Kor, smiling, tired, drained. In a good humor we rappelled off and drove out to Gallup for a steak.

It was colder on the second morning. Venus Needle was fluted with three summits and one great dihedral up its front face. At 250 feet, it was a bit higher than Cleo. A legend that Kor had unearthed said that the summit had been a test of marksmanship for ancient warriors. The objective was to shoot an arrow that would land neatly on the summit—just—without sliding off.

The first pitch went quickly and well; a 5.8 scrabble up a dirty crack. When I gained the rather nice belay stance, Kor launched himself at the final 130-foot dihedral. Dirt and sand rained down as he turned the first overhang. Then there were only muted sound effects. Occasionally he made himself understood. I was putting tension on the wrong rope. We were both going to die.

Finally it was over. I climbed up to find Kor wedged in a cleft separating the summits. The highest summit was anticlimactic—no arrows. Two Navajos who had been silently watching us climbed into their pickup and drove away. Layton and I, spent, the intensity and the fear dispelled, roped down, got in the Ford, and drove back to Boulder.

Layton Kor climbs Cleopatra's Needle, a fearsomely thin sandstone spire in western New Mexico.
Photograph Layton Kor Collection

Kor's route up Steamboat Rock ascends its steep east face above the Green River and Echo Park.
Photograph Stewart M. Green

The bulk of my climbing in the desert was on the spires and pinnacles. Steamboat Rock in Dinosaur National Monument, with Mike Covington and Brian Marts in 1965, was an exception. Steamboat was no pinnacle—it was a wall. The climb followed a single straight crack system for some 700 overhanging feet. It turned out to be an extremely difficult and risky climb. Mike Covington had been working in Steamboat Springs and discovered the climb, and tells the story of the first ascent.

Steamboat Rock

Michael Covington

Prior to doing the climb, Brian Marts and I had done a reconnaissance of Steamboat Rock and had picked out a crack system that appeared continuous from bottom to top. We estimated it to be between 600 and 700 feet high, and it looked extremely steep. I was working in Steamboat Springs at the time, and somebody mentioned to me that if I wanted to climb something hard, Steamboat Rock was the place. The main problem we noted on the reconnaissance was going to be getting us and our gear across the river, which was wide at this point, just below the confluence of the Green and Yampa.

Layton Kor aid climbs out a big roof on the East Face of Steamboat Rock in Dinosaur National Monument.
Photograph Michael Covington/Layton Kor Collection

For the ascent, a friend in Steamboat lent us a small raft, which led to a comical situation. Layton decided to take the gear across first. He loaded up the raft with all our stuff, climbed in, and the raft promptly sank! The crowd of tourists who had gathered to watch the proceedings thought this was hilarious. We retrieved the raft, but it was punctured, so an alternative solution had to be found.

Eventually Brian Marts experimented with wading into the river. He found that though wide, it was shallow in parts, and he eventually found a place where we could wade all the way across.

It was midday by the time we and all the gear were over, but we decided to get as far as we could that day and commenced fixing ropes. It was blisteringly hot during the afternoon, and the rock was steep and continually overhanging. By the end of the day we had fixed two ropes and descended to spend the night in the campsite.

Next morning, we were up early to wade the river. It was freezing cold in the dawn shadows. Once across, it took a long time to ascend the fixed ropes because all we had with us was one pair of Hiebeler ascenders. One of us would go up, and then slide them down the rope for the next person. It took us until mid-morning to reach our high point.

The climbing on the lower section of the wall was hard direct aid and Layton, who led the whole climb, used numerous knifeblades following a compact and incipient fracture.

In the middle of the climb we came across a wonderful eagle's nest located dead center on a flat ledge. We admired the eagle that had built it for its remarkable craftsmanship.

The roof of the eagle's nest alcove was a huge overhang which Layton led, traversing right on direct aid for 75 feet. It was an enormous roof. Finally he disappeared over the lip and set up a belay higher up the wall. Brian went next on the haul line. It was an incredible situation when I lowered him out. He kept going out, and out, and out. Finally he was all the way out and used the Hiebelers to move up to Layton. I sent the haul sack out and then followed the aid with him belaying me on the other rope while I removed the pins. At one point he was belaying while I was seconding, and he was also belaying Layton, who was too impatient to wait for me to arrive and had started off leading the next pitch.

As I reached the edge of the overhang I heard Layton shouting to me to hurry, because I had all the gear and he was out. He was on bad pins and not very happy about it, and the belay anchors were not the best either. It was a desperate situation. Brian was able to get the haul line to me and I tied on as much gear as I could and sent it up to Kor. He was able to make it past the bad section and set up another belay higher on the wall where we joined him, just below the last pitch.

Down below, there were some people on the river in a raft. The wall was so overhanging that Layton shouted to us that if he fell off on the next pitch, he'd land right in the raft. "Hey, Covington," he shouted, "tell those people to get out of the way in case I fall." I was so tense that without thinking I leaned over and started to shout down. It took me a moment before I realized I was being teased.

A few moments later Layton actually took a fall, about 15 feet. He ended up well out in space kicking and struggling. Brian and I were in a corner and couldn't see him too well. Brian said, "I'm not sure but I think he just fell." Because of the drag on the rope passing through numerous pitons, all Brian had felt was a small tug on the rope. Meanwhile Layton was flopping about in midair trying to get back on the rock. Eventually he did so, climbed straight back, and finished the climb. To the best of my knowledge our route on Steamboat Rock has never been repeated.

Wild aid climbing up a wide slot on South Sister.

1966 took me to the Three Sisters, a group of pinnacles some 400 feet high in Monument Valley, where Larry Dalke, Dick Erb, and I made the first ascent of the South Sister. On another occasion I climbed the North Sister, that was a serious undertaking. On the lower section of the North Sister there was a traverse that involved knifeblades and a bolt or two to get over to the main crack. Then a long 3-inch crack took us farther up the wall. Near the top there was some hard free climbing and some strange artificial climbing necessitating drilling holes in the rock and pounding pitons into the holes.

Descending the North Sister was the scariest part of the climb. A 150-foot rappel took us down the center of the face to a small ledge in the middle of nowhere, with no cracks. It was getting late and we were fighting time. I didn't have any bolts with me, so I drilled two holes and pounded in two Chouinard ¾-inch stubby angles. My partner rappelled down to me and I was concerned that the rappel rope might hang up in the loose rocks of the top. We were lucky. It didn't. We carefully pulled down the ropes and rethreaded

them through slings connected to the two pitons for the next rappel, which took us to the ground.

The third of Mark Powell's classic desert ascents of the late fifties was Spider Rock in Canyon de Chelly in northern Arizona. Close to 600 feet high, Spider Rock is one of the highest and most imposing of the desert towers. It was the first tower that Powell and his party climbed, prompting Wilson to later write, "We knew almost nothing about climbing on sandstone . . . we felt that we would not only be pioneering a new route but also writing a new chapter in the history of rock climbing in the Southwest."

Spider Rock was my favorite climb in the desert and over the years I climbed it twice, once with Harvey Carter, and once with Larry Dalke. On my first climb, with Harvey, we had limited knowledge about the spire, but something inside us seemed to tell us we were in for a fantastic climb.

Heavily laden with technical gear, Harvey and I left the canyon rim and rapidly worked our way down the broken trail that led toward Spider Rock. The descent was just long enough to allow our curiosity to play games with any doubts we might have had.

It was still early as we crossed a dry streambed and rounded the corner of a subsidiary canyon, revealing our objective. Harvey and I were impressed indeed. Spider Rock from ground level looked just as bold and sinister as it had appeared from the rim overlook.

Excitedly, we tied on the rope and soon Harvey disappeared into a deep chimney, a back and knee fissure that separated the two towers of Spider Rock.

Real difficulties presented themselves some 40 feet above the chimney, where we found the soft rock honeycombed with expansion bolt holes left by an earlier unsuccessful party. Apparently they too had had difficulties getting anything solid into the rotten crack.

Above the honeycombed section I reached a point in the crack where I was having a terrible time finding a piton placement. I tried everything I had, but nothing would hold. Finally, I reached as high as I could in the crack. I couldn't see what I was doing, and more by feel I managed to drive a Bong deep into a rotten pocket. I didn't trust it but it was the best thing I had found up to this point. Gritting my teeth, saying to myself, "Come on, Layton, there's a lot more climbing to come. Try it." I clipped in, gingerly transferred my weight to it, and it held. Eventually I managed to struggle up until I was standing on the Bong, and then was able to step into a 5.7 chimney that led easily up to a belay ledge.

Narrow slots and overhanging cracks led us higher and higher into the upper recesses of the tower. At the end of a long direct aid pitch, we arrived at the infamous "Black Hole," a dark cove, the floor of which was filled with large blocks of broken sandstone—the very place where one would not want to spend a night.

An expansion bolt ladder led out of the overhanging left wall of the Black Hole to a crack system higher up. It looked strenuous, and, after climbing it, due to the steep angle,

Spider Rock, in Arizona's Canyon de Chelly National Monument, is not only one of the world's tallest sandstone towers but is also illegal to climb.
Photograph Stewart M. Green

we decided to leave a fixed rope for the descent. It looked as though a rappel would leave us hanging in midair, far out from the rock.

Partway up the bolt ladder we were confronted with a dilemma. One of the expansion bolts had fallen out. After some experimentation, tied-off nested pitons in the empty bolt hole solved the problem. Soon we reached a large ledge used by the Californian pioneers as a bivouac site. We were three-quarters of the way up the climb.

Rest, water, a little nourishment and a very exposed, awkward corner above occupied the next hour of our lives. Oblivious to anything other than the immediate problems, we followed a steep crack to where three bolts led up a blank headwall. Loose rock was followed by several overlapping tiers, and it was all over. True to our earlier anticipation, it had been an incredible climb; the most enjoyable I would ever do in the Desert Southwest.

Congratulating ourselves over and over, we entered our names in the summit register. Unfortunately the light was going fast, leaving little time for luxuriating on the summit. Moving quickly, a number of vertical rappels took us down to the fixed line and back into the Black Hole.

It was considerably darker inside the Black Hole than outside. Confusion reigned, and we were unable to see to arrange the ropes for the next rappel. Reluctantly, we settled into our accommodations for the night. Spider Rock was an unkind host. With an arm wrapped around one block, and a leg wrapped around another, I spent one of my more uncomfortable desert nights.

The following morning after making the final rappels to the ground, Harvey and I began the hike back up to the rim where we had left the car. Under normal conditions, the hike takes about 45 minutes. That morning, in my weakened and dehydrated condition, it took me a full 2½ hours to plod wearily back up the trail. Arriving back at the car, with a bottle of pop in each hand we said goodbye to the generous Canyon de Chelly.

A number of years passed and the desire to climb Spider Rock again began to build up. Eventually, climbing fever won out and I returned to Canyon de Chelly, this time with Larry Dalke. I trusted Larry as much as any person I ever climbed with, and always felt comforted when he was leading above me, knowing that he could climb the pitch as quickly and safely as I could. Despite Larry's tremendous ability, he maintained a high degree of humility, a characteristic that was respected and appreciated by all who knew him. On this second ascent of Spider Rock our conditioning, coupled with my previous knowledge of the route, enabled us to reach the summit by noon, just 5 hours after starting the climb. During the ascent we noticed that some tourists at the Spider Rock overlook had spotted us and seemingly had become our informers. I was making the last rappel to the ground when I saw a ranger hiking up toward us. He was armed, and had a camera in his hand. I reached the bottom of the rappel and the ranger was waiting. He

Layton Kor leads a pitch on Spider Rock, one of the best climbs in the canyon country.
Photograph Harvey T. Carter/Layton Kor Collection

83

wasn't friendly. One of the first things he told me was that anything we said could be used against us in court.

When Larry arrived, the ranger made the two of us pose next to the "evidence," our climbing gear, and he took a photograph. After this he bundled us into his jeep and drove us down to the ranger station. On the long 12-mile ride out we had plenty of time to think. I figured we'd had it and that they were going to hang us both.

At the station the ranger handed us over to the chief ranger, who took us into his office. His first words were, "Do you boys want to get a lawyer before we start to talk?" "Do we need one?" I answered, figuring that our only chance was to plead ignorance. "That all depends on what you say in the next few minutes," the ranger replied. "Well," I said, "I don't think we were doing any harm. It's a beautiful spire and as rock climbers we really wanted to climb it, but not with any intention of upsetting anybody."

The chief ranger sat thinking this over for a few moments, and then, to my surprise, said, "Well, did you enjoy the climb?" With this question the mood changed and we all relaxed. He decided to be lenient with us, but he did say in no uncertain terms that we should spread the word that if anyone else was caught climbing Spider Rock they would certainly be prosecuted, and there was no doubt in my mind that this was exactly what he would do. When Larry and I returned to Boulder we had some color prints made of our photographs of the climb and sent them to him in appreciation. Out of respect for the local people's feelings, and the promise we had made to the ranger, I never returned to Spider Rock again.

On another occasion, Chuck Pratt climbed Spider Rock and after the climb was at the nearby trading post having a beer. A group of local Indians were present, and they knew that Pratt had climbed the spire. Legend has it that a Spider Woman lives on top of Spider Rock. Just opposite is another spire called Whispering Rock. If any of the children are naughty, so the legend goes, Whispering Rock whispers over to Spider Rock and Spider Woman descends from her lair, catches the naughty children, carries them back up, and eats them. The rocks at the top of Spider Rock have been bleached white by the sun and resemble the bones of the naughty children. One of the Indians in the trading post came up to Pratt and asked if he had just climbed Spider Rock. Pratt nodded. The Indian, acting as spokesman for the group, said, "What did you find up there?" Pratt thought for a minute, and, feeling that local people were probably superstitious, decided that he'd better go along with the legend. "Well," Pratt replied, "we found some white bones on top." At this the assembled Indians cracked up. They knew perfectly well that the story was merely a legend and that there weren't children's bones on top of the spire.

The desert was always a special place for me during the sixties, such a mixture of experiences: the wild car rides following obscure back roads seeking uncertain destinations; the adventure of first ascents, of treading where no human had been before; the

magnificent geometry of sandstone obelisks reaching to the sky, pointing me toward unknown destinations.

Though not aware of it then, at the same time that I was pursuing the summits of obscure desert pinnacles, I was also growing up, finding out who I really was, exploring myself at the same time that I explored canyon labyrinths, and redefining priorities. In retrospect, looking back at those days, at the person I used to be, I have mixed feelings. There are times today when, as I mentioned earlier, they seem like wasted years. In my headlong rush to experience everything the desert had to offer, to discover its secrets and treat its untouched summits, I was unmindful of higher, more spiritual outlets for my energies. I was not a spiritual person in those days. My goals were the goals of this world and I pursued them with such single-minded passion, dallying en route with the parties, drugs, and women that were integral aspects of the climbing scene in the sixties, that there was no room for anything else.

On the other hand, I cannot deny that these adventurous worldly experiences contributed to who I am, and the desert climbs were an important part of my development. I can only speculate about the person I might be today if I had missed these experiences—a multitude of desert climbs forever etched in my memory.

The desert climbs were indeed special. These were the formative years and in much the same way that the wind erodes the sandstone, shaping it imperceptibly into new forms, so the experience of climbing in the desert was subtly working its magic on me, rounding off the sharp edges of my personality, softening the jagged corners, soothing, calming, maturing, making me the person I now am; a person not with regrets, but with a different perspective transformed by the passage of time.

The Black Canyon of the Gunnison, protected as a national park, is one of the deepest and narrowest gorges in North America.

Photograph Stewart M. Green

4

BLACK CANYON OF THE GUNNISON

The Black Canyon, a gorge of the Gunnison River in Western Colorado, is notable for its narrowness, depth, ruggedness, and great expanses of sheer walls. At its deepest and most spectacular section, the rims of the canyon are only 1,300 feet apart, while it ranges from 1,700 to 2,700 feet deep. Composed of granite, schist, and gneiss, the walls are streaked by organic acids, forming abstract designs. Except at midday, its lower reaches are shrouded in gloomy twilight, making the name Black Canyon particularly appropriate.

I first learned of the Black Canyon from a climbing friend from Boulder, Bob LaGrange. At the time, 1962, he had just returned from a sightseeing trip, had color slides of the canyon, and was bubbling over with enthusiasm at its climbing possibilities. A careful study of the photographs revealed giant granite cliffs larger than either of us had climbed before. The very next weekend we loaded the car with a large assortment of technical gear and tore off on the 7-hour trip to the South Rim.

A day and a half later, with the use of forty pitons, one expansion bolt, and a bivouac, we had completed the first ascent of a 1,700-foot route we called the *Black Buttress*.

The first problem to be overcome in climbing in the Black Canyon is finding one's way down to the base of the climbs. Not all the gullies that lead down into the canyon are reasonable. They vary from easy scree and boulder descents, to slippery, grassy troughs that end in sheer cliffs that would require many rappels to reach the bottom. Once down in the bottom, depending on the climb chosen, a second obstacle to be negotiated is the river that snakes its way through the canyon and that at high water can be impassable.

In the early sixties we had the Black Canyon to ourselves. It was a remote place, and unknown to other climbers. The only other people we would see would be the occasional fisherman.

A major feature of the canyon is a tremendous cliff more than 2,000 feet high named the Painted Wall for the intricate patterns painted on it by intrusive bands of pegmatite. The second climb I did in the Black Canyon was the East Ridge of the Painted Wall with Jim Disney. We had no idea how hard the climb was going to be and we carried far more gear with us than we needed. This slowed us down and caused us to bivouac unnecessarily.

The first 500 feet were the hardest, very steep climbing involving direct aid, and also difficult free climbing on an exposed face. There were also routefinding problems in the lower section. Then, in complete contrast, the ridge became easy for the next 500 feet and we climbed unroped.

The amount of time that we had taken getting down into the canyon to the bottom of the climb, plus the technical climbing on the lower section and the fact that we were carrying so much gear, put us below the final headwall just as it began to get dark. Fortunately we were on a spacious ledge, a comfortable place to bivy. We even found brushwood on the ledge and we were able to start a fire and heat up a can of beans that we had with us. With the addition of a loaf of bread, the supper menu was hot bean sandwiches.

Next day we topped out early in the morning, happy that we had been able to find a route up the edge of the Painted Wall.

On another occasion in the Black Canyon we were descending a 1,500-foot brush and scree gully and came to an abrupt drop-off. Below us a boulder half the size of a house was neatly plugged between two vertical walls, blocking our way. There was no choice but to rappel. My companion, Brian Marts, the same person I had climbed Steamboat Rock with, roped down first. I followed, wondering if it would be possible to climb back up past that giant chockstone in case of retreat.

Feeling committed we continued our descent, deeper into the canyon, toward the base of our climb. Old tin cans and other debris that had been thrown off the rim above unpleasantly changed the scenery at this point.

Weeks before I had carefully studied our proposed first ascent from the north rim of the canyon, but wasn't sure that there was a climbable route up the 1,800-foot pillar we were approaching.

By any standards 1 p.m. is a late start, but it didn't make much difference as there was no way we were going to make it to the top of the wall without a bivouac.

On the lower section of the pillar we found ourselves immediately in the thick of things battling with a large detached flake. It began with back and knee climbing and as I worked my way higher the gap between the flake and the wall became wider until I could barely span it. A section of 5.9 with no protection followed, taking away any fun I'd been having. A dangerous exit at the top, followed by a short traverse to a belay ledge, pushed my ragged nerves to the limit.

Layton Kor nalls tricky crack systems high on the first ascent of the *Diagonal Wall* on North Chasm View Wall.

Above, we changed crack systems, working our way to the right across some marvelous slab pitches leading to a broken area. The lateness of the day and the polished slabs above dictated a bivouac. Brian was an easygoing companion and I felt relaxed in his company. I was glad that he was experienced for we had chosen a serious line, no place for a beginner.

I rarely sleep well on bivouacs and this one was no exception. Tossing and turning during the night, I knew I would make up for it as usual with 15 hours in the sack when we returned home. During waking moments I occupied myself wondering about the deteriorating weather and wondering even more about the slabs above our tiny perch.

Morning arrived and with it a damp mist. "Don't worry, Brian, it rarely rains here," I encouraged my companion. Not the only time I was to make this foolish prognostication in the Black Canyon.

Our gear sorted, the carabiners and pitons wrapped around me, resembling a mustached bandolero I started climbing. A light drizzle accompanied me up the steep slabs above. Despite the moisture, it was as enjoyable as climbing can get.

Then, the wall demanded we pay the paymaster. The slabs banked up steeply to eighty degrees or so and heavy rain began falling. A severe thunderstorm engulfed us. Within moments we were saturated and I was forced to begin the crux pitch with water pouring out of my parka sleeves and the bottom of my pants.

A4 climbing followed; several knifeblades, RURPs, an expansion bolt at a blank spot. More RURPs and knifeblades higher up. Suddenly one pulled. The downward call deposited me 20 feet lower. Oh, dear, now it must be done all over again.

We were more than happy to leave that unpleasant rope length behind.

The rain continued for the rest of the day and almost before we realized it, darkness was on us. A hundred and twenty feet of vertical rock separated us from the canyon rim. Rather than face a long wet bivouac, we opted to go on. With a small flashlight gripped between my teeth I nailed my way piton after piton upward. Arriving, I flashed the light on the watch on my wrist. 10 p.m. It was all over.

Brian struggled up the pitch and joined me. Thankful to have escaped the canyon's dark clutches, we climbed into his Volkswagen and departed the area. He drove and I slumped asleep in the passenger seat until my sleep was frighteningly disturbed by a dream in which I saw our car plunging off the edge of the road. Waking up in panic, I frantically grabbed the steering wheel and tried to wrestle it from Brian's grasp in my half-awake attempts to ward off the imagined disaster. As we struggled for possession of the steering wheel, with the car weaving all over the road, Brian hollered, "Layton! Wake up! It's all right! You're having a nightmare!"

The next climb in the Black Canyon was a route we called the *Shining Buttress* that I did with Huntley Ingalls in September 1962. This climb followed a pillar diagonally across from S.O.B. Gully, the normal descent route into the canyon. As Huntley's account describes, the ascent was notable for a particularly dangerous incident.

Shining Buttress

Huntley Ingalls

Time to arise. It was still night in the silent juniper and piñon forest of Chasm View. Layton and Larry Dalke were already up but I lacked their enthusiasm. My head felt like old cement soaked in stale pickle juice. Nothing seemed worth the torments of early morning resurrection. Kor was different, known for his restlessness the night before a big climb, pitching, tossing, and frequently asking for the time.

Disinclination aside, plans were now reality and, caught up in their machinery, I was committed No out. No postponement now. Layton and I would attempt the first ascent of the *Shining Buttress* in the Black Canyon Narrows. We were prepared to spend 3 nights on the climb. Larry, generously, had agreed to drive around to the other side and meet us at the rim.

The Black Canyon is an archetypal place. In the late afternoon, seen from Chasm View, it resembles a Gore engraving painted by Bierstadt. The sun highlights its rims, spires, and ancient juniper with gold. The intermediate abyss is luminous blue-gray merging into the near black gloom of its depths . . . 2,000 feet below. Deep down the rapids' speed and tumult are muted by distance. Even all this magic and wonder could not enliven my gray, drained spirits. Layton and Larry were almost ready. After forcing myself to move, a cold cheerless breakfast preceded the mechanical routine of preparations.

In the dark we slouched heavily across sand and rock. Upon entering a precipitous gully, the interminable sliding, struggling descent began. Fighting for balance, struggling to hold down runaway speed, battling obnoxious thorn bushes, the descent did nothing to raise my spirits.

The first gray light of dawn slowly crept over the Black Canyon. Its buttresses emerged like ancient myths embracing concrete form. Would our climb provide Kor and I with similar transmutation?

Down, finally, the chaotic, rugged edge of the river confronted us. Would I survive my efforts to follow Kor's tremendous leaps over rushing water to land precariously atop wet boulders? Miraculously, it worked. Standing at the foot of the *Shining Buttress* with that distinctive feeling of dread and anticipation one feels just before a major climb, we commenced our final preparations.

Suddenly, Kor let out a roar. We had forgotten the bolt kit.

"We'll do it anyway!!" he shouted to the canyon walls.

Another epic in the making?

In the deep shadows the first three pitches were 5.5–5.8. Vertical cracks and blocky overhangs. The dark, untouched rock was fractured and loose. Both cold from the early morning and hot from my exertions, I struggled to find the kinesthetic counterpoint which would make the climbing enjoyable.

After 250 feet the first sunlight touched us and a section of easy scrambling took us by surprise. The wall is so huge that what appears smooth when the entire sweep is viewed from a distance was proving tractable on a human scale.

As we passed, dry bushes gave off a dusty smell.

Soon, the slender patch of sunlight was behind, replaced by foreboding shadow. In its depths the Black Canyon is a sparsely colored place. Its dark gray rock absorbs light and color. Even the blue sky is constricted and the surrounding leaden grayness feels like an encumbering weight.

Layton Kor leads a pitch in the Black Canyon.

Two more pitches of cracks and scrambling brought us to the base of an enormous sloping slab about a quarter the way up the buttress. Moving easily up the slab, we approached a vertical, sinister, dirty salmon-colored pegmatite band—one of the most dangerous features of Black Canyon climbing. Fractured. Friable. Protection unreliable—sometimes a mere placebo.

The first pitch was moderate, ending on a good ledge. Then about 50 feet up a shallow vertical chimney, Layton attempted to place an angle piton behind a thick flake. There was a sudden crack and I was shocked to see a massive boulder grinding down the wall and Layton falling with it! Holding on to the rope, I leaped from my belay stance for I was directly in its path. The boulder broke into pieces and flew in all directions. Now I was intensely alert and experiencing the time dilation that race car drivers have reported in emergencies. There seemed plenty of time to dodge the blocks, but I was worried about holding Layton. The prospect of both of us plummeting to the bottom of the wall flashed through my mind. Then I saw him stop. By sheer luck his foot had hit a projection and arrested his fall. Now I had only to dodge the flying rock. Scampering about the ledge sideways, left and right, I ducked a typewriter-sized block as it shot over my head. Then, all was still. Both Layton and I were unscathed. Contemplating our good fortune, we paused, listening to the rocks crash and resound into the depths of the canyon 600 feet below. Larry had witnessed the incident from the rim and said later he thought we were finished.

Examining the rope carefully I was surprised to find it untouched. Shaken, but determined to continue, Layton continued the lead, making an unprotected 70-foot traverse left across appalling rottenness. When my turn came the rock felt like petrified bread crumbs. I could feel it fracturing under my feet. I experienced the unpleasant feeling of being in over my head, facing an elemental struggle for life.

The next pitch, almost as dangerous, led up a vertical trough filled with unsound blocks, which we followed to a difficult slab left for 40 feet to a worrisome belay in slings. Then a short, but very strenuous pitch, climbed vertical and overhanging rock with great exposure. Hard put to follow, I felt my arms and fingers turning numb. Once again, as I had so many times in the past, I found Kor's ability on this type of terrain quite unbelievable.

As we climbed higher, the sun shone brightly on the other side of the canyon and far below turned river pools into cheerful gray-green jade, partially relieving our oppression.

Fourth-class scrambling, easy except for thorn bushes, finally led into sunlight on a spacious ledge. Joy! Like emerging into life. All our miseries and uncertainties fell away.

Two-thirds of the way up the buttress a spectacular catwalk ramp gradually ascended to the left and broadened into grassy terraces. If we followed it, giving up the direct line on the buttress, we could reach the rim before nightfall. In the aftermath of the rockfall, not feeling overly enthusiastic about a bivouac, we viewed this exit with a mixture of relief and disappointment.

The easy way out was irresistible and we followed it carrying the rope in coils. So as not to let us off too lightly, the buttress steepened once again. A friction traverse, a touchy corner, a chimney, broken climbing about 5.5. It seemed endless. Always one more obstacle to surmount. As the sun dipped low toward the horizon, finally the last pitch . . . a 5.8 overhanging flared chimney, complete with thorn bush.

Arriving at the rim, Larry was there to meet us. We had been on the wall for 11 hours.

Stopping at a small restaurant on the way back, Layton and I smiled on overhearing a waitress say to one of the customers, "I heard a rumor that two men climbed up the Black Canyon today."

The following year, 1963, I had an excellent season in Yosemite, making the first ascent of the *West Buttress* of El Cap, and the third ascent of *The Nose*. In August I had been up to the Logan Mountains in Canada with Jim McCarthy, Royal Robbins, and Dick McCracken and made the first ascent of the Southeast Face of Proboscis. Returning to Colorado in excellent climbing shape, I made plans for a new route in the Black Canyon, which, as Tex Bossier's account describes, we hoped might be Colorado's first Grade VI.

The Narrows of the Black Canyon, just up from North Chasm View Wall, is the narrowest section of the gorge.
Photograph
Stewart M. Green

Chasm View Wall

Tex Bossier

The big old house on University Avenue was witnessing its usual activity—climbing talk. As the Camp 4 of Boulder, the Climber's Ranch of Colorado, Komito's house was the focal point of the local climbing scene. Four climbers were there that evening in 1963 and we were talking rock—big rock. Will Bassett, a preppy from the East, was a solid mountaineer from the Dartmouth Outing Club. Good as Bassett was, however, the premier Easterner of the era was in attendance, the Godfather of the Gunks, the legendary Jim McCarthy. I was there as well. Recently 18, I was just out of high school. McCarthy and I were each about 5'9" and sitting on his shoulders I was able to look directly into the eyes of the fourth person there that evening—Layton Kor.

Kor had only recently returned from a successful trip to Yosemite. He had wanted to stay in the Valley longer but had run out of partners. The original burnout man, Kor was indisputably the most powerful and dynamic climber in America at the time.

Discussions that evening centered around the development of big wall climbing: the first ascent of Half Dome, Harding and the boys on The Nose of El Cap. Layton told stories of his recent climbs in the Valley, and McCarthy expounded on the finer points of technique in the vertical world of the Gunks. Talk eventually focused on the fact that there weren't any Grade VI routes in the United States outside of Yosemite. Wyoming, teeming with magnificent climbs, was stretching to label a Grade V. The much sought after and infamous Diamond of our own Colorado had turned out to be a Grade V. Indeed, just a month earlier Kor and Robbins had put up a new route on The Diamond in a single day.

Clearly we faced a serious situation and in the true spirit of Colorado patriotism, Layton turned the conversation to the Black Canyon of the Gunnison. I had first heard of the place when Huntley Ingalls described a climb he and Kor had done there a year before, directly opposite the wall Kor was now describing—Chasm View Wall. "It's this really big wall with a ramp diagonalling up and right for about two-thirds of the way, then inverting to narrow cracks and big overhangs spaced by wide chimneys. Once we get into the overhangs we're committed. The only way off is up." It didn't take much for Kor to convince us. If McCarthy and Bassett were going, I certainly wasn't going to stay home.

Bassett was the terrified soul who shared the blue '57 Ford with Layton for the drive to the Black Canyon. Details of these infamous commutes have been adequately documented elsewhere. Suffice it to say that Bassett's expression on disembarking at the Black Canyon, with pale sweating face and glazed staring eyes, testified that this one had been no exception. Actually, Kor might have been considered a good driver—if no other cars had been allowed to share the same road.

After leaving much earlier and arriving much later, Mac and I joined Will and Layton at the canyon's rim. Sitting around the campfire that evening, we discussed our tactics. These were the days before chalk, Friends, yo-yoing, or chopping holds. The two major ethical dilemmas of the day were expansion bolts, and siege vs. alpine-style ascents. We had taken oaths that the first Grade VI in Colorado deserved our commitment to a classic ascent. Despite knowing that we would pass through bands of rotten rock, we planned not to degrade our attempt with unnecessary or extensive bolting.

Along with high ethics, we were armed with the latest Yosemite big wall techniques and equipment. Our hardware racks were laden with Chouinard chrome moly pitons ranging from RURPs to 4-inch Bongs, and we had the new jumar handles. We planned to use basically the same method employed by Fitschen, Frost, Pratt, and Robbins on the second and continuous ascent of The Nose

The *South Face* route pioneered by Layton Kor and Larry Dalke, now free climbed as *The Cruise*, follows cracks right of the prominent Nose on North Chasm View Wall.

Photograph Stewart M. Green

(Royal hadn't developed his jumar sack hauling method yet). The leader established a strong, multiple anchor, tied off the haul line, and belayed the second. The two remaining climbers took turns jumaring the haul line. The most novel aspect of this method was the way the hauler attached the sack. It was suspended by a long piece of 1-inch webbing attached to a heavy leather belt (⅛-inch thick and 6 inches wide) and hung about 3 feet below one's feet. The theory was that the belt spread the load but I vividly recall feeling like I was being cut in half on a long steep jumar.

Early next morning, standing at the Chasm View overlook and staring at the 1,800-foot-high wall as Kor described the route, I experienced that interesting medical phenomenon involving the rearranging of internal organs—namely my heart was in my throat. The Black Canyon of the Gunnison is a dramatic place and in the summer of 1963 only two or three routes had been climbed, none of which were as serious as Chasm View.

Fear and doubt began to sink in. Bassett, perhaps still suffering from Kor's driving, was mute. McCarthy reflected on the value of life as a married man. I still had 3 years to go before my twenty-first birthday. Despite all the grand talk on classic vs. siege climbing, we had been wise enough to bring along some extra ropes. After all, we reasoned, the Californians were sieging climbs and there really wasn't any overwhelming reason that the first Grade VI in Colorado had to be alpine style—let the second ascent partly do that. Camping on the North Rim that night, we agreed to give the climb our best effort but opted to fix as many ropes as seemed reasonable.

Layton and I insisted that we celebrate our last night before the climb with Swisher Sweet cigars. Now there are cheap cigars and there are cheap cigars, but to the aficionado the element responsible for Swisher's success is that they taste like candy when chewed. Unknown to the others, we had brought along cigar exploding devices. Bassett declined, but Jim was game for a cigar. Kor and I had difficulty restraining ourselves as his cigar burned further and further down, but finally the thing exploded with a loud bang, mushrooming the end. Layton and I rolled helplessly with laughter but fortunately Jim had a good sense of humor. The tension was dispelled and we had something else to think about besides the climb.

Next morning we hiked down to the bottom of the canyon. From its base, the wall didn't appear as frightening as it had from the South Rim. It was very steep, but the ramp leading up and right for 1,200 feet served to ease the angle.

The climbing on the ramp was relatively straightforward and almost all free. We spent more time on this section than the difficulty warranted, but fixing the lines and mastering the hauling took time.

The weather had been cloudy and ominous all day, but Layton assured us that it never rained in the Black Canyon. The locals wouldn't recognize rain if they saw it, he assured us. Our plan was to climb the ramp the first day, bivouac, and then weave our way through the overhangs for a projected 2 more days. My level of excitement was steadily growing as we neared the end of the ramp and the daylight hours waned. We were approaching what was for me a major psychological barrier—my first bivouac. I was fearful about sitting on a ledge all night long on a big wall. It seems odd thinking about it now, but at the time I had so little experience that I didn't know how I'd react.

At the end of the ramp we found a series of small ledges, none large enough to accommodate more than one person. Kor was at the highest point, McCarthy just a few feet above me, and Bassett over to the left about 10 feet. In mockery of Layton's predictions, it started to rain, gently at first, but it was obviously going to get worse. The more we berated him, the more Layton laughed. We were in good spirits and enjoying every minute of it, until the fancy bivouac gear Komito had supplied us with began to leak. Kor jumared up to the highest anchors and managed to spread his hammock under an overhang. (We all had the European fishnet kind, expecting to need them on the ledgeless upper wall.) Layton and his transistor radio stayed dry that night while the rain soaked the rest of us.

Next morning, as light became perceptible, we were engulfed in a dramatic whirlwind of dancing clouds. Shafts of light shone vertically upward from the depths of the canyon, while other masses swirled and skipped in wave patterns. We sat on our perches awed as light beams and rainbows mingled with mist. They were below us. They were with us—we could reach out and touch them. They were over our heads. The clouds died as the power of the sun burned through and we began to take stock. Everything (except Layton) was sopping wet. Bassett, whose health had been fading, was feeling worse. We decided to head down the fixed lines and return in a few days if the weather improved.

Two days later we were back at our high point with the overhang-littered headwall looming above us. The pitch immediately above our bivouac, where the ram inverted, turned out to be the most difficult and dangerous pitch on the climb. As we stood there looking up at the rotten jumble, Layton turned around and with his little Cheshire cat grin said, "You'd better let me take this lead, Jim, I'm not married." It was McCarthy's lead but in the interest of speed he deferred to Layton. The lead took Layton 6½ hours, and Jim 1½ hours to clean.

By early morning, Bassett, running a fever, and feeling worse, decided to go down. He agreed to clean the fixed ropes as he went, which we would retrieve from the canyon later. McCarthy, Kor, and I jumared to the anchor above the horror pitch. We were committed. The rest of the wall was extremely steep, with numerous hanging belays and overhanging sections. One section near the top stands out particularly in my mind. Jim and I were suspended in belay seats. Above us Layton had led a complicated zigzag pitch through narrow chimneys and overhangs, finally anchoring near a big ledge. It was my turn to jumar the haul line. I attached my jumars, tied several huge knots immediately under them, connected two small prusik slings, received my third screamed but barely perceptible assurance from Layton that the anchors were good, and told McCarthy he could let me out. I had good reason for these mental crutches. By the time I hung 150 feet directly below Kor, I was at least 30 feet out from the rock. There was no doubt in my mind as I looked down through my feet at the river 2,000 feet below that I chose life.

It didn't take us long after that to reach the top. Kor said it was harder than The Diamond. McCarthy stated it was harder than Proboscis, which he had recently climbed. We decided it probably was that Grade VI we went to climb.

In retrospect, the Chasm View Wall was a good climb and the experience is now part of me, but it wasn't a Grade VI.

After the Chasm View climb I returned to the Black Canyon many times during the mid-sixties, always to do new routes. Routes like the *Porcelain Arête* with John Kerr, the *Russian Arête* with Larry Dalke, the *South Face* of Chasm View with Dalke, the *Rosy Arête* with Bob Culp, the *Diagonal Wall* with Wayne Goss, and the west flank of the Painted Wall with Dalke, Wayne Goss, and Mike Covington. Downstream from the *Russian Arête* Goss and I also climbed another long diagonal crack splitting a huge face, requiring 1½ days and a bivouac.

Having climbed both flanks of the Painted Wall, I had been treated to extraordinary views of the main wall. Fractured by centuries of weathering, the rock looked loose, unstable, and constantly overhanging. Finally, with Larry Dalke and Bob Culp, we mounted an attempt on the main wall. The result was an epic of major proportions.

We started up the center of the wall from the top of a grassy terrace and immediately encountered rotten rock, worse than anything I had previously climbed in the canyon. After a number of desperately loose pitches, we arrived underneath a massive overhang. Bob Culp recounts what happened next:

> The ceiling went way off to the left and then up. It was Kor's lead. He went nailing around the overhang and was busy on the pitch for 2 or 3 hours. Dalke and I were hanging in slings dozing and freezing . . . a storm was moving in, and it was getting late in the afternoon. It was a long pitch, continuously overhanging, and ended up nowhere, just a couple of pins on more overhanging wall. Kor had done two or three RURP placements in a row. In some places he had done sky hooks in a row. It was a fiercely difficult pitch.
>
> When my turn came to jumar, there was no rope left to lower me out. Kor had run out the full length of the rope around the corner, leaving me with about a 30-foot pendulum. I put my jumars on, tied the pack on, turned off my mind, and jumped. I took a fantastic pendulum and ended up way out from the rock. There I was hanging on the rope with Kor cackling down, "You should see the expression on your face."

The next section of the wall looked even worse—rotten and continually overhanging. Larry led up a little way and said he didn't think it would go. I made an attempt and after an hour had made little progress. Culp and Dalke finally persuaded me that retreat was the prudent thing and we prepared to rappel. Culp's account continues:

> The sickening thing was that, to get off, we had to rappel from the two bad anchor pins clear to the end of the hauling line, which ended up 20 feet from the wall. From there, the plan was to pendulum in underneath a big ceiling, and we had no idea if it could be done. Kor took off first. We just hung there watching. He rappelled down, then disappeared under the ceiling. He pendulumed back out, and then he swung back under and grabbed onto something, apparently a pin, and eventually secured himself. It was one of the most horrifying descents I've ever made.

The edge of the Painted Wall frames the lower Black Canyon and Gunnison River in one of America's best adventure climbing areas.
Photograph Stewart M. Green

I returned once more to attempt to complete this route with Larry Dalke. The expansion bolt drill that we had with us malfunctioned and once again we were turned back. This was my last attempt on the Painted Wall and its ascent was to elude me.

In retrospect the main feeling I have about climbing in the Black Canyon is the sense of freedom that resulted from having a whole new area to explore, an area that made Eldorado Canyon seem almost insignificant by comparison.

GLENWOOD CANYON

On our drives to the Desert Southwest we passed many times through Glenwood Canyon, an impressive place with high limestone cliffs. The walls of the main canyon seemed too rotten, but the numerous side canyons seemed to offer relatively more compact and climbable sections of cliff. The most promising area we were able to locate was a massive wall above Grizzly Creek.

Bob Culp joined me for the first exploration of the constantly brittle rock of the Grizzly Creek wall. Seven hours climbing up a series of thin crack systems in a pronounced corner provided the first ascent route.

Some distance to the right of the route I did with Culp is a large horizontal overhang capping a large corner system in the middle of the face. I returned on another occasion with Larry Dalke and we climbed a route that went up to and around the left side of the roof, which we called the Bear Paw.

The most difficult section of the face lies to the left of both these routes where the face overhangs continually for some 600 feet. My partner for the first attempt to find a route up it was Bob LaGrange. Seventy-five feet of direct aid on terribly rotten rock was as far as we managed on this first try.

Later, I returned with Huntley Ingalls and with considerable difficulty pushed the route another 75 feet higher, reaching a section of even worse rock where we could find placements for neither pitons nor expansion bolts. At this point, only 150 feet up, we rappelled off and abandoned the climb. I named it the *Cima de Fantissimo* because of its similarity to photos I'd seen of Dolomite climbs, but Huntley had his own ideas and disparagingly called it the Mudwall.

The Mudwall off Glenwood Canyon offers a long, classic Kor route up loose rock.
Photograph Jeff Achey

Layton Kor climbs *Many Bands,* a new
route in Glenwood Canyon in 1986.

Photograph Ed Webster

5

YOSEMITE VALLEY

While I was climbing in the Tetons in the early sixties, I had heard the local climbers jokingly refer to Yosemite as "The Gulch," compared to the striking alpine peaks above Jackson Hole. But I also met Royal Robbins in the Tetons. He talked enthusiastically about the beauties of Yosemite, and said, "Layton, you're going to have to come out and visit us and try some of the Valley climbs for yourself."

Sometime later I travelled to Yosemite with Jack Turner. We drove through the tunnel that leads into the Valley, and were presented with a panorama of the most impressive rock walls I had ever seen. I felt two kinds of awe: the sheer physical presence of the walls, and also the reputations associated with the climbs. At the time Yosemite climbs were without doubt the hardest in America, possibly in the world. Stories of legendary ascents had filtered through to Boulder and I had been duly impressed hearing of Harding's epic bolting session all night long up the final headwall on the first ascent of *The Nose* of El Cap.

Some of the classics at the time were the *Lost Arrow Chimney,* the *Steck-Salathé* on the North Face of Sentinel Rock, the *Northwest Face* of Half Dome, and the El Cap climbs. On my first visit I was not ready for the biggest undertakings and settled for the *North Face* of Sentinel. I was apprehensive even about this "standard" Valley climb. Before leaving Boulder I had talked with Dave Rearick about it and his, "It was even harder than I expected," coupled with Chouinard's "My arms were tired at the end of every pitch," coming from such superb climbers, was enough to have me worried before we began. I found the climb hard, indeed, but our ascent was uneventful. For 11 hours Turner and I worked our way up the strenuous cracks, liebacks, flared chimneys, and delicate slabs of a rock wall that thoroughly exercised our abilities. We were not disappointed by this great classic and from it came confidence that started me in the direction that was to eventually culminate in the major big walls.

After Sentinel, I returned to Boulder and then almost immediately went back to the Valley with Bob Culp. Our objective was the *Lost Arrow Chimney.* Properly intimidated by the prospect of such a long climb, we were up before dawn and the sun was just rising as we made our way up small rock outcrops, past occasional trees and sandy, brush-covered benches. To our left was the foaming white water that hurtles down from Yosemite Falls and a heavy mist kept us company on our approach to the base of the wall.

El Capitan, the biggest granite monolith in the world, looms above
Yosemite Valley in Yosemite National Park.
Photograph Stewart M. Green

Layton Kor stems up *Lost Arrow Chimney* in Yosemite Valley.
Photograph Bob Culp/Layton Kor Collection

The first ascent of the *Lost Arrow Chimney* in 1947 had taken John Salathé and Anton Nelson 5 days and was an impressive achievement for the time. Culp and I hoped to be able to do the climb in 1 long day, which was the way it was sometimes being climbed in 1962.

Strenuous cracks, polished grooves, and squeeze chimneys confronted us right from the word go, some of which were wet and slippery with green moss: not the type of climbing I was accustomed to in Colorado. Neither Bob nor I were having a good day. We climbed awkwardly, seeming to expend more energy than was necessary. We had not yet refined our technique to deal with the smooth Yosemite granite. These flared, rounded cracks demanded constant exertion. Part of our energy was needed just to stay inside the crack, the rest to make upward movement. Any relaxing would result in our popping out and sliding down the wall below.

Just below the notch separating the Lost Arrow Spire from the main face, we arrived at the Harding Hole. The plan was that Bob, being considerably thinner than me, would squeeze through the hole and save us the time and effort of doing a strenuous artificial pitch above. Unfortunately, he couldn't fit through, and, needless to say, neither could I. We had no choice but to nail our way up the overhang into the notch.

Steve Roper had given me a selection of pitons for the Lost Arrow Tip. In addition to being an excellent climber, he was extremely well organized. He knew precisely which pitons were necessary to climb the final section. He had provided me with fifteen pitons; some were old Cassin soft ones that had been sawn off into different lengths. It was as though he had been up and measured the cracks very carefully. He had even told me which piton to use where. It worked out right on the button, with one exception. Just below the bolt ladder that leads to the summit, there was a place where the crack flared nastily. So many pitons had been beaten in previously that it was a real problem to find a solid placement. I spent 45 minutes attempting to nest pitons before I could work out an arrangement that would hold my weight. Finally, I ended up with a 2-inch angle placed sideways, and knifeblades stacked around it. It was 9 p.m. by the time we reached the top of the pinnacle, and 2 a.m. by the time we eventually trudged wearily into Camp 4 feeling like two coal miners after an extra shift.

I was impressed with how strenuous and difficult the climb had been, and was even more impressed when Chuck Pratt and Frank Sacherer climbed the route all free in 1964. At the time I thought that if the *Lost Arrow Chimney* was as hard as I had found it, then I could only guess of the difficulties that the major routes in the Valley presented.

After 2 days' rest, I went up with Mort Hemple to repeat the *Steck-Salathé* on Sentinel, the same route I had done earlier with Jack Turner. This route was always a favorite of mine and I climbed it four times over the years.

One thing I learned about the *Steck-Salathé* was that I needed to have a small partner with me able to lead a particularly tight slot known as the Narrows, which was the hardest pitch for me on the climb. This sinister place starts with a back and knee chimney, and then one wall closes in and forms an overhang. On my first ascent with Jack Turner, I had somehow led this pitch and had had a terrible time of it. I was stuck in the Narrows for at least half an hour involved in a vicious struggle. At one point my chest was stuck in the narrow section of the chimney, a virtual granite prison, and my legs and feet were flailing wildly in midair in the wider section below. After this experience, I never led the pitch again. I always made sure I had a partner small enough to lead it. On a later ascent with Chuck Pratt, he led the pitch, anchored part of the rope, and dropped a loop down for me to use as a hand line. With Pratt pulling as hard as he could on the rope that went to my waist, and with me pulling as hard as I could on the hand line, I barely made it. Had my weight of 185 pounds increased over the years, I would not have been able to continue doing this fine climb, at least not via the Narrows.

Over and above the climbing, Yosemite was a wondrous place to spend time. I never tired of the magnificent scenery, of the moss-covered oak trees set in broad meadows through which the clear Merced River wound its way, the many waterfalls plunging down white granite faces, the side excursions to Tuolumne Meadows, the swimming hole at the lower end of the Valley and the boulders we used as diving platforms. These, coupled with Yosemite's more civilized amenities and the social life of Camp 4, made the Valley not just a climbing area, but a way of life.

After the *Steck-Salathé*, another classic I had my eye on was the *Chouinard-Frost* route on the West Face of Sentinel. On my first attempt with Ed Cooper, we retreated in the face of a storm low down the face, but left a gallon of water on the ledge for the next attempt. Cooper wasn't available when the weather cleared, so I returned with Jim Baldwin, who had climbed the *Dihedral Wall* with Cooper. Picking up the water as we passed, we made good progress on the lower section of the wall. The sixth pitch was the notorious expanding flake, of which the guidebook says, "Can be rated A1 or A5, depending on whether the climber pops." Fortunately, it was Jim's turn to lead. He was an expert aid climber and the pitch didn't look too bad. I felt comfortable, securely anchored to four pins on my hanging belay, watching him nail horizontally left. It took me by surprise when his second pin popped and abruptly deposited him 20 feet down the vertical wall. I held him without any trouble, and without wasting any time, he climbed straight back up and tried it again. He hammered in the first piton. Stood in it. Hammered in the second piton, and once again the flake expanded. The pin he was standing on pulled, and again he went flying 20 feet down the wall. I expected him to ask if I wanted to try it after this,

Jim Baldwin works across an expanding flake traverse on the *West Face* of Sentinel Rock.

but no. He composed himself, went straight back up again, and this time succeeded. I was impressed by his coolness and determination.

When my turn came to second the pitch, I was sweating and nervous, sure, given that the pitch was a traverse, that I was going to strip all the pitons and take the same fall that he had taken. Fortunately the expanding action of the flake seemed to work in reverse and the pitons were solid as I crossed and removed them behind me.

A short pitch took us to the base of the notorious Dogleg Cracks. I'd heard a good deal about them from Yvon Chouinard, who had told me they were two of the hardest he'd experienced. The first one was a 150-foot, 4-inch jam crack. I ran the rope out and couldn't get enough protection in to feel comfortable. Part of the problem was that it was so strenuous that it was hard to stop and place protection. I marked my upward progress by the sound of Jim's voice calling up to remind me of the amount of rope left. The second Dogleg was infinitely easier because the crack was exactly the width of my size 12½ shoe, which jammed perfectly between heel and toe, allowing me to wiggle up with far less effort than I expected. At this point darkness overtook us and we pulled out our hammocks for a hanging bivouac as there were no ledges in sight.

During the night, I was sound asleep, when, somehow, a knot shifted and worked its way through a carabiner. I abruptly dropped 2 feet down the face. I had no idea what had happened and felt petrified with fear. It took me a long time to satisfy myself that the system was secure and that it was all right to go back to sleep again.

The biggest climb I did during my first season in Yosemite was the *Northwest Face* of Half Dome with Bob Kamps. In 1962 it was the only route on the face. Later, Robbins was to put up the *Direct,* and *Tis-sa-ack.* Bob and I bivouacked directly underneath the face the night before the climb. In the half light the brooding wall hung over us reminding us that as a Grade VI it wasn't to be taken lightly.

Early next morning we made our way up prekicked steps in the steep snowfield that was banked against the face and went to work. Mixed free and artificial climbing carried us up to broken flakes and ledges several hundred feet up the wall. The dirt-filled cracks and rotten rock in this section were anything but fun. Fortunately, somewhat higher, in the vicinity of the Robbins Traverse, the rock improved, became more compact, and the climbing became much more enjoyable.

We spent the night bivouacked on a narrow flake about three-quarters of the way up the wall. When we were settling in I put pressure on the flake and it shifted. It was an unnerving situation spending the night on top of a flake that might suddenly detach and tumble down the wall, taking us with it.

The next day we eventually reached the famous undercling pitch, which started up some vegetation-filled cracks to a flake that juts out to the left. Where most people have to make a succession of undercling moves out to the left, my height enabled me to reach high over the top of the flake and eliminate the hard moves.

The Zig Zags were all I had expected them to be. Compact. Elegant. Beautiful climbing.

With the *Northwest Face* of Half Dome behind me, and with a new degree of confidence based on the fact that I hadn't found it overwhelming, inevitably my thoughts turned to the ultimate wall—El Capitan.

· · ·

There were three existing routes on El Cap at the time: *The Nose,* the *Salathé Wall,* and the *Dihedral Wall.* To repeat any of these would have been an achievement, but I have always been more interested in new routes. There was plenty of unclimbed rock on El Cap and I spent many hours examining the face from the meadows down below. There seemed to be a continuous crack system up the West Buttress, following a prominent pillar in an area of rock that had not been climbed.

I enlisted Eric Beck as my climbing partner and in April we began work on the face. The lower, slabby section of the wall began with some thin delicate flakes, which we handled with care. Somewhat higher, as the slabs steepened, we reached a protruding corner that contained dry, bushy vegetation, and enjoyable climbing turned to grunging. Eric and I spent several days fixing ropes up the steep slabs.

On a day when we weren't climbing, I was preparing gear in Camp 4 when Steve Roper approached and informed me that he was to be my new climbing partner for the West Buttress. "What's the deal?" I asked. "Where's Eric?" With a grin Roper answered, "Eric sold me his interest in the climb for ten dollars and a Bong Bong."

I accepted this switch in climbing partners philosophically, feeling quite happy with my new companion, for Roper was one of the most organized people I have ever climbed with. He had a keen mind for detail and knew exactly what was going on. His account of the climb captures the flavor of the first ascent of a Yosemite big wall in the early sixties.

The West Buttress

Steve Roper

When I first met Kor, in the autumn of 1960, it was the time of year when the burnt-out resident climbers of Camp 4 were doing short routes and telling themselves that winter was imminent. So when Kor showed up and aggressively paced the campsites in search of partners for big routes, I cringed. I had already enjoyed a good year, after all. But, as I soon learned, Kor was a persuasive fellow, and we went to make the third ascent of the north buttress of Lower Cathedral Rock. This climb was notorious for its intimidating aid pitches, and on one of these I saw Kor at his finest. Whistling "Bolero" incessantly, he soared upward with such professionalism and verve that I had no idea of the pitch's difficulty. Cleaning, I found nested pins, tied-off pins, knifeblades mashed into seams, and pins packed behind creaky flakes. I was impressed.

On March 20 a postcard of El Cap, postmarked Yosemite, arrived at my house. "Come to the Valley, dad, to join me in the snow. I am hot to do something. Will be waiting for you." This telegraphic prose lured me away from my job in mid-April and into an adventure that kindles my memory equally with the climb of The Nose. (Kor, Glen Denny, and I managed to climb this superb route at the end of May.)

Layton Kor takes a nap on a sunny ledge on the *West Buttress.*
Photograph Steve Roper/Layton Kor Collection

Steve Roper dines on chips and cinnamon-nut twirls on a bivouac ledge on the *West Buttress.*

The weather in the Valley during the spring of 1963 was abysmal and Kor was restless. Already famous for this quality, he seemed especially determined and agitated, roaming the soggy campground or the more comfortable lodge, asking, "How about a climb, dad, even a short one?" He stalked the floor of Yosemite Valley relentlessly. On one of his wanderings Kor studied a route that seemed not only worthy of his skills but, more importantly for this time of year, dry. The West Buttress of El Capitan is not as high as The Nose, nor is it as imposing, but it had caught the eye of earlier climbers because it so boldly separated two outstanding walls: the *Salathé Wall* and the West Face. Yvon Chouinard had a possible line in May 1961; he and I had made a desultory attempt on the lower section. Later, Chouinard returned with Fred Wright, but they made yet another halfhearted try. Basically, the West Buttress remained virgin, and Kor wanted it badly.

Every Yosemite climber of the early sixties knew of Kor's prowess on the rock, but a few neophytes were blissfully unaware of his powers of persuasion. To climb with Kor was to be in the company of a master, and when the master called upon you—well, there was no possibility of refusal. Living in the Valley in early April was a fine climber named Eric Beck. Talented, but somewhat intimidated by Yosemite's walls, Beck had planned a modest schedule for the year: a slow progression of increasingly difficult ascents. El Cap, the dream of us all, lay in Beck's future. Or so he thought.

Kor lured Beck to the West Buttress as easily as the Pied Piper ensnared the children of Hamelin. Visions of glory buzzed through Beck's brain as Kor foretold of hanging belays and bivouacs in the midst of acres of gleaming white granite. Mesmerized, Beck sat with a glazed grin as the master vividly described the nubile nymphs who would flock to his quarters following the successful climb. In a moment of weakness, forgetting his vow to climb with moderation, and mindless of the fact that his quarters consisted of a leaky tarp covering a fetid mummy bag, Beck agreed to try the buttress.

Later, Beck was to claim that it had not been a mistake to accompany Kor on the lower section of the West Buttress; rather, it had been an education. The weather being rotten, the pair decided to string ropes for a while before cutting loose and striking out for the rim. But it was hard going, and after several climbing days spread out over a fortnight, Beck realized that he was out of his league, mentally if not physically. The climbing was vertiginous and agonizingly slow. The hanging belays were spectacular, to be sure, but they were also scary. Rappelling the fixed ropes each afternoon also proved less than enjoyable.

Kor, meanwhile, was enjoying himself immensely: His main concern was whether Beck would have the mental fortitude to continue. But Kor had long been accustomed to climbing partners less committed than himself, and he knew someone else could be coerced if Beck came to his senses, which he did in early May.

Jim Harper was next; he lasted a day, as did Kor's third partner, Ed Cooper. Beck went up once again in a futile attempt to conquer his fears. Now it was my turn, for I had recently arrived in the Valley to get in shape for The Nose. I too fell prey to the soft ministrations of Kor, and I too was lured unwillingly to the West Buttress. But I had to go; after all, it was a training exercise for The Nose.

The weather was still unstable, or so Kor and I oftentimes assured ourselves at dawn as we trembled—not just from the cold—in our bags. Occasionally we drove in dead silence to the parking area at the base of El Cap, only to turn back and, chattering like escaped prisoners, head joyously toward the cafeteria. A few times we trudged sullenly up the talus to the start of the fixed ropes, only to turn back for petty reasons. I was the instigator of most of these retreats, but I noticed that Kor too seemed subdued. It was a big, big wall. A few times we jumared to the top of the fixed lines and advanced the route a few more pitches.

Sometimes we would drive down to El Cap Meadow to check out the route for the hundredth time. Watching Kor's unabated enthusiasm on afternoons like this, I realized I was along for the ride; Kor was unquestionably the driving force. Although keeping up the proverbial brave front, I was leery of the West Buttress for the simple reason that its secrets were still to be dealt with. And they would have to be dealt with, half the time, by none other than myself. There could be no consultations with Harding or Robbins or Pratt about this route. I realized at last why the big boys were the big boys. And Kor was obviously one of them; that fact, at least, calmed me tremendously.

Feeling uneasy about the blatant use of fixed ropes in an era where such aids were beginning to be frowned upon by our peers, Kor insisted that we soon push for the top. Tired of the repetitious jumaring and queasy nights in Camp 4, I agreed. On May 15 we began the final push, figuring the upper half would take only 3 days, a correct guess as it turned out. Kor was strangely silent as we smoothly ascended the ropes toward the high point, now some 1,200 feet above the talus. As dawn arrived, we were nearing the upper anchors, the silence punctuated only by our rasping breath and ritual curses.

I will never forget the overall feeling of the next 3 days. I cannot conjure up the individual pitches—thankfully, I must add—but certain segments have permeated my consciousness. One incident, a trivial one, still amuses me. There I was, nervously affixed to a vast plate of granite by strings and spikes. Kor arrived at my hanging belay station bristling with an enormous rack of iron. Without pausing he clambered over me as if I were a mere set of handholds and footholds. The iron rudely caressed my body; flailing limbs knocked my glasses askew. Seconds later, his feet treading my hair, he was driving a piton, asking for my remaining iron, and attaching the haul rope. I gazed at him in wonderment.

Layton Kor nails a flake on the *West Buttress*.
Photograph Steve Roper/Layton Kor Collection

The climbing on the West Buttress was demanding but not particularly dangerous. Cracks appeared whenever necessary, except in a very few places. One section, which we named the Grand Traverse, ranked then—and perhaps still does—as one of the most striking passages in Yosemite. Not incredibly difficult, it typified the wondrous quality of the West Buttress.

Near sunset of the second day we found ourselves close to the rim, huddled on tiny bivouac ledges separated by 40 feet or so. Kor settled onto the higher ledge in the twilight. From my perch I watched the Ribbon Fall Amphitheater turn golden, an entrancing sight. Kor, always uneasy when alone, rappelled to my ledge for social reasons. My reverie disturbed, we talked and shared jokes as dusk descended upon the Valley. As nightfall arrived, Kor reluctantly swung hand over hand back to his lonely granite aerie.

With the first ascent of the *West Buttress* accomplished, next on the agenda was the third ascent of *The Nose* with Glen Denny and Steve Roper. *The Nose* had had only two previous ascents by 1963: the first ascent by Harding and party in 1958, and the second ascent, which was the first continuous ascent, by Fitschen, Frost, Robbins, and Pratt, in 1960, taking 6½ days. Our hope was to make the third ascent. Glen Denny continues with his account of the climb.

Steve Roper gives Layton Kor a belay on a seaside cliff at Mickey's Beach after climbing at Yosemite in 1962.

Photograph Joe McKeown

The Nose

Glen Denny

Kor was one of the many characters who hung out in Camp 4 in the early sixties. He had a unique drive, a nervous energy. More extreme than anyone else in those days, he couldn't sit still on a climb, and hardly even on the ground.

Kor would arrive in the Valley early in the season when it was still late winter, before most of the Californians would consider going up on the walls. Most of the Valley climbers had the typical California attitude—"Why go up in bad conditions and be miserable. We'll wait another month and enjoy ourselves." When Kor arrived there would still be snow on the ground.

Layton Kor does an aid traverse high on the *West Buttress.* Photograph Steve Roper/ Layton Kor Collection

Kor would hunt around for partners day after day, but generally the Valley layabouts weren't interested. He reminded me of the way that Fred Beckey operates. Where Beckey would be more subtle, and pretend that he wasn't too eager, Kor was always direct. He wanted to climb and he needed somebody to climb with. He was like a working politician, always looking for people to aid in the cause. If he didn't find someone to climb with, then, perhaps as a consolation prize, he would seek female companionship to while away the hours.

During the winter of 1962 Layton exchanged letters with both myself and Roper.

KOR TO ROPER 2/17/63

Steve,

Get to the Valley soon. You, Glen and I must do the Nose this Spring. I've never felt sure if I was up to it or not before, but I am now. I'm ready for anything. Will do SIXES like mad to get into shape for the Nose. I think the three of us could be the finest team out for that route.

I've just bought a cagoule and elephant's foot, plus other items. I am also working out steady with weights to get into the very best possible shape.

I really want to do that climb man. I think it's the most beautiful thing in the world—white granite for hundreds and hundreds of feet. What could be finer than to spend our strength, minds and desire towards the greatest thing in the world—the Nose of El Capitan.

I'll be in the Valley April 1st ready to go. We just must do this route now while we are all young and full of strength and desire. The three of us all want this very bad and the time is right—later it may not be (partners, regulation, weather, could stop us later on). So let's do it this Spring.

best regards,
Write soon,
Kor

KOR TO ROPER 2/23/63

Roper—

Got the letter. Glad to hear you're as hot for the Nose as I am. As you said, we'll be the fastest "direct aid team" going.

As I see things now, I'll be in Yosemite April 1st without fail. My weights, the boulders, and new routes (firsts) in Eldorado are keeping me in superb shape. I have been climbing every day that I possibly can, even in bad weather.

The water and food amounts I'll leave to you as you are without question the expert on these things. No matter what we take on the wall, we will still suffer, but I don't care, for the Nose I'll go through anything.

The Sentinel climbs drive me wild. The *West Face* and the *Chouinard-Frost* routes are the most beautiful things around.

We just must do the North Face of Higher Cath. Rock and push it through the overhangs to the summit.

Also the Quarter Dome really sounds great. I hear it's a fine route. Have you given any thought to a new route on Half Dome. I would like to give it a try anyway. This summer man, I'm going to go all out on everything. Join me,

more letters May,
regards,
Kor

The three of us were excited at the prospect of The Nose, but awed by the history of the climb. Fitschen, Frost, Robbins, and Pratt were the very best climbers of the day in Yosemite, and they had taken a week for the ascent. We viewed it as an ambitious undertaking and felt truly psyched up. Steve Roper joined us to make a team of three. We felt strong and well prepared.

We hoped to be able to do it in a fast time, and a major point of debate for us was whether or not to go for Dolt Tower on the first day, because there aren't any good ledges between Sickle Ledge and Dolt Tower. We decided to go all out for Dolt Tower, chancing the prospect of a night in slings in the Stove Legs if we didn't make it.

There was no thought of pushing the free climbing standards on this ascent. Our mental state was that just to get to the top using direct aid was hard enough. Rescue on El Cap was unheard of and our plan was to climb safely, without sticking our necks out, keeping plenty in reserve. We took food and water for 5 days.

The previous parties had suffered from the heat and to avoid this we decked ourselves out from head to toe in white clothes, including little white sailor caps to reflect the sun as much as possible. Ironically, it rained for the last 2 days on the climb.

Layton had a hard time of it when it came to his turn to haul. Not in terms of the physical demands of hauling, but coping with being alone on a ledge, just he and the bags. For hour after hour. He would constantly call up questions about how we were doing. He could see perfectly well what was happening, but the relative inactivity was frustrating. He wanted to be up on the pitch climbing.

As it turned out, our planning and organization paid off, enabling us to complete the climb in 3¼ days, quite a bit faster than the second ascent. All three of us were experienced, competent aid climbers. We swung leads and teamwork was the determining factor in the speed of the ascent. We probably had a better selection of Chouinard chrome moly pitons than the second ascent party, but we were using essentially the same hauling system, as Robbins had not yet invented his jumar hauling system.

That same June, shortly after climbing The Nose, Kor and I climbed a new route on the North Face of Sentinel. Everybody wanted to get a route on Sentinel in those days. There were plenty of lines and it certainly was one of the classic features in the Valley.

I led an aid pitch in the middle part of the wall and arranged myself in a sling belay as there was no ledge. It was an awkward situation and I felt quite precarious dangling there with a thousand feet of nothing underneath me. Layton seconded the pitch at his usual fast rate, and, full of enthusiasm, climbed past and over me like a human windmill. I had carefully arranged everything neatly, and Layton's progress created minor havoc. I wanted to explain my arrangement but he wasn't listening, just grabbed what he needed, stood on my knee, on my shoulder, on my head, and took off up the next pitch leaving me feeling like a cyclone had just gone through.

At the top of the pitch, he belayed and observed my progress. I don't consider myself a slow climber, but as I climbed, I could tell that he was getting antsy. As I neared the belay he began to engage in one of his noted plays. He started to tell me how bad the next pitch looked, trying to talk me into letting him lead it. "You're looking a bit tired, Glen. And it's getting late. Maybe I should lead the next one?" he tried. I said to him, "Now, Layton, you know what the etiquette is. You get to lead some and I get to lead some."

He was really disappointed when I prevailed and led the next pitch.

I found Layton an extremely trustworthy and compatible partner. He wasn't temperamental. He would not get angry or flip out over small things. He was unflappable, but his speed was something else.

When we climbed together in 1963 I had no intimations of Layton's spiritual side. Either it didn't exist, or he kept it well hidden. He was not a reflective person in those days, but was very present tense, seemingly living for the moment. If he thought about the future it seemed to be in terms of the next climb. I was taken by surprise later in the sixties to hear of his religious conversion. I would have expected someone who would experience such a conversion to be opposite to Kor's character. In the Valley he was generally considered the most all-out climber of the bunch of us. Climbing was such a priority for him in those days that it was difficult to imagine him with another major interest.

After the ascents of the *West Buttress* and *The Nose* of El Cap in 1963, I had spent enough time in the Valley, and done enough climbing, that I was no longer perceived as an outsider. Tom Frost was working on a climbing article at the time and I remember him saying to me, "You're a Yosemite climber, aren't you, Layton?" It made me feel like I finally belonged to this elite group. Yosemite had taken many young climbers in under its stone wings, and carefully honed their abilities, allowing them to go to other areas and do the hardest climbs with ease. It seemed that everyone who came out of the Valley could climb 5.9, which at the time was at the top of the alpine scale.

One of the pupils who had graduated with top honors from the Yosemite school was Chuck Pratt. He had been involved in a large number of difficult ascents and I counted myself fortunate to have done a number of these with him. Chuck was one of the smoothest climbers I have ever seen. Where I had to exert maximum effort, he seemed to just melt through problems. His effortless upward progress on hard rock reminded me of a fish swimming fluidly upstream. We had climbed the North Face of Higher Cathedral Rock together and Chuck's next interest was the second ascent of the *Royal Arches Direct.* He had been partway up this climb on an earlier attempt with Bob Kamps, but wet conditions had forced a retreat. Having listened to Chuck's description of his earlier attempt, I knew I was getting involved in something far more difficult than a run-of-the-mill Yosemite rock climb. Our predecessors, Royal Robbins and Joe Fitschen, had spent 3 days on the first ascent of this 1,200-foot climb. The crux section, climbing over the Arch itself, had required many hours with several leader falls.

The night before the climb came the Yosemite ritual, one I did many times throughout the years. On a picnic bench amidst the Camp 4 boulders we sorted our gear: rows of pitons of different sizes, a large sling of carabiners, direct aid slings, two ropes, and not to forget the tie-off loops, hammers, swami belts, a quart-and-a-half of water per man per day, and food to our liking. Finally, a bulging duffel bag ready to go.

Then darkness and I retreat to my cave in the boulders. "Hope the bears don't come around tonight." Toss. Turn. Sweaty palms. Visions of desperate situations interrupt sleep—visions, of course, which generally never come true (except on this particular climb).

Morning. Chuck and I locate the starting point at the base of the Royal Arches. (Fitting that Royal should be the first to climb *Royal Arches Direct*.) Problems begin just a short distance up. On the sharp end, with a good deal of rope out, I search for protection and settle for a little black RURP in a shallow fracture. A token gesture, but I feel better. Then hand over hand up a fragile vine growing out of the Arch.

Then Chuck leads, difficult climbing to a sling belay from five pitons driven straight into decomposed granite. As I approach he disconcertingly informs me that he is unhappy with his anchors. As I pass I add several more.

From the last questionable aid piton I step out of my slings, reach up and begin liebacking the rounded edge of the arch we've been following. Brittle flakes break off in my hand. I almost fall. Fear engulfs me. The pitons below, including Chuck's anchors, aren't good enough to hold a fall. A ragged, trembling "Chuuuu . . . . uck" parts from my lips. My partner-in-fear later tells me it felt like his heart stopped.

The pitch ends at an expansion bolt, and the nasty section finally over with, we arrive at a small ledge. One rope length between us and the crux pitch. Chuck heads upward attempting to wedge pitons end-to-end in a bad width crack. They won't hold his weight. Tries again. Pitons pull out again. Pratt gets upset, I go through fingernails like a lawn-mower going through grass. He gives up on direct aid and liebacks the arch. Fifty feet to the right he goes, feet above hands, upside down, no protection. The slab is wet and slippery. Incredibly hard. I shout congratulations, pendulum across and join him.

Then it's my turn: an A4 nail-up over the Arch. Old-style RURPs left in place. Much easier now after Royal tore moss and vegetation off on the first ascent. One-and-a-half hours later we reach the top of the Arch and a huge tree at the base of the final wall. Home for the night. Food. Water. Little sleep. Sunrise. Re-sort gear.

Then Pratt does a brilliant lead. Climbing the tree for 50 feet he adroitly steps back onto the cliff, eliminating a grungy direct aid pitch.

Higher. Chuck is leading. A shaky pin pulls. He falls. Tries again. Falls again. I've never seen Pratt fall before. My fingernails are now gone. On his third try he succeeds, and the main difficulties are over. We reach the rim. One-and-a-half days of our lives gone forever. Never again. Down to Camp 4 to find beer to wash our fears away.

In response to a request for an article describing one of our climbs together, Chuck Pratt responded with the following letter.

YOSEMITE

Chuck Pratt

Well, Layton, old friend,

It's time to sit down at the typewriter and say something about climbing with you in the granite gulch that was home to so many of us in the sixties.

What can I say about the man I consider to be the best rock climber of his generation? Maybe I just said it. Not a statement to make lightly, but one I can defend easily. I already can hear the nitpickers at work: "Sacherer had more finesse in $3\frac{1}{2}$-inch jamcracks"; "Harding had more obsessive endurance"; Robbins pioneered more Grade VIs"; and so on. Not to diminish the contributions made by many climbers of that generation, I still feel that in sheer overall ability to step off the ground and climb to the top of a rock wall, you had no equal. It didn't matter that the rock was granite, sandstone, limestone, or quartz; that it was solid, rotten, or the dried mud of the desert spires. Nor did it seem to matter that the rock was covered with ice, snow, or pigeon droppings; or that the rock was in California, Colorado, New York, or Canada. I never saw anything stop you or even slow you down. By comparison, most of the rest of us must have seemed agonizingly slow to you, but you were patient enough to climb with us anyway.

Climbing with you was a virtual guarantee of success. I recall the attitude around Camp 4 was that if you were going climbing with Layton, you would not only get to the top, but be back in time to climb something else, even if it meant that Layton had to take over the lead from his babbling partner and haul him to the top. Only climbing with Royal could I have been as certain of success, but with this difference: On those extremely rare occasions when Royal would fall, I could stop him. It is one of the blessings for which I am most grateful out of that whole era—that I never had to try to hold you in a leader fall. TM Herbert used to refer to you—always affectionately—as "200 pounds of swinging meat."

Considering your size, it was all the more amazing that you could move so fast on a climb. How fast were you? Do you remember this little incident from our climb of the North Face of Higher Cathedral Spire? You were cleaning some long aid pitch up to an awkward, cramped sling belay. When you reached me, you handed me a sling to clip into the anchor for you to stand in. Without hesitating, you stood in it before I even got it clipped in. It was the closest I ever came to having to catch you in a fall. It wasn't your carelessness or inattention, it was simply your . . . speed.

Later on the same climb, I discovered a problem that I must have shared with most of your climbing partners—reaching a bivy ledge that would have accommodated two average-size people. Remember who spent the night in slings? Next morning you were off in a typical frenzy, finishing the lead while I was still waking up.

You were always in a hurry, Layton, at everything. Fast at climbing, at driving, at eating. Even walking, you moved with that characteristic posture I could recognize at a hundred yards—body tilted slightly forward at the waist as though you were leaning into a wind only you feel, moving at a gait somewhere between a walk and a run. I can't picture a more bizarre pairing of climbers, on the ground at least, than the two of us trying to walk together, the energetic giant and the slow gnome. In a few steps you would outdistance me by 10 feet; the technique I had to develop to keep up with you can only be described as "scuttling." But we did seem to make a good climbing team.

Now that I'm trying to remember the climbs we did, there were more than I thought: Higher Spire, Sentinel North Wall, Middle Cathedral Rock, *Arches Direct,* routes on Glacier Point Apron; I doubt that I can remember all of them, but I recall even our failures with a certain fondness. Our one El Cap climb ended on the first pitch, when in your unbounded enthusiasm, you continued to pull on the hauling bag after it was jammed under an overhang until you pulled the entire top of the bag almost completely off. The few remaining threads would not have survived the remaining 2,500 feet, so we just went somewhere else to play, grateful that it happened where it did.

And Higher Cathedral Rock, where the seat of your climbing pants disintegrated so badly that after a couple of pitches you had nothing but a couple of tubes on your legs.

Then after twice failing to climb some long face on Middle Rock, I talked you into trying it with me. That way I had the insurance, the guarantee. And we would have made it that time, except somewhere up there after 2 days of really ugly mixed climbing I found myself aid climbing some dirt hummocks 20 feet away from a third-class walk-up to the summit, all for the sake of some idiotic purist notion of a plumb-line to the top. The sense of absurdity was more than I could handle, so we gave it up. I think you realized it much earlier and were just humoring me, or were just too polite to wake up a sleepwalker who thinks he knows where he's going.

Your response to all these fiascos was one of brief disappointment followed by a long period of hilarity, another quality that made climbing with you so appealing. There were some very serious climbers in Yosemite, then as now, and if I had been with one of them there probably would have been recriminations, arguments, an attempt to establish blame; but your enthusiasm for the sport wouldn't allow a couple of aborted climbs to discourage you. Make no mistake, in addition to being the fastest, the tallest, the most energetic climber I've met, you were also the most enthusiastic. Think of all the climbing partners you've burned up. I think only Fred Beckey has gone through more partners than you have, but he's been at it much longer.

I remember the stories that drifted out of Boulder long before we ever met: of some hyperkinetic giant roaming the streets trying to find someone—anyone—who had two hands and the mental capacity of at least a moron who was willing to learn how to belay; of a red-eyed obsessive who climbed faster than was humanly possible. For years we thought you were a myth created by Colorado climbers to sabotage our self-esteem. Not until Steve Roper and I finally met you and climbed some of your routes were we convinced that you really did exist. From then on we awaited your arrival in Yosemite as a natural phenomenon, an event like a tornado or an earthquake, and the time we spent climbing remains among the best memories I have of the years spent in Yosemite.

Keep the Faith,
Chuck

6

EIGER DIRECT

My first connection with the Eiger Direct was as an observer. In 1964 I attended an American Alpine Club banquet in Boston. John Harlin was the guest speaker that evening and showed photographs that he had taken on the lower section of the wall on a reconnaissance trip. The photographs gave me some idea of what was involved in climbing the Eiger in winter. Prior to this occasion I had heard on the climbers' grapevine that John and a number of other European "northwallers" were interested in such a project; and what an undertaking it would be—a direct line up one of the most difficult and dangerous rock and ice walls in the Alps.

My next connection with the project was more direct. Arriving in Europe in the fall of 1965, I went directly to Leysin, Switzerland. This lovely little village was nestled high on the side of a mountain and was accessible by either a narrow winding road or a steeply inclined cog railway.

In addition to being at the base of a ski and rock climbing area, Leysin was the home of the American school and college, and was the base for John Harlin's International School of Modern Mountaineering. Royal Robbins, Mick Burke, and Don Whillans were all employed in Leysin when I arrived. With all that climbing talent under one roof, Leysin was the ideal place for someone needing climbing companions.

After a few days John Harlin and I became reacquainted and the inevitable question followed: Would I perhaps be interested in joining him on the direct winter ascent of the Eiger? I had thought about the possibility before John asked, and wasn't certain if I had any business getting involved in so risky an enterprise. Despite the voice of caution, something inside me seemed to say go ahead, and I said yes immediately. Dougal Haston, the well-known Scottish climber, was already committed, so we had our three-man team.

Harlin was an extremely accomplished climber. I did some rock climbing with him near Leysin and in my estimation he was capable of climbing the very hardest routes in Yosemite at the time. His ability on mixed climbing was phenomenal. He moved like a cat on the steep ice, beautifully balanced. As we were to find out, there was never any doubt that Harlin was the natural leader.

Both Harlin and Haston had climbed the Eiger before, so I was really the beginner in the group.

John was the master organizer. To have any kind of reasonable chance of success it was essential that we be superbly equipped for the climb, and he had rounded up large

The moon rises over the formidable North Wall of the Eiger on a cold afternoon.
Photograph Chris Bonington/Layton Kor Collection

The Eiger crew, from left, Layton Kor, Dougal Haston, and John Harlin, and their mountain of gear to climb the big wall.
Photograph Chris Bonington/Layton Kor Collection

quantities of free equipment from various manufacturers. It was also essential that we be able to devote a substantial amount of time to the climb, and, as none of us were independently wealthy, John had worked out a deal with the *Daily Telegraph* in London to finance the expenses of the venture in return for preferential coverage of the event. Though he declined to be a member of the climbing team, Chris Bonington was to come along on the lower section of the face and take photographs for the *Telegraph*.

John's approach to the climb in terms of sponsorship and organization was more characteristic of a Himalayan expedition than an alpine climb. Once on the face, however, the plan was to make an "alpine-style" ascent, climbing in one long continuous push, without sieging and without stringing fixed ropes all the way up. John estimated that it would take approximately 12 days.

In early February we moved from Leysin to Grindlewald. Fritz Von Almen, the proprietor of the hotel of Kleine Scheidegg, beneath the North Face of the Eiger, had given us reduced-rate accommodations, and the Mammut Rope Company was providing as much free rope as we needed.

The *Daily Telegraph* agreed to cover the cost of a helicopter reconnaissance flight to check conditions. Herman Geiger, the famous Swiss mountain pilot, flew the helicopter for us and this excursion, which lasted only a short time, was to be one of the most exciting rides of my life.

John, Dougal, and I climbed into the whirring machine and in a few brief moments were heading up toward the face. As we approached the huge mountain wall clad in snow and ice from top to bottom, the helicopter became alive with nervous laughter, reflecting the uneasiness that had been building up in us during the past few days.

The reconnaissance flight was successful and enabled us to take a series of photographs that we later examined for a feasible route.

Unfortunately, the weather of this time was unsettled. Brief spells of 1 or 2 good days would inevitably be followed by storm; John paid close attention to the weather forecasts as time slipped by and the 10-day clear spell we needed showed little sign of materializing.

We had no difficulty passing the waiting time as the heavy snowstorms provided us with superb powder skiing. Unfortunately, one afternoon John took a fall and dislocated his shoulder. It was a terrible shock and I thought we were going to lose our climb before it started. Medical attention for John was promptly sought and the doctor said he would take at least a week to recover. As the weather still hadn't improved, we decided to return temporarily to Leysin.

A few days later we were in Leysin organizing equipment when out of the blue Chris Bonington phoned Harlin and startled him by telling him that a team of eight Germans had already started on the Direct. We dropped everything, jammed all the gear into the vans, and headed straight for Grindlewald.

As soon as we arrived, Chris told us that the Germans were well organized, well equipped and certainly to be taken seriously. They were using siege tactics with two lead climbers going ahead, fixing ropes, while the other six followed behind hauling gear. It seemed that their plan was to fix ropes up the whole, or most of, the face and establish well-supplied intermediate camps in snow caves before finally making the summit push.

John Harlin scopes out the Eiger Nordwand from Kleine Scheidegg.
Photograph Chris Bonington/Layton Kor Collection

John's shoulder was still troubling him, so it was agreed that Dougal and I would go up first. The logical starting point was a steep ice gully where the Germans had already placed fixed ropes. Haston and I started up, using the fixed ropes, but after several pitches continued climbing without them. The gully had some very steep sections, ice bulges of seventy-five to eighty-five degrees. Jorg Lehne, the German team leader, later stated that these ice gullies were more difficult than anything they had encountered on the North Face of the Triolet, one of the hardest ice climbs in the Alps.

At this point in time, none of the Germans were on the face. After fixing these lower pitches they had returned to their headquarters, a small hotel on a knoll above Kleine Scheidegg.

We hadn't progressed very far up the lower section of the wall before I realized what a gifted climber Dougal was. He had been seasoned on the winter ice gullies of the Scottish highlands, and it really showed. His previous experience had developed in him a relaxed, almost businesslike way of doing things.

Dougal began leading an uncomfortably steep, iced-up inside corner. It was very impressive from below, yet he made it look so easy. I jerked the camera from my pocket and took several photographs, only to later discover that I had no film in the camera!

By the end of the first day we drew close to the First Band, a 300-foot vertical section of rock about 2,000 feet up the face. I was leading at the time, front pointing on ice covered with soft snow. With the snow balling up under my crampons, occasionally I would slip an inch or two before they would catch. It was during this unnerving situation that I happened to look up at the window that looks out onto the face from the railway tunnel inside the Eiger and noticed a woman tourist. Her face was pressed against the glass and she was regarding us with an expression of morbid fear. The look in her eyes unsettled me for some minutes and brought home the reality of where we were. After Bonington's

Layton Kor leads one of the hard aid pitches on the winter directessima on the Eiger Nordwand.
Photograph Chris Bonington/Layton Kor Collection

Layton Kor racks up to lead an aid pitch on one of the steep buttresses.
Photograph Chris Bonington/Layton Kor Collection

phone call things had happened almost too quickly and it had been one mad scramble to get to Grindlewald and onto the face; suddenly here I was on my first real climb in the Alps, 2,000 feet up the Eiger, and in winter.

By this time we were about 500 feet above where the German fixed lines ended. As there was still daylight we decided to press on and try to fix ropes partway up the First Band. The Band was composed of typical Eiger limestone, compact with no real crack systems, small holes here and there, and incipient fractures. I was compelled to use knifeblades and RURPs, and numerous tied-off pitons. Occasionally I'd find a small hole in the limestone into which I could drive a tiny Chouinard angle piton, which would ring perfectly as it went in—as good a placement as you could hope for.

Inevitably, it began to snow. Small spindrift avalanches funneled down the gullies, engulfing us. I rigged a sling belay on the vertical wall and waited patiently for Dougal to follow. As I hung there in the belay, avalanches periodically buffeted us. It was powder snow though, and didn't hurt, but had we been in the middle of an ice field it would have been a serious situation. Secured to our direct aid pitons, we were reasonably safe. Nevertheless, the fluffy white stuff found its way into our clothing and before long we were uncomfortably cold.

The storm worsened and the avalanches intensified. It was time to bail out. We rappelled back down to the bottom of the Band and chopped out a platform in the ice to bivouac for the night. By this time a ground blizzard had developed on the face and visibility was zero. We spent an absolutely miserable night. The ice platform we had made for ourselves was tiny, perhaps 12 inches by 20. As the night wore interminably on, our body heat rounded the icy edge of the ledge and we would periodically slide off and end up hanging from the ropes. It was one of my worst bivouacs in the mountains.

Next morning the storm continued unabated. We descended through it and reached Kleine Scheidegg totally spent.

While Dougal and I were on the wall, John and Chris had met with Jorg Lehne and Peter Haag, the leaders of the German team. It had been worked out that up to Death Bivouac, about two-thirds of the way up the face, both groups would follow independent lines—after that we would see.

Toward the end of February the weather improved and both we and the Germans returned to the face. The Germans were first back up and there was definitely a competitive atmosphere between the two teams. The newspapers really built up this aspect of the climb.

To make it possible to endure long periods of time on the face, both we and the Germans established a series of ice caves. Life in them was relatively

Dougal Haston melts water in a snow bivouac cave while John Harlin looks on.
Photograph Chris Bonington/Layton Kor Collection

cozy compared to the conditions we experienced out on the face. Tarps were spread on the floor, and neat shelves were chopped in the walls to store our gear: food, cooking equipment, and other necessities. Everything had its respective place, ice axes and crampons were stuck into the walls of the cave. We even had a small whisk broom, which we used to meticulously dust the snow off our boots and clothes as we entered. It was important that we kept a tidy house. The Germans were luckier than we were when it came to locating accommodations and they invariably stumbled on large natural ice caves, one of which they named the Ice Palace. We, not being so fortunate, often had to hack caves out of the hard snow, and, consequently, ours were smaller and more cramped.

The extreme weather continued and 8 days passed before we were able to return to the face. Climbing again with Dougal, we continued working our way up the First Band on continually difficult direct aid. We were making good progress and had most of the First Band behind us when our enemies, snow and avalanches, returned. I descended to Kleine Scheidegg while Dougal and Chris stayed on enlarging the snow cave, where they spent the night.

The weather was variable the next few days, but on one of the fine days I was able to return to the First Band, and, climbing with John, was able to finish this section.

Above the First Band, John and Dougal teamed up and dealt with the next section of difficult mixed climbing. Lack of protection and long runouts made the climbing very serious.

Meanwhile, the German climbers were also making excellent progress. At this point our two teams were climbing side by side. The press jumped on this and one newspaper printed "Against the Germans." Above the caption was a photograph of John, Dougal, and myself.

The weather soon deteriorated again and another retreat was called for. Retreat in these situations was generally a relief, leading to good food, a warm bed with clean sheets, and local people to socialize with. During the bad weather spells I enjoyed myself more down below.

On March 4 the weather improved with blue sky overhead, and Chris Bonington and I were to keep one another company on the face. Apart from the obvious merits of his climbing record, Chris was completely at home in the mountains and was able to relax and enjoy any situation, even on the Eiger. We hauled supplies between the First and Second Bands and at the end of the day we arrived at a tiny snow cave where Haston and Harlin had bivouacked the night before. A quick glance told me I couldn't be comfortable in it by myself, let alone two of us.

A little while later, there I was, crunched between the hard snow that formed the outer shell, the hoarfrost-covered limestone on the inside, and the low ceiling above, unable to move around much. Lying there in a most uncomfortable position, feeling that somehow I had been cheated, the first thought that came into my mind was "Man, what a miserable place this is!" At this point Chris, who was tucked further back into the cave, and who was no better off than I, looked over at me and with the most satisfied smile said, "Layton, this is going to be a great bivouac."

Next day, John and Dougal climbed the Second Band and, unable to find a good place for an ice cave, hacked out a skimpy bivouac ledge in the ice. The next day a long stint of climbing up the Second Ice Field following the edge of the Flatiron took us to Death Bivouac. John and Dougal were climbing together, and Chris Bonington and I were bringing up the rear, hauling supplies. We reached the top of the Second Icefield in pitch darkness and I was still coming up the ropes as John and Dougal were excavating an ice cave.

Layton Kor leads up the snow-plastered face of the Eiger.
Photograph Chris Bonington/Layton Kor Collection

The ice cave was precarious. We had tunneled into a bulging mushroom of ice and in the side of the cave was a small hole looking straight down the ice field. It felt as though the whole structure could slough off at any moment and give us the most incredible ride of our lives.

The period that we were on the face was one of the most extreme winters that Grindlewald had seen. I am doubtful that had the Germans not been on the face, and had we not eventually teamed up with them, that we would have been able to climb it alone, particularly had we adopted the alpine-style tactics that John had originally planned. The fixed rope method that we used has been employed by most subsequent parties.

As we were finding out, the Germans were all excellent climbers. They received their sponsorship from the Belser Company, a Stuttgart publishing firm, who had provided them with a Swiss ground manager and public relations man, Harri Frey. I was told they received their weather forecasts on the face via a transistor radio from a Stuttgart rock 'n' roll station. Occasionally I would be in the vicinity of their snow cave and see the radio antenna poking out, sweeping from side to side trying to pick up the signal.

After the first few days, once we had adjusted to each others' presence on the face, relations between the two groups were friendly and the Germans would periodically invite us over to their spacious cave for coffee. We, unfortunately, were not able to return the invitation due to the small size of our cave.

After our late arrival at Death Bivouac the previous night, it was afternoon of the following day by the time we had reorganized and made the ice cave habitable. The weather was clear and Dougal and I set off upward to make what use we could of the remaining daylight. Dougal cut beautiful steps up the steep black ice of the Third Ice Field. I appreciated how neatly they accommodated the front halves of my large feet. Above, I took off on a difficult mixed pitch that led onto the crest of a ridge leading to a massive buttress of rock between us and the Spider. We named it the Central Pillar. At its base we met up with Peter Haag and Gunther Strobel, who had climbed up directly from their snow cave. We discussed the alternatives. The Germans favored a chimney blocked by a huge, unstable-looking bulge of snow to the right of the Pillar, while Dougal and I were more interested in a more difficult-looking, but seemingly safer traverse round the base of the Pillar to the left, leading into a gully that led up toward the Spider.

After completing our inspection of what lay ahead, it was time to descend. Darkness was approaching as Dougal and I rappelled downward to rejoin John and Chris for the night in the Death Bivouac snow cave. We were optimistic that the next day would see good progress being made.

Morning brought yet another snowstorm. Disappointed, John and Dougal decided to wait it out in the cave, while Chris and I descended to Scheidegg. By now we were becoming accomplished rappellists, once making the entire descent from Death Bivouac

Layton Kor traverses across mixed terrain to a fixed rope on the Eiger.
Photograph Chris Bonington/Layton Kor Collection

down to Kleine Scheidegg in 2 hours. The storm persisted and John and Dougal ended up spending 5 days in the Death Bivouac snow cave. On the fifth day they too descended, and we all regrouped in Von Almen's hotel.

Two days later the weather improved and Bonington and I made our way back up the fixed ropes, intent on pushing the route past the Central Pillar up to the Spider. Chris's role as photographer had been modified somewhat and he was for now functioning in all respects as a member of the climbing team. We reached the snow cave at Death Bivouac late in the day and next morning ascended the fixed ropes to our high point directly underneath the Pillar. Chris Bonington's account of the climb tells what happened next.

CENTRAL PILLAR

Chris Bonington

The morning dawned fine. Layton and I set out early, but not early enough to beat the Germans, who were already at work in the corner system to the right of the Pillar.

"If you can't get across the Pillar, we've had it," I commented to Layton. "You'll have a dobbing match to get past those buggers."

"Don't worry, it'll go alright," he replied, quietly confident.

I climbed up the fixed rope Layton and Dougal had left in place earlier. Jorg Lehne, looking rather like a wartime storm trooper, was paying out the rope to Karl Golikow, who was out in front on their line.

"Morning, Jorg. Do you think Karl will get up?" I asked.

"Maybe. We do not like the snow bulge. It could be dangerous. What will you do?"

"We're going round the side. There's a better groove on the other side of the Pillar."

"Ah, but the bottom of the Pillar looks very difficult. I don't think it is possible."

"To Layton, anything is possible," I replied with less confidence than I tried to put into my voice.

Layton came up and joined me at this point—gone was the cumbersome, rather diffident backwoods-man from the States, gone the nervously tense companion of the previous day. He was now sure-moving and confident. He went straight into the lead, kicked up a few feet of snow to the foot of the rocks, hammered in a peg, clipped in a carabiner and etrier and stepped up. A short pause; gloved hands, searching, had found another placement for a peg, nudged one into the crack, topped it with half a dozen sure blows and repeated the previous process. He knew exactly what he was doing and where to find the right placements for his pitons by glancing at the rock rather than by trying a dozen different places. He then knew how hard to hammer the piton into the crack—not too hard, yet sufficiently to hold his weight. He was a craftsman, superbly adapted to this highly specialized form of climbing.

He reached the line of weakness that stretched round the base of the Pillar. From below it had looked easy-angled, but now I could see that this was a relative term. It was still desperately steep, and loose into the bargain. Clusters of icicles clung to every crevice in the rock, and Layton had to clear each one away before finding placements for his pegs. I don't think any of our own team, or that of the Germans, could have completed that traverse without drilling a succession of holes for bolts, but Layton, making maximum use of his long reach, and uncanny ability to place pitons, got across it, using the cracks and crannies that nature had provided in the rock.

This type of climbing is slow progress, and the morning slipped by as he moved and swung deliberately from etrier to etrier. I talked in a desultory fashion to Jorg Lehne, gazing down at Scheidegg, now 6,000 feet below us, and watching the cavorting black specks of the skiers as they gamboled in their world of bright sunshine.

A cry came down from above. Layton had managed to get round the side of the Pillar, had pulled the rope in, and now it was my turn to follow up his pitch using jumars, and removing the pitons. Following Layton, this could be desperately difficult, because they were placed so very far apart. I found him perched on a narrow ledge he had cut out of the ice. Above, an ice runnel ran between steep rock walls to an even steeper ice field. It looked hard. I belayed myself and Layton set out once again. At this stage, I had no intention of doing any leading—I had come along in an emergency, was getting some extra pictures, and was happy to hold Layton's rope.

But Layton was no longer moving with confidence. He, a master on rock, had little experience on snow and ice. He messed around, trying to put in an ice screw—a knack that he hadn't yet learned. But at last he got it in, climbed another few feet, cutting steps in the wrong places and getting tangled with his crampons.

"Can't get a bloody peg in," he muttered.

I was getting worried. You can't afford to fall off on ice; the ice screw runners are of doubtful value, and would almost certainly pull out. If he had a long fall, I might also be pulled from my stance, since his belay pegs seemed none too sound.

"Do you want me to have a go?" I offered. "At your present rate, I don't think you'll get up before dark."

"Okay, this just isn't my scene."

And so I found myself out in front, for the first time on the climb—something I had never intended to do. I couldn't help but get a thrill of excitement, mingled with apprehension. It looked a long, hard ice pitch, harder than anything I had ever attempted before.

Layton Kor catches his breath on a chilly belay ledge high on the Eiger.

After I had climbed down, I watched Chris lead the steep ice pitch that had given me trouble. He climbed brilliantly, without any hesitation at all. He placed one protection piton midway, but it was a token gesture and certainly wouldn't have held a fall. I was very impressed.

While Chris and I had been climbing up the left side of the Central Pillar, the Germans had bogged down, unable to climb past the unstable mass of snow in the right-hand chimney. Chris and I rappelled down to spend the night in the snow cave at Death Bivouac, and there met up with Karl Golikow and Jorg Lehne. Various possibilities were discussed, including Karl and Jorg jumaring our fixed rope after Chris and me the next day.

Next morning the discussion continued and it was finally decided that Chris would descend. Meanwhile, Karl and I would join forces, jumar back up the fixed rope, and climbing as a team finish the pitch at the top of the Pillar together. Jorg would jumar behind us, but would wait in the Spider for Harlin to arrive and discuss the details and implications of the climb becoming a joint venture between the Americans and the Germans.

Chris presented this turn of events over the radio to John, who was not too happy initially to hear that the two teams had joined forces in this manner on such a crucial section of the climb. In any event, the decision was made. Golikow and I would share the rope together. Karl was a wonderful fellow, always smiling. Although his English was limited, he had one favorite phrase, which he frequently repeated: "Layton, it's a hard life." How right he was.

Karl and I jumared the ropes and after reaching the top of them, he led a spooky-looking pitch to the top of the Pillar. It was a narrow funnel of ice inside a decomposed limestone trough and I felt nervous perched there on my tiny stance contemplating 3,000 or so feet of wintery emptiness beneath me as he led the rope upward, finding only one protection piton on the pitch.

That evening it was Karl's birthday and I was invited over as a guest for the celebration in the Germans' snow hole. The other German team members down below sang "Happy Birthday" over the radio, and Jorg Lehne responded in festive vein by shooting off some flares. Amid the celebrations it was decided that Jorg and I would climb together the next day and hope to push the route through to the Spider.

To our disappointment the top of the Pillar provided nothing in the way of a bivouac site, just a narrow arête. We had no choice other than to keep pushing on. In front of us was an overhanging headwall blocking the way to the Spider. I spent the rest of the day nailing my way up this steep, brittle section of cliff, reaching a point that I estimated to be perhaps two rope lengths below the Spider. Time ran out and once again we rappelled back to the Death Bivouac snow caves.

A winter sunrise bathes the Eiger Nordwand in rich light.
Photograph Chris Bonington/Layton Kor Collection.

Next morning Jorg and I left the Death Bivouac together and jumared up the Central Pillar to the high point. Jorg insisted on leading the next pitch, which was direct aid, leaving me to lead the following pitch, which looked like difficult ice climbing. I knew the ice was coming up, so I offered to lead the rock if Jorg would swap places with me and lead the ice. With a twinkle he replied, "Layton, I too like the rock." So it ended up with Jorg on the rock and me on the ice gully, which formed the lower right-hand leg of the ice field known as the Spider.

This 100-foot section was the most serious rope length I was to lead on the climb. The rock was sheathed in an armor of ice, not thick enough to cut steps in, so I gingerly balanced my way up on front points. "Bonington, where are you now that I need you?" At the top I turned and looked down at the rope running 75 feet down to Jorg without a single piece of protection between us. My nerves were on edge and finally I found a place where I could cluster some Chouinard knifeblades behind a flake. Higher up I placed an expansion bolt and set up a sling belay on a slab at the beginning of the Spider. This point was to be the highest I was to reach on the climb.

Meanwhile, John and Dougal were jumaring up the fixed ropes to the Death Bivouac snow caves. I rappelled down and joined them, leaving Jorg preparing a bivouac site in the Spider. As I descended, Karl jumared up to join Jorg.

Meeting John and Dougal at Death Bivouac, we were disappointed to hear over the radio that the weather forecast for the next day was bad. As usual, I volunteered to descend to Kleine Scheidegg and pick up some things we would need for the final push. As I descended, John and Dougal remained, considering jumaring up the fixed ropes that afternoon to assess the situation in the Spider.

Shortly after I left, John and Dougal received a revised weather forecast over the radio telling them that the bad weather would probably not arrive until the end of the following day. They also heard that one of the Germans had reached the next feature above the Spider, the Fly. The implication was that the Germans were now in a position where a summit push was imminent. With these two pieces of information in hand, John and Dougal decided to go up the fixed ropes straight away and join Jorg Lehne in the Spider. Dougal set off first.

Meanwhile, at Scheidegg, Peter Gillman, a reporter for the *Daily Telegraph*, was watching events through Von Almen's telescope. Out of nowhere, he saw a red object falling down the face. It happened very quickly and the falling object disappeared from view in the vicinity of the Third Ice Field.

Very concerned, Bonington and I embarked on a search. From the top of one of the ski lifts we skied a traversing line across the base of the face to the bottom of the fixed ropes. As we approached we could see pieces of equipment scattered about. At first we were relieved, thinking that it probably was a piece of equipment that Peter had seen falling. Then Chris saw a blue rucksack beside a dark shape in the snow. At first I thought it was a bivouac sack, but as we approached closer the dreadful reality became apparent. It was John's body. Chris and I sat sobbing in the snow as the awful, undeniable realization that John was dead sank in.

Later, we learned what had happened. Dougal had jumared the fixed rope up the Central Pillar, and had waited in the Spider for John—expecting him to arrive within half an hour. After 2 hours John had not arrived. Desperately worried, Dougal then began jumaring up toward the Fly, where the Germans had a radio, to talk to Scheidegg and see if he could find anything out. As he jumared up, he saw one of the Germans, Roland Votteler, jumaring up the Spider below him. Dougal descended and Roland gave him the terrible news of John's death.

We were all heartbroken at this disastrous turn of events. Everyone was

John Harlin at a belay stance on the Eiger.
Photograph Chris Bonington/Layton Kor Collection

in a state of shock and emotional turmoil. The first response was that we should all abandon the climb. High on the face, it was Dougal who initiated the process that culminated in the decision to continue. He reasoned that the team was now poised in a position to finally achieve John's greatest dream. What could pay him greater tribute than to go on and complete the climb? If completed, the route would be his memorial—the John Harlin route. If we retreated, his death would have been for nothing. The decision was finally made between Dougal and the German climbers in the Spider to continue, climbing as an international rope, united by Harlin's spirit.

As Dougal and the Germans began working on their final push upward, I also made my decision. I would go back up the face and attempt to join them for the summit push.

Later, after many strenuous hours of jumaring, I reached Death Bivouac once again, and met Peter Haag. We discussed the situation and agreed to push on together, up the Central Pillar to the Spider. Just as we were preparing to move out, Karl Golikow and Rolf Rosenzopf came rappelling down the final section of the Pillar just above us. We were dismayed to find out that they had stripped the fixed ropes behind them leading up to the Fly. Their rationale was that the fixed ropes were badly worn and that it was risking another accident for anyone to go back up them. It was decided that those above would go on, while everyone below would turn back.

At the time it was a great disappointment to be frustrated in this way in my plan to join Dougal and the Germans for the final push. I had gone through a great deal of psychological stress in the immediate aftermath of John's death, and it had not been easy making the decision to go back up the face once again. Having put all of this psychological and physical energy into getting back up to Death Bivouac, it was a major disappointment to find that Karl and Rolf had stripped the fixed ropes, making further upward progress impossible.

In retrospect, the good that came out of this situation was the later realization that if I had continued up, and been subjected to the horrendous conditions that Dougal and the Germans confronted on the summit push, there is a good chance that I would have lost my toes to frostbite, as happened to the German climbers.

The final push to the summit of the Eiger achieved by Dougal and the Germans is one of the all-time epic stories in mountaineering history. It was a nightmare for them above the Spider, where they ran into the fiercest storm of the climb, a wild blizzard. They were barely able to deal with the extreme situation and the climb became a grim struggle for survival.

Finally they reached the summit, paying a dear price in frostbitten extremities. The John Harlin route now existed on the North Face of the Eiger for all time.

Once everyone was back at Kleine Scheidegg, my smiling German friend Karl Golikow, with whom I had shared two rope lengths below the Spider, approached me. Putting his arm round my shoulder he stated, "Layton, it's an easy life." It was all over.

The Eiger was the most unusual climbing experience of my climbing career. I was thrust so quickly into it, an international situation involving strangers and competition. At times it had the feeling of being a circus, at others a media event. Not the kind of circumstances I relished, and I was never again to become involved in such a situation.

For a long time afterwards I periodically felt depressed. Harlin was gone and that hurt. We had talked and had plans for other climbs we wanted to do together in the future. John wanted to go on to do climbs in other mountain areas. Without his inspiration and companionship, those plans faded.

7

THE ALPS

A little land with big mountains." This caption, located under a photograph of a large mountain range in the Alps, had stayed with me from my earliest climbing days. It conjured up visions of the endless climbing opportunities that Europe had to offer.

With the Eiger ordeal over, and winter long gone, frolicking spring weather was knocking at the door. I began to think about finally visiting some of the Alpine areas that I first began dreaming of some 10 years earlier, pouring over climbing books in the Boulder library.

One of the first major areas to shed its winter snows was the golden walls of the Italian Dolomites. I had been strongly affected by the many photographs I had seen of climbers on those horrendously steep climbs and was eager to experience them firsthand.

Italy in the springtime can be blisteringly hot and the best way to experience that heat is by hitchhiking cross-country. Added to this is the small problem of the Italian auto. I soon found, when I was able to get a ride, that they weren't designed for the tall American. With knees pressed uncomfortably close to my chest, I politely suffocated in the backseats of their toy cars.

The Tre Cima Di Laverado group is one of the rock climbers' meccas in Italy. Books and periodicals abound with exciting accounts of adventures that have taken place on the walls of these towers.

The north face of the Cima Grande, the central peak of the Tres Cima, was one of the most sought after classic north face climbs in the Alps in the sixties, a climb I had had my eye on for a long time.

With my heart and mind ready and willing, all I needed was a companion who would agree to tie on the opposite end of the rope. The campground by the Laverado hut was teeming with climbers and mountain enthusiasts, but unfortunately for me, most of them didn't speak English.

"The British are coming . . ." Their accents gave them away and my problem was solved by the friendly sounds of a group of English climbers hiking past my campsite. I struck up a conversation, hoping that one of them might be interested in the Cima Grande. A stocky, friendly young fellow by the name of Geoff Hamriding agreed to join me on the *Comici* route.

Next morning, out of respect for the great climb awaiting us, our start was a very early one. In semidarkness we stumbled along the broken scree slope to the foot of the

The Tre Cima di Lavaredo are three distinct peaks—Cima Piccola, Cima Grande, and Cima Ovest—that offer some of the best climbing in the Dolomites.

wall. Two insignificant people to attack the north face alone? Hardly, for we had been hearing voices and the first light revealed climbers everywhere lining up at the bottom of the different routes. Quickly we climbed unroped up a broken tower to a spacious ledge at the beginning of the difficulties. The view upward was sobering. The wall rose vertically for the next 750 feet.

Sweaty palms, greasy fingers, and possibly residue from the rubber boots of countless climbers made the holds on the first pitch a slippery ordeal. This was not the case on the second pitch, suggesting that perhaps many parties had become demoralized at this point and rappelled.

One thing was certain as we progressed upward, we wouldn't get lost. It was simply a matter of following the protruding heads of innumerable pitons. At times only the tips of our fingers and the front edges of our klettershoes touched the rock as we balanced our way up the vertical wall.

At a small but substantial belay stance some 500 feet above the ground, out of curiosity I extracted one of the too many belay pitons. It was old, primitive, handmade of soft steel, some 7 to 8 inches long, and rusty into the bargain; an ancient reminder of the countless ascents this famous climb had received over the years.

Above the vertical section, a short traverse took us to the final chimney system. Here Geoff took over the sharp end of the rope and speedily led the remaining pitches to the ringband, a distinctive ledge that runs all the way round the top of the Cima Grande. We skipped the summit and began the descent, dodging the falling rocks that some yodeling Italians high above were kindly kicking off.

My campsite in the valley below was one of the few things I found in Italy that was free. Home Sweet Home was a cave in the boulders, its limestone ceiling perforated with tiny holes: great for piton placements but also perfect rain drains, saturating me and my equipment.

The small restaurant at the nearby Laverado hut provided an occasional needed change from cooking outside, but at the same time taught me something I might never have suspected, were not Italy and spaghetti synonymous. I was served a large plate of pasta on top of which was the equivalent of two tablespoons of runny tomato sauce— not enough to even flavor the noodles! A real letdown after my salivating visions of a spicy, thick, robust sauce.

One particular evening, with the restaurant filled to capacity, the air pulsating with the noise of many languages, an unusually large Italian climber appeared. In his hand he held the head of a piton that had broken off under his weight, sending him on a terrifying 100-foot plunge down one of the vertical walls. He was happy to be still in the land of the living and proudly showed his souvenir to everyone in the restaurant.

Dick Shori, an American from Baton Rouge spending the summer in Europe as a math exchange student, showed up at the Laverado hut. We laughed, swapped stories about climbing in the States, and shook hands, committing ourselves to do the *Direct Cima Grande* the following day. The guidebook, *Selected Climbs in the Dolomites,* had the following to say about our proposed adventure.

"By the N. Face Direct (Brandler-Hasse, 1958). Most of the pegs are in place (230– 250). The overhanging section is about 400 feet with pitches of at least 120 feet. It is one of the most formidable routes in the Dolomites 1,600 feet Grade VI superior."

Next morning the bottom of the face yielded an unwanted surprise. We were third in line for the *Direct*. Off to the right at the bottom of the *Saxonweg* route was another party, and to the right of them on the *Comici* two more parties were lined up. Was this Grand Central Station? Were we not at the base of one of the steepest walls in the Dolomites, starting a Grade VI superior route? Like a couple of warm bodies in an unemployment line, we took our turn.

Difficult free climbing with occasional stretches of aid carried us upward. At first I was concerned that the party above might slow us down, but we were never to catch up with them. They stayed a consistent rope length ahead of us throughout the climb. Europe, as I was finding out, did indeed have many fine climbers able to do big climbs in fast times.

Although Shori had done little direct aid he was an excellent climber and his happy smile throughout the climb indicated that he wasn't having any trouble.

Off to the right at our level on the *Saxonweg* route, two German climbers seemed to be stuck, unable to make upward progress. Although we were unable to understand what they were saying, the tone of their shouts left little doubt that they were in an unenviable predicament.

The next 400-foot overhanging section was the crux of the climb. At the end of the difficulties after continually strenuous climbing, we reached a scree-covered ledge. Waiting for us were the two Germans we had been following. It was an unusual and unexpected end to the climb when one of the Germans proudly informed us that while he was here on the *Direct Cima Grande,* his wife was in Munich having a baby!

A few days later Denny Morehouse suggested that we try the *Couzy* route on the North Face of the Cima Ouest. I had not given the *Couzy* much thought and was more

Layton Kor leads a pitch on the *Brandler-Hasse Route* up the
steep North Face of the Cima Grande in the Dolomites.

145

interested in the Swiss route on the same face. "Climb the French route?" I replied. "Aye, Layton, it will be something we can really get our teeth into." Little did I appreciate at the time the literal truth of his statement, for we were to find some sections of rock on our proposed climb so soft and decomposed that a person could have done just that.

The *Couzy,* named after the late, great French alpinist Jean Couzy, was put up in 1959 by Rene Desmaison and Pierre Mazeaud. Desmaison was France's best artificial climber and this was his masterpiece. For 7 days they labored on the overhanging wall, trailing a long line that reached the ground and their support party. Each evening they pulled up food and supplies for the following day. Nylon hammocks were their sleeping beds.

Denny, coming from Great Britain, knew his way around the Dolomites, which were his summer home. He had already climbed the *Direct Cima Grande* and was interested in only the most difficult climbs.

"Layton, we'll need a little extra gear for the *Couzy,*" he informed me. "We'll certainly have to bivouac." One of the extra pieces of gear was his belay seat, which he proudly showed me. At first glance it looked like a swing seat that had been stolen from a children's playground. It was made of thin board, approximately 7 by 14 inches, with a hole drilled in each corner. A strand of rope some 2 feet long was threaded through each hole. The ropes came to a loop and all four were held by a carabiner, which could then be clipped into a piton. This unlikely contraption served as a miniature belay platform.

"Boy, that's going to be fun to use," I thought to myself.

We arrived at the base of our route the next morning at the same time as the sun, the difference being that it had a good reason to be there. I somehow wasn't surprised not to find a waiting line. We had the climb to ourselves.

Like a couple of army generals, seasoned tacticians, we discussed the plan of attack. It was agreed that I would lead the first six pitches, Denny the next six, and so on.

Only 20 feet up the wall I found myself anxiously looking for protection on the rottenest rock I'd climbed in the area. It gave me a good indication of how often this particular climb was done. Had there been a lot of traffic most of the loose rock would have been pulled off. We were more than willing to go onto direct aid and leave that teetering rock pile behind. Reaching a white pillar, we belayed alongside it. The view upward made me wonder if we were in the right place. Directly above, the cliff overhung furiously, continuing that way for the next 800 feet.

Consulting the guidebook, the description of the next section could have been extracted from the nightmare of a climber in anguish. It read, "Above is a wide overhanging crack running diagonally left. To begin with this crack is cut by several roofs and 100 feet higher it changes to an overhanging diedre, the top of which is closed by a delicate overhang. (A3 belay seat above the overhang.)"

Working my way up from one fixed piton to the next, I finally arrived at a carabiner hanging from the tip of an overhang. Happy with my find I continued up the strenuous crack and soon found yet another carabiner at the lip of another overhang. Before the pitch was over we had added nine carabiners to our already large collection.

We later found out what had happened. The previous party had decided to retreat. The face was too steep to rappel down, so they were forced to reverse the climbing process. The last man down was not able to reach back above the overhangs and retrieve the carabiners.

Before the end of this steep section, we had one more surprise in the form of a 6-foot blank section with nothing but a large hole in the rock. Apparently some pitons had fallen out. I ended up nesting a conglomeration of pitons next to a wooden block to pass this tricky section.

As the climb progressed, the opportunity for me to use Denny's belay seat never materialized. My climbing companion was so cluttered with slings, special harnesses, and other technical paraphernalia, all connected to the belay board, that it was impractical for him to get it loose. I was destined to spend the rest of the climb hanging from my thin, circulation-hampering belay slings.

For the remainder of the day we continued climbing, following the tangible proof that others had indeed passed this way—the long row of fixed pitons. It was nearly dark when we reached a small ledge nestled in the overhangs. This tiny perch, about a foot wide and 3 feet long, was the only one we had seen in hours that was large enough to sit on. A rope strung from one end of the ledge to the other served as a barrier to prevent us leaning too far forward during the night. Securely anchored we turned our attention to the thing we needed most—water. The hot sun reflecting off the yellow walls had taken its toll and we had brought far too little. We settled down for the night in an uncomfortably erect position with water dominating our thoughts. A little later, however, had it not been for our position, we could have had all the water we wanted. It began to rain! We could see the silver droplets falling 25 feet out from our ledge, a reminder that tomorrow our battle with the overhangs would continue.

The following morning we organized ourselves as best as our cramped position allowed and turned our attention to the problem of how to get off the wall. From the right-hand edge of the ledge the line of pitons continued that would serve as our lifeline to the top. We started climbing on rock similar to that of the previous day, but due to our water deficiency we moved much slower.

A short distance higher we arrived at a diagonal crack containing many wooden blocks. The old cord hanging from them had a disconcertingly bleached appearance. Each time I clipped in and applied weight, they squeaked frighteningly, I was definitely finding

Layton Kor aids out a big overhang on the *Brandler-Hasse Route* on the Cima Grande.

this climb more serious than other technically harder aid climbs in the Tres Cima area. The poor quality of the rock, the overhanging nature of the route, and the unthinkable problem of retreat added up to a climb-and-a-half.

Eventually we arrived at the last pitch of the overhanging section, the most difficult and spectacular of the entire climb. Directly above our heads was the biggest overhang on the route. In places it jutted out horizontally for 15 feet. In silence appropriate to the seriousness of the situation I worked my way right, following a decomposed limestone trough. Beneath the ceiling I was surprised that some of the pitons didn't pull out at first touch. The traverse took me to a point where the overhang was narrowest. Taking a short rest to examine the problem confronting me, I noticed a new feature of the climbing that served only to make me even more apprehensive. Our predecessors had hammered small round blocks of wood into natural holes in the roof, an inch or so in diameter, and then had driven pitons into the blocks, forcing them tight against the sides of the holes. The end result was a sort of wooden expansion piton, one of the most unique pieces of climbing engineering I had ever seen.

Unique or not, it was indescribably scary clipping into those strange improvisations and swinging out under the overhang. Dangling not a moment longer than I had to, at long last I pulled over the lip, climbed a few feet higher, and set up a sling belay in the most exposed position I'd ever experienced. While Denny was engaged in his private struggle below, I tried the best my nerves would allow to enjoy that unreal place. Entire sections of the wall below were not to be seen. They just curved out of sight. A rock dropped from that position would have landed some 50 feet or more out from the bottom of the face.

Denny joined me and easy fifth-class climbing took us up the compact gray wall above. Seventy-five feet more and we reached a large scree terrace. The difficulties were over. We had done it! The summit was still several hundred feet above, but we couldn't have cared less. Feeling like two lost souls emerging from the desert, we followed the scree ledge to easier terrain and began our search for water.

After this successful visit to the Dolomites. I returned to Leysin and headed up to the Tour d'Ai and the Tour Mayen, the two peaks above the village. Colorful alpine flowers, fluted limestone slabs, and old abandoned cabins brightened the hike up to the cliffs.

Although the Tour d'Ai and the Tour Mayen are not large by alpine standards, they both possess an interesting feature. They are guarded by limestone bands varying in height from 100 feet at the lower end, to the 700-foot North Face of the Tour Mayen.

Leysin was my base camp for nearly a year and I visited this excellent little climbing area on many occasions. I needed only the urge and a climbing companion, and I was off.

There were rumors about an unclimbed route on the East Face of the Tour d'Ai. This side of the mountain consisted of a long vertical cliff broken in its center by a massive dark cave, the most prominent feature of the entire face. I had heard that a number of Swiss parties had attempted to climb this section of the wall. They had reached the vicinity of the cave, and then had retreated. Don Whillans, the noted British climber, who was also living in Leysin at the time, agreed that the climb was worth a try.

I had heard many stories about Whillans before coming to Europe. He was noted for his ability to climb extreme pitches on-sight, often without protection. A mountain journal discussing one of his climbs, *Forked Lightning Crack,* described his lead and commented, "It was bald and bold."

We made our way up the lower section of the route uneventfully, and found ourselves a rope length away from the cave. On belay, safeguarding Whillans as he seconded the previous pitch, I had a chance to study the overhang directly above my head. It looked uncomfortably strenuous to say the least. I noticed two or three vintage pitons tucked in the overhang, relics undoubtedly of the Swiss attempts.

Don joined me and took over the lead. I pointed out the pitons thinking that since he'd never been here and therefore didn't know what was above the overhang, he'd want some protection.

Whillans reached up, grabbed a large hold under the overhang, and pulled himself up like a gymnast on a chinning bar. Paying absolutely no attention to the pitons, he worked his way out around the overhang and disappeared out of sight above. When my turn came to follow, I found out that the difficulty was not the overhang but a polished slab above. It was all I could do to keep from falling off backward. Nothing had changed: It was "bald and bold."

We had arrived at our objective. The cave was perhaps 30 feet wide by 50 feet high and felt like a damp dungeon. It wasn't hard to see why the other parties had lost interest at this point. Direct aid was required, and as this was more my cup of tea than Whillans's, I began nailing up the brittle side of the cave. By the time I reached its top, it was nearly dark. Leysin was calling. We rappelled off leaving a fixed rope in place.

Next day we returned and with the help of the fixed rope rapidly reached our high point. Even then it took the remainder of the day to climb the final 200 feet—testimony to the difficulties of this short climb. Whillans decided the climb deserved a fitting British name, and called it "Plum Duff."

In Leysin, home, for the most part, was the Club Vagabond, a hostelry catering to tourists, ski groups, and somehow even attracting the climbing crowd. I worked at the Club sporadically, doing such important jobs as washing dishes, carrying out the garbage, chopping ice off the step (just the kind of exercise I needed!), and babysitting Fougere, a sister hotel lower down the mountain. A bearded young American from Salt Lake City by the name of Court Richards was working there too. It took me a considerable amount

Layton Kor at a hanging belay on the Tour Mayen in the Swiss Alps.

of time to convince him that what we needed to be doing was "this new route" on the North Face of the Mayen.

Through the years I've found myself in many strange situations, but none quite like the Mayen. As we hauled our equipment in to the 700-foot face, I noticed some odd-looking chunks of metal lying around in the rubble at the base. I didn't give them much thought until cannon fire in the valley below began ringing in our ears. It suddenly dawned on us that we were in the target area of a Swiss Army artillery range and the metal was shrapnel. We tore out of there as fast as our already tired legs would allow, over the saddle between the two peaks, and back to Leysin.

Only later, when things had quieted down, did we return to the Mayen for a climb that took parts of 2 days and carried with it the occasional vision of being blown out of our direct aid slings by a well-aimed shell.

During my stay at Leysin, I met a young American named Rick Sylvester who had just finished a mountaineering course at the International School of Modern Mountaineering. As the following account describes, Rick then joined me for a climbing trip to the Dolomites.

Layton Kor hangs it all out on the Plum Duff Tour in Switzerland.

Photograph Don Whillans/Layton Kor Collection

The Dolies

Rick Sylvester

The sign read, "Venezia—86 kms."

"Oh, Rick. Venice!" Rhoda's eyes lit up. "So close."

A voice from the backseat, Kor. "Hey, man, I know this Grade VI. Really neat."

We left the girls at the trailhead for 2 days. The climb was . . . "really neat."

My marriage broke up a couple of weeks later.

The first four climbing partners I shared a rope with were Don Whillans, Dougal Haston, Yvon Chouinard, and Layton Kor. I guess one could characterize my introduction to mountaineering as a baptism by fire. Sure, there were a couple of fellow students from the International School of Modern Mountaineering tied on too, but admitting that dilutes the impact, and that might be wrong, for impact there certainly was.

I'd finished a year of graduate school abroad at the University of Stockholm. After a month of sightseeing, my wife Rhoda and I ended up in Leysin, a Swiss village that was the site of the climbing school where I was signed up to take a beginning course.

I entered Leysin with somewhat mixed emotions. Three months earlier, John Harlin, the school's director and founder, had fallen 4,000 feet down the Eiger's North Face. My thoughts ran something like, "If that's what happened to an experienced expert, then what's in store for me, a mere novice?" Of course I knew that I was unlikely to be exposed to such a severe situation. But still.

There were many things I learned that summer, but looking back I've often thought that climbing might have been the least of them. For, more than just learning a new skill or sport, it proved to be an initiation into a new way of life with its own special subculture; one, though I didn't know it at the time, I was never wholly to leave. The climbers I met at Leysin were unlike anyone I'd encountered before, sort of mountain bohemians if you will. Each seemed to possess a definite and unique personality. Years later a climbing and skiing friend, Adrian Rosenthal, would observe that whereas the skiers and groovy singles he knew in California all seemed somehow similar, each climber he knew appeared wildly individualistic. Perhaps it's the nature of the endeavor; the hard rock and ice wears away the outer layers until the kernel is exposed. My high school and college acquaintances seemed more or less like variations on the same theme, but Whillans, Haston, Burke, Chouinard, and Kor stood out as striking originals. Clearly out of the mainstream, they seemed like characters from a book, larger than life, filled with life. I was reminded of protagonists from Hemingway novels, like *The Sun Also Rises, To Have and Have Not;* existential castaways all. (Sartre was popular then.) Alongside the likes of Kor and Whillans I felt like the Alan Bates observer bearing witness to Anthony Quinn's Zorba.

I ended up taking not one, but two sessions of instruction that summer at Leysin, the second due to the fact that half of the first had been weathered out. Much of the time I was nearly catatonic with fear and apprehension, but deep down I knew this climbing life was somehow for me.

The second session had ended and Rhoda and I were hanging around Leysin. I was sitting on the bed in Whillans's room in the Club Vagabond looking through some of his climbing books. Don was out teaching or perhaps getting an early start on the evening's debaucheries. I'd just pulled another volume off his shelf when Rhoda came in.

"Layton Kor's downstairs looking for someone to climb with."

Kor had been making daily sorties to the rocks above the village. He'd been applying his prodigious energy to putting up numerous new routes on the three major limestone formations, where, rumor had it, he seemed intent on doing every conceivable line. Tales of incredible first ascents marked by thin hard nailing over horribly exposed cave roofs filled the bar in the evening. My inexperienced mind created images far worse than reality . . . or perhaps not.

Rhoda was anxious to resume the Grand Tour, to get on with the essential business of following the well-beaten tourist path through the museums and assorted whatnot of RomeParisLondon. In turning me on to the possibility of climbing with Kor, she figured he was merely looking for someone for another afternoon route above the village. So did I, but Layton had grander ideas. He had a list of climbs, mostly Grade VI's with big reputations, that he wanted to work through in the Dolomites, or Dolies as the English and subsequently everyone else came to call them. Somehow Layton knew I had wheels, in this case a used Morris Oxford I'd picked up for $200 just before leaving Sweden, and he wanted to know if I was interested in climbing with him in the Dolies for a week or so. Looking at him, I secretly wondered what would happen were he ever to fall.

Climbing novice that I was I nevertheless had heard something of Kor, both the climber and the person. Already renowned at that time, he was reputed to be a dynamo, a mover, a restless climber of unlimited energy and drive. He was said to have the strongest set of hands in climbing, supposedly the result of his work as a stonemason. Way ahead of his time, a veritable Bob Beamon of mountaineering, he had scaled routes and sections of pitches free that wouldn't be repeated for years. And his aid climbing was spoken about in equally awed terms. A few years later, Lito Tejada-Flores, on his return from the third ascent of Fitzroy via new line, would remark about the so-called big plum down there, the East Buttress: "In good weather four Layton Kors on speed might be able to do it in 5 days."

But, what interested me even more than his climbing prowess at that time was what I'd heard about Kor the person. Someone remarked that if Layton was at a party that was boring for him, rather than making any of the conventional gestures of politeness he'd just wander into the next room, or leave. I got this picture in my mind of a total non-compromiser, someone with no time for pretense or artificiality. Having been enamored of Ibsen in college, I perhaps saw in Kor the opposite of Peer Gynt, the personification of Brandt. Here was truly someone too dynamic and up-front, too filled with energy to be willing or able to put up with life's small hypocrisies and dishonesties. Kor was someone who wouldn't give in. He was someone who'd rather be out doing things, who heard and acknowledged vital voices calling, "Climb!" In short, it was the way I hoped to be, though I was not fully aware of it at the time.

At any rate we, meaning Rhoda and I in the front seat and Layton and his French girlfriend in the backseat, were soon on our way to the Dolies. I recall a lot of giggling emanating from that backseat. Someone was having a good time, whereas next to me I felt less pleasant vibrations from another who'd rather be sightseeing in RomeParisLondon. And so the kilometers rolled by.

The first "Six" on Layton's list was, unfortunately, perhaps the hardest of any route we were to attempt. The *Maestri* on the Roda di Vael, 450 meters in height, V+ A3, was certainly the most intimidating. A classic route, hard and mostly artificial, it had required 6 days for Maestri's first ascent. These details I learned subsequently. At the time all I knew was that the route was hard . . . and scary.

We set out on the approach from the hut. Such a couple we made: Mutt and Jeff. Kor forged ahead in his silly knickers and cloddy-looking Kronhofers and I trudged behind in my equally silly knickers and heavy mountain boots. A dank day. The sky was leaden and gray, appearing overcast as it often does with first light before the sun rises. I was "breathing air like razor blades between deathly black and deathly white." The cliff rose ominously. Like most limestone it was vertical at the minimum. It would have been off-putting to many experienced climbers, not to mention a raw novice whose then greatest climbing achievement was the lowly Aiguille de l'M at Chamonix.

My emotions were already in a tizzy when the final coup de grace occurred. Close to the base I started, struck by drops of water, though the effect was more as if they were drops of acid. After my initial surprise, a ray of hope shone through. Possible salvation, a last-minute reprieve: rain? In other words, we (or more accurately, I) might not have to climb.

"Nope. They're just drips off the summit overhang. You know, the top of this route probably leans out at least 40 feet from the base."

I looked up. The summit disappeared in grayness. Halfway up was a striking feature, an ominous triangular-shaped roof. Talk about previsualization—the idea that before you can do something you must be able to picture yourself doing it—there was no way I could picture myself dealing with that feature.

We roped up and Kor led the first pitch. Exact details are vague in memory. I think it was mixed, a combination of free and aid. I remember that Kor encountered some trouble at a couple of spots (the reader, of course, knows what goes through the mind of the fearful novice when he sees the expert leader slow down). At last the shout, "C'mon up!"

Nothing went right. What's dim in memory is the exact feature that gave me trouble—a sort of cleft at the base. What is vivid is that I couldn't get up it. I couldn't even get off the ground. The rock was painfully cold to my fingers, and the chill seeped into my heart. A lieback was required. Over the years I've come to recognize liebacks as one of my foremost nemeses (others include face climbing, smearing, hard jamming, la de da da), requiring as they do strength, aggressiveness, daring, skill, and technique. Further, I was weighed down with pack and hard hat, items I hadn't been forced to climb with at ISMM. They seemed to exert an added burden many multiples their actual weight. I resented Layton for having made a donkey of me with them, lessening my already slim chances.

Time passed, lots of it. The first move was a killer. In half an hour I literally hadn't gotten off the ground. In fact, by that time, I wasn't at all sure I wanted to. After all, what was there to look forward to above?

And there was a need to hurry. Though most parties doing the route then bivied, we'd brought no gear for that purpose.

Embarrassment also added to my problems. "What must Kor be thinking?" was what I was thinking. By now he must be fuming, or at the least ruminating that he'd made a big mistake. "Came all this way and this bozo can't even get off the ground. Can't climb at all." Kor knew I was a wrestler, and earlier, as justification for taking a novice like me along, had made some mention of having once climbed with a wrestler and knew that they were strong. Clearly there were weak wrestlers too.

Finally, after even more time had passed in fruitless endeavor, came a shout, impatient and with perhaps a touch of anger.

"C'mon, man! It's only 5.7!"

An admonishment wasn't unexpected by then, but not one in that particular form. I doubt I can convey the full effect that statement had on me. Today the announcement, "C'mon, man! It's only 5.15c!" would have less impact. Fifth-class climbing had been something we ISMM students had barely heard mentioned. As a result, it had assumed mythical proportions. It was another dimension. And not only was this fifth class, it was upper fifth class. And there was this madman yelling down at me, both his tone and content clearly conveying the absolute inconceivability that anyone could be experiencing the slightest bit of trouble at such a standard. Yet, there I was, unable to get off the ground, with the rock cold, loathing the claustrophobia-causing hard hat and the pack pulling me back, and all the time that continual pitter-patter from the curtain of drips 40 feet behind.

Somehow I eventually got up the first pitch. Kor must have pulled. I remember at one point he commanded, "Climb the rope!" For me that remark ranked with his previous "5.7" one. Climb an 11-millimeter line? Impossible. The ropes I had enough trouble with in gym classes, the ones specifically designed for climbing, were five times as thick, and not covered in a slippery smooth sheath.

Layton turned out to be a realist. We rappelled off. I don't remember if it was at the top of that pitch or if we did one more, but at my rate of progress there was no way we were going to climb the face without a bivy. I recall Kor being emphatic, if not a bit sarcastic, that the route wasn't worth doing with a bivy. It was academic, however, for there was probably scarce chance I could have made it, bivy or not. I was glad to be leaving, not to mention alive, but it didn't make for a great start to our trip and I smarted at what might be going through Kor's mind.

Following the *Maestri,* we travelled through the Dolomites for a few days doing some short routes. After my ignominious failure a major personal victory occurred when I successfully followed Layton up the *Franceschi* route on the Cinque Torri (Five Towers), the hardest route by far that I had climbed at that time. Then followed the Southwest Ridge of the Torre Delago in the Vajolet Towers—classic climbing, steep, but with plenty of holds and an outrageous "a cheval" near the top. I was grateful for this departure from the mind-boggling "Sixes" on Layton's list and for the first time experienced the pure joy of climbing, the sensuality of physical movement, that old ballet on the vertical. I was learning, improving, and getting used to the exposure. More important was the evaporation of my secret fear, that due to me Kor wouldn't succeed at a single route on his list and the whole trip would be an ascentless, embarrassing fiasco.

It was after this route that I committed my great transgression, opting for the final Six on Layton's list, rather than for Rhoda's Venice. And by so doing, I showed my true colors, made my choice—climbing instead of RomeParisLondon. Perhaps this fuelled the fires that led to Rhoda's mutiny and the beginning of the end of our marriage.

We arrived at the remote Brenta, an area the guidebook describes as "isolated from the main Dolomite region . . . the most westerly of all the Dolomite groups." The areas we drove through heading there had a feeling akin to many of our sparsely populated mountain regions here in North America. We passed a few poor villages, stark contrasts to Cortina and its like. In the afternoon we parked at the trailhead.

Our goal was the Cima d'Ambiez, requiring a longish approach to a hut from which we would set out early the next morning. Layton and I left the girls at the remote trailhead with not even a village to wander about in and certainly a stark contrast to being pushed along in a gondola down some Venetian canal. We set off hiking, an approach filled with philosophical banter, things too true to set down here—well, talk about the problems of dealing with women anyway. We reached the Agostini hut as darkness fell. Due more to poverty than only American wilderness ethic, we intended to sleep outside the hut, but a drizzle began, necessitating both of us crawling into Layton's bivy sack. Naturally, we had no real tent. As the condensation started and as my mind began questioning if this was going to work, a woman who turned out to be the guardian came out and invited us to use the hut, free. I was struck by the kindness of her offer.

The hut wasn't crowded and we had no trouble finding space on the long dormitory bunk where up to twenty can sleep side by side. There was a feeling of intimacy, warmth and camaraderie, and safety too. It was my first taste of mountain hut life and I've idealized it ever since.

It didn't take long the next morning to reach the cliff's base. But Layton was having trouble locating the start of the route. It was a novel experience to witness this seemingly infallible climbing machine clearly perplexed. The Cima d'Ambiez was a broad cliff offering no obvious line. Naturally I was no help; I didn't even know what we were looking for. I'd long since realized I was along for one purpose—the belay. Hopefully it was one I could fulfill.

Layton became agitated. There was no time to waste. I gathered it was a hard route we were supposed to be doing, perhaps the hardest of the entire trip. It had a decent reputation, supposedly not done often. We eventually traversed a little ways out on a broad ledge. Still far from certain we'd found the route's start, Layton began nailing a right-facing corner. He hurried, turning on the speed. Twenty feet up. Twenty-five. Suddenly, almost before I could register it, he was falling. And a moment later I was rising. It was that

6'5" 200-pound lanky body against my 5'6" 130 pounds. It was the fastest I ever gained several feet at the base of a climb, far surpassing my efforts on the *Maestri*.

A hurriedly placed 2-inch Bong had pulled. Although I'd left the ground, I held the fall, stopping Layton a few feet short of the deck. I'd fulfilled my function, earned my way, perhaps even earned some small niche in the annals of mountaineering history. Having held a Kor fall had to be some kind of distinction. Surely that might qualify me my place.

The fall provided Layton with the impetus he needed to find the correct start. A lack of fixed pegs in the crack confirmed his doubts that this wasn't it. Several hundred feet farther left turned out to be where we should have been. We relocated and started again. Steep, sustained free climbing was the order of the day. It was my first experience with what at the time seemed absurdly thin and continuous climbing. I suppose I grabbed some pegs but still managed to eke out sections requiring more successive hard moves than I'd ever made before. When I wasn't too gripped, I almost enjoyed the climbing. My confidence that the rope could really be trusted also improved. Of course, Layton did all the leading, keeping a tight rope, if not applying outright tension.

"Hey, not so tight! I can climb this without help." I was definitely coming along. I wasn't the same person as on the *Maestri* a week earlier. Only Layton didn't know it. He didn't seem to perceive my great improvement. How disappointing.

"This is the mountains, man. Weather comes in quick. You've always got to hurry."

The sky was perfectly blue, not a cloud. More tugs on my swami belt, but I really could make the moves. Old relativity was at work. Once past the bulging crux, the remainder, though harder than anything I'd ever climbed before, didn't seem so bad. The angle dropped back on the last pitches and we found ourselves on the summit early, probably not much after noon. From there, it was all downhill.

Shortly after the Dolies, I ended up soloing the Matterhorn, an ascent that, but for the time and climbs with Layton, would have been way beyond me. On returning to Leysin, filled with the headiness of having been both literally and figuratively the highest in my life, I announced the victory to Rhoda. "I'm leaving you," was her reply. Yes, from there it was all downhill.

The Cinque Torri, or "Five Towers," are a popular climbing area in the Dolomites.
Photograph Stewart M. Green

Europe was full of surprises. One day, out of the blue, Yvon Chouinard arrived in Leysin. As always, he was fit and ready to go climbing.

We decided to warm up (or so we thought) on a route on the Tour d'Ai. The climb followed a pillar that formed the corner between the East and North Faces. The weather was fine when we started but partway up it began to snow. By the time we reached the summit the rock was coated white. It was one of those freak snowstorms that occasionally come out of nowhere in the Alps.

Yvon's main interest was to do a major ice climb in the Chamonix–Mont Blanc area. He already had the climb picked out: the 3,000-foot Swiss route on the North Face of Les Courtes. Definitely a serious undertaking.

When we arrived, Chamonix was teeming with tourists from all over Europe. A favorite vacation spot, it was also a climbing center for the great alpine routes. After a binge of wandering through stores and climbing shops, we eventually wound up ice-bouldering in crampons on the broken glacier above Chamonix. Some of the local guides were also there and it was embarrassing comparing their performance to mine. They casually walked around on the steep ice as if they had been born with their crampons on.

A téléphérique ride began our venture in fine style, transporting us swiftly from the valley high up into the exhilarating atmosphere of the mountains. Yvon and I had saved ourselves a long walk.

From the téléphérique station we followed a well-marked trail for several hours to the Argentière hut. It was beautifully situated on the opposite side of the Argentière glacier from the peaks and we were able to take in the entire panorama of the north faces of the Triolet, Courtes, Droites, and Aiguille Verte. When the sun hits these peaks at a certain angle they emit a glassy sparkle, appearing even more intimidating than normal.

That evening at midnight, when most people are climbing into their beds, we were climbing out of ours. It was standard starting time for the big ice climbs. Lack of sleep had left me feeling pathetic as we stumbled through the darkness and began the long trudge up the glacier to the base of Les Courtes. By the light of headlamps we began moving together up the first steep snowfield. Roped together, we did not belay, wanting to save all the time we possibly could. After a thousand feet or so of this progress, a high-angle ice bulge on our left brought our soloing to an abrupt halt. It was time to start belaying.

Two rock pitons in a small pillar backed me up as I watched Yvon tiptoe on crampon points up and across the steep bulge—the crux of the climb. I felt fortunate to be in the company of this superb climber whose abilities enabled him to handle difficult ice climbing in such an easygoing manner.

For the next 2,000 feet we repeated the same procedure over and over. A short ice axe in one hand. A taped ice piton in the other. Front point for 75 feet. Chop a large foothold for balance. Place one ice screw. Continue front pointing until the rope runs out. Chop a small belay ledge. Place one ice screw and one ice piton for belay anchors. Bring the second man up. Repeat. Repeat. Repeat.

By the time we reached the top the sun was long gone. Worried about avalanches, we headed down. Descending the other side of the mountain proved to be the most risky part of our venture. Entire sections of snow were sloughing off, carrying large chunks of rock with them to crash and disappear in the gullies below. Arriving at another hut, the guardian informed us that two weeks earlier two German climbers had been killed in an avalanche on the same descent.

8

DIAMOND IN WINTER

n Colorado in the winter of 1967, despite the traumatic experience of the Eiger Direct, my appetite for winter climbing had still not been satisfied. This time, without the media fanfare that had accompanied the Eiger, I headed up to my old haunt, the East Face of Longs Peak, with Wayne Goss and Bob Culp, intent on making the first winter ascent of The Diamond via a new route.

We arrived at the shelter cabin about 2:30 p.m. on March 4 to find superb conditions dominating the surroundings below the East Face of Longs Peak. Bob Culp and Wayne Goss, my two rope mates standing nearby, agreed that to call this winter climbing, when conditions were almost summer-like, was a bit unfair.

Close behind was our helpful support party, consisting of Dany Smith, John Pinamont, and Tom Ruetz, all members of Boulder's Rocky Mountain Rescue Group. It was thanks to them that the crushing loads with our climbing gear had reached the cabin.

After a short rest, we watched as the openings in the mist gave us a view of the colorful, vertical Diamond. Happy with the prospect of a winter first, we all dug into the monumental task of shoveling snow out of the cabin. Before long, steam rose from cookers and soon hot soup, meat, and pots of warm drinks kept us happy until the cold drove deep into our sleeping bags. As usual I had trouble sleeping, and to add to my misery the wind picked up and the howling noise remained all through the night. By morning 6 inches of snow had fallen and our winter had returned.

Before feeling the effects of our light breakfast, we left our support party and began hiking through the fresh snow to the bottom of the East Face. An hour later we ascended Lambs Slide and were at the beginning of Broadway. Culp, who had not been feeling well up to this point, became most uncomfortable with a sore throat. Knowing that this was no place for anyone who was ill, Bob left immediately for the shelter cabin. Wayne and I roped up at this point; to go any further without protection would have been unwise. After the first rope length of traversing we could see that the white band we were on was little more than a steep snow bank of unstable snow. At the end of every lead we were forced to burrow deep into the snow to reach rock for piton anchors. After about 2 hours of dangerous wading and one close call with an avalanche that sloughed off inches below us, we reached our bivouac site below The Diamond. It was very late so we began digging out a cave with a cooking pot as we had dropped our shovel during the traverse of Broadway. Cold and near-darkness kept us at a fair pace till finally we reached the rocky floor

Climbers cross Broadway below The Diamond in a snowstorm before its first winter ascent.

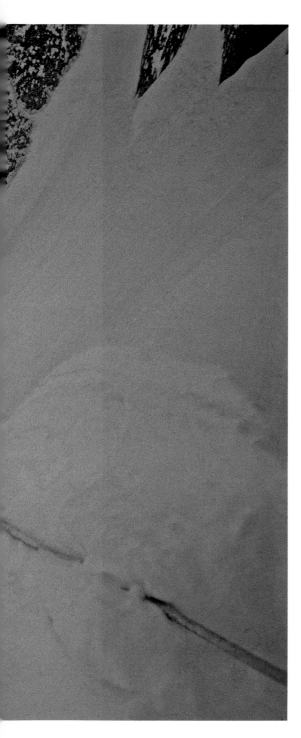

and large amounts of bivy gear left by Bob and Wayne on an earlier attempt. After sorting out the mess and rigging a hammock above the bivouac to keep out the storm, we retired to our bags completely spent. Again our cooker sent out the blue flames that promised much-needed food and liquids. After our snack, sleep followed. Around three o'clock, a piton that supported the hammock above gave way—leaving us half-buried in the new snow. Once again our soup pot was put to work and peaceful rest seemed hours away.

The morning arrived too soon and the weather was still quite bad. We gobbled down some food, stuffed our packs full of gear, tied on the 150-foot ropes, and worked our way through the snow to the beginning of our new route a hundred feet away. The climb began with mixed climbing across steep slabs plastered in snow. Our very first rope length took us an hour-and-a-half and ended on a tiny stance in the middle of nowhere. As we were directly above the North Chimney, the powerful wind from the bottom of the East Face funneled up the walls carrying sharp snow crystals, which forced us to put on our ski goggles.

Wayne quickly led the next pitch, climbing up a slippery groove well over seventy degrees. After he had anchored the ropes and pulled up the packs. I prusiked up, removing the pitons until we both shared the same ledge. Still no improvement in the weather, and our two-way radio, which the Park Service had been kind enough to lend us, promised even worse conditions for the next day.

Preferring to try again in a day or so (after all, who could want to climb in bad weather?), we were soon on our way down the wall, leaving fixed ropes behind us until we had reached the easy snow slope at the bottom of the North Chimney.

The next couple of days we spent at the shelter cabin, mostly listening to the transistor radio and eating. The

Layton Kor aid climbs in frigid conditions on the first ascent of the *Enos Mills Wall*.

weather remained windy and cold, and our food supply dwindled till finally we all packed out toward Boulder for fresh supplies.

Just a day later Wayne and I returned to Longs. We spent the entire day hiking from the parking lot until finally the last fixed ropes carried us to our bivouac on Broadway. The weather had improved considerably and our bivouac that night was quite fun. We rose early the next morning convinced we would get our wall and soon were together at the beginning of the ropes.

I snapped the jumars onto the fixed line, applied my weight, and watched loose snow free itself from the long red rope leading to our high point. After finishing the diagonal struggle I slid the handles down the rope to Wayne and soon we shared the tiny perch, where days before bad weather had forced us to retreat.

After organizing our equipment we ascended the third rope length of the climb. This vertical step, which was entirely artificial, ended on a mossy ledge in a snow-filled corner 130 feet above. Several sound anchors gave mental rest as Goss rapidly nailed his way up another exciting pitch deep into unknown terrain. An occasional gust of wind and the feather-like snow that followed made us happy with our warm clothing. After Wayne had rigged another sling belay 80 feet above, he hauled up the packs while I removed the belay pitons that provided security on the dangerously steep wall.

Wayne Goss tests an aid piton high on The Diamond.

It was always nice to be moving, for while in motion the warmth seeped through our systems and chased out the cold and misery we endured on the silent stances. About noon I began the fifth lead of the climb. This airy experience followed a wide crack on the edge of a 100-foot pillar. I had nearly reached its top when a protruding piton tore a large hole in my down jacket. Unable to stop, I continued struggling up the bad-width crack until some small footholds provided rest. The now-useless down spiraled like falling leaves toward Goss, who hung in slings 75 feet below. It was very late in the day when I left the comfort of a 2-foot ledge on top of the pillar and began hammering long pins deep into the ninety-degree wall. If we were lucky a bivouac ledge awaited us at the end of the lead.

A hundred feet up, the rock became rotten and the smooth diagonal overhangs stopped all progress. I was trying desperately to place a piton on my left, when the tiny angle holding my weight popped out and a terrifying 20-foot plunge into the dusk followed. When it ended I was swinging upside down, squinting toward Goss, whose bright smile showed it had been an easy catch.

I quickly climbed hand over hand up the rope, drove a larger piton into the same crack, and once again studied the traverse to the left. A thin sling hooked over a tiny knob held my weight, while I nervously placed a poor piton upside down beneath the roof. Using this for balance, I left the little security I had and tiptoed on the very edge of my double boots across a slab that ended in an overhanging snow-filled corner. It had turned completely dark as I hung from my tortured fingers, placing several pitons to secure the belay.

"Lightning" Goss, who was in remarkable shape, removed all the pitons in just a few minutes, and soon headlamps cast out two beams halfway up The Diamond.

"Just above us is the bivouac," I told Wayne, not really sure of anything except how lousy I felt. As Wayne belayed I sighted along the flickering light, which cut into the darkness, yielding a 1½-inch crack. Three pitons put me on a small snow shelf 15 feet above Wayne and with the last of my energy I stamped out a small ledge in the snow. Again I placed the necessary belay anchors and began hauling up the packs, which felt like three mailbags full of lead. Soon a bright shower of sparks lit up the large piton on which Wayne was hammering, and before long he pulled out the last piton of the day. I slowly worked my way into the sleeping bag while Wayne, without a word, dug through the packs removing food, cooking gear, and other items we would need for the night. After joining me in idle comfort, he fired up the stove to provide us with the only food we could consume, hot raspberry Jell-O.

Even though we had to remain sitting all night, it was warm, reasonably comfortable, and we only woke up occasionally to change positions. Morning arrived with the sun gods and their yellow warmth, which we thankfully absorbed along with more hot Jell-O.

Looking down an exposed dihedral on the *Enos Mills Wall.*

Stiff swollen fingers kept us from smiling as we sorted out the mess from the night before. After things were a bit straightened out, more pounding, which inserted our metal spikes, carried us up a huge overhanging open book above the bivouac. A hundred and twenty feet up I crawled into another sling belay, a position that was overhanging Goss and the bivouac site by 10 feet. We carefully nailed the last 70 feet of the open book up, to, and over a 3-foot roof; then belayed 30 feet above in slings from a horizontal crack system. This thin brittle crack cut all the way across The Diamond to the well-known Table Ledge. The view at this point was quite spectacular as everything below to Broadway was overhanging.

Layton Kor waits for the morning sun to warm up a freezing bivouac.

Artificial climbing on The Diamond in winter, as we were finding out, is a slow and delicate process, and our snail-like pace was almost sure to provide us with another bivy on the wall. The next rope length was even more rotten and every well-placed piton sent granular, red rock dashing all over the mountain. After I had climbed another 130 feet, the last 10 of which consisted of a horizontal traverse on "spooky" knifeblades, I set up the fifth hanging belay of the climb. While Wayne removed the pitons I viewed the crack system 40 feet to the left where I had joined the master of technical climbing, Royal Robbins, on a 1-day ascent of the wall.

Once again darkness set in and as our headlamps were giving us trouble, we almost expected a night in slings on the blank wall. Both Wayne and I agreed to make the top if at all possible, as we were still worried about the unsettled weather. Fifty feet above, another large roof provided a strenuous 10 minutes and a spectacular view into the depth. Above the overhang the crack widened and an occasional free move was needed to eliminate the

The Diamond, lying above 13,000 feet, is an exposed alpine environment during the winter.

use of expansion bolts, as our biggest pitons (4 inches) were not large enough. After many minutes of struggling with rope slings and my headlamp cord I somehow managed to force several pitons deep into the icy crack, setting up the last belay of the climb. Wayne soon shared my position at the hanging "spaghetti gardens."

After a few minutes' rest we changed places and I led into the night with a blinking headlamp until the wild blast of the wind told me it was all over. We arrived at the top of the wall at about 10 p.m. and bivouacked on the spot. The wind kept us awake most of the night and our short walk to the summit of Longs the next morning was a tiring, breathless undertaking. Even that was soon over and I shook hands with my tremendous partner for the first winter ascent of The Diamond—an experience we would long remember.

Galen Rowell at a hanging belay on the *Salathé Wall.*

9

SALATHÉ

The last major climb I did in Yosemite was the *Salathé Wall* with Galen Rowell. Galen was an auto mechanic at the time, living in Berkeley. He was an excellent, strong Yosemite climber with muscle to spare. We arranged that Galen would lead all the hard free cracks, and I would lead the hard nailing. As his account of the climb tells, this arrangement was to work out admirably.

Salathé Wall

Galen Rowell

In the early sixties, Layton Kor was the only one of us who really seemed to enjoy climbing the big walls. At the time, Camp 4 was inhabited by trailers, dogs, and climbers, with priorities considered in that order by the National Park Service. Layton was an obvious exception among the scrawny group of college dropouts who literally lived in fear of the big walls they so badly wanted to climb.

Steve Roper described their situation best: "Caught between two influential ways of life, i.e., the parental ideal that one must go to college and become successful, and the instinctive desire of all animals to be free and wild and to do what they want, these climbers give the impression that they are waiting, patiently waiting, for some unlikely and ill-defined miracle to transform them from their free, yet unhappy and wretched existence into an existence of security, complacency, and pseudo-happiness."

Layton was a definite anomaly. At a time when out-of-state climbers were not accepted by the xenophobic tribe that inhabited Camp 4, he became an instant insider. His presence was so powerful, his personal integrity so obvious, that he escaped most all the infighting and petty jealousies of the times.

Layton and Royal Robbins both stood apart from the social pressures of Camp 4. They managed to get up a tremendous number of climbs while climbers of nearly the same technical ability sat out their days in camp or made short, relatively insignificant climbs that did nothing to further the Valley's potential as the greatest pure rock climbing area in the world.

The two men had nearly opposite mental attitudes, however. Robbins saw his triumphs as intellectual, the result of applying his imagination to the sport. He willed his body to follow his mind's course, which was freer than that of others, partly because it was not constrained by academia. Robbins had dropped out of school earlier and more decisively than most of the Yosemite crowd. Where he saw a clear course toward self-education, other climbers were still paralyzed by real and imagined ties with academia.

One night I ate a Number 31—a hamburger with chips for 45 cents—in Yosemite Lodge with a group of four college dropouts. All, unknown to each other, were National Merit Scholars, a situation with the odds exceeding any of their considerable mathematical abilities. Yet this foursome was somehow unable to self-actualize their powerful imaginations in the way that Robbins and Kor could.

Layton remained apart from the mental agony that characterized Camp 4, making jokes with short punch lines to poke fun at those who took life too seriously. When Robbins made a multi-day first ascent on the north wall of Sentinel Rock, he wrote that the sunrise was "better than Mozart." Layton climbed a new route next to Robbins's, returned to Camp 4, and described the sunrise as "not as good as Fats Domino."

When Layton invited me to climb the feared West Face of Sentinel with him in March 1963, I was proud to be chosen as his partner. As we walked to the base, I thought about how I had passed muster by leading a hard jam crack with him a few days before. Or had I?

Walking up the trail, head bent low so as not to be terrified by the shadow of Sentinel looming in the moonlight, I remembered the conversations of other climbers around the fireplace in the Yosemite Lodge lounge:

"Robbins is the best in the world. Just look at the routes he's done!"

"Pratt's a better climber."

"But he does his best climbs with guys like Royal. I think Kor's the best. He gets up anything with anybody. He just goes through camp and picks up anyone who can belay him and drags the guy up route after route, Kor wears out partners several times a month."

Layton Kor aid climbs up thin cracks on a lower pitch on the *Salathé Wall.*
Photograph Galen Rowell/Layton Kor Collection

I had been picked up in Camp 4. Somewhere in the back of my mind I feared death on Sentinel, and I made a mental inventory of my possessions and what my parents would think and who would call them. But I feared not doing Sentinel far more than death. I was absolutely fixed on not turning back, on supporting Layton, on doing my share of leading if he let me.

On the way out of camp I had to skip every third step or so to keep up with Layton's enormous gait. I was 5'8" to his 6'5". His pace remained rapid through the forest, across the thick, frosted grass of a meadow, over a bridge and up the steep switchbacks of the Four Mile Trail under Sentinel Rock.

I thought of the day before, and how Layton had asked Eric Beck to climb the West Face with him. The West Face was almost virgin territory, unexplored except by a few rock gods like Robbins, Chouinard, and

Frost. Everyone dreaded a long jam crack with a twist in it midway up the wall. Beck, not one to be martyred, replied, "Do you wish to see my blood run from the Dogleg Cracks?"

Beck liked to call life 5.6—just hard enough to need protection, but not very interesting. A year earlier on a cold April morning Layton had similarly dragged Beck onto Middle Cathedral Rock, where they made an astounding 1-day first ascent of a hard Grade IV.

Sweat poured down my brow as I tried to keep up with Layton. I held his tall frame just far enough in front of me to block the view of the narrow face. I planned to walk up to the wall without looking up, and to start climbing without looking down. That way I'd be committed before I got too terrified.

Fear was a normal part of climbing conversation in those days, so I told Layton just how I felt. He said he was scared too, both of the climb and the fact that he felt sick. It was his first mention of not feeling well.

We arrived minutes later at the base and uncoiled the ropes. Suddenly Layton said, "We're going back."

As a consolation we climbed Sentinel by the *Steck-Salathé Route* a few days later. Layton didn't fit through the Narrows, an extremely tight chimney. I stood above him, put the rope over my shoulder in a crouch, then stood up with great force whenever he yelled, "Pull," at the end of a total exhale.

In June 1967 the man who had asked me to climb the *Salathé* with him was quite different from the boisterous Layton of the early days. He'd stopped his incessant pacing, but the look of a caged lion was still in his eyes. At the first bivouac on Heart Ledge he told me of his frustration on the Eiger, how the Europeans thought he was a quitter each time he descended thousands of

Galen Rowell cleans a pitch high on the headwall of the *Salathé Wall*.

Layton Kor leads wide cracks on the *Salathé Wall*.
Photograph Galen Rowell/Layton Kor Collection

feet to the Kleine Scheidegg Hotel, and how he actually did far more work going up and down than the other climbers who hung heroically in bivouacs each night, to the delight of the media.

Then came the accident. A broken fixed rope sent John Harlin to his death. The Germans stripped some of the fixed ropes high on the face and Layton was cut off from the summit team. He watched them finish the climb without him.

Layton Kor hangs in aiders below a roof high on the *Salathé Wall*.

Photograph Galen Rowell/Layton Kor Collection

Layton expressed no bitterness, but his pain was obvious. He had lost a friend, a climb, and a connection to the other climbers as well.

Layton was quieter than I had ever seen. Occasionally he would rage about, as if to prove that he was his old self, but he acted like a man who had lost the love of his life. I didn't understand what was happening. I expected life in the Valley to go on forever, with no beginning and no end, just people climbing together, joyfully scaring themselves. I saw myself and Layton as part of a flow that I expected to continue as long as I lived.

Layton had seen a different world, one of finality and agony, and it had changed him. If we had done the *Salathé* a year before, he would have wanted all the best leads. We would have argued for them until he found a polite excuse to devour as much of the route for himself as possible and a way for me to save face. This time he just wanted to get up the route. He asked if I could lead all the free climbing. The stores were out of my favorite Pivetta Spiders, and the only decent shoes I had were a pair of leather mountain boots I used for High Sierra climbs. I said yes, confident that once on the wall he would take over as usual.

At that time there were many more aid pitches than free pitches. With his extreme reach, Layton could cruise up aid cracks with far fewer placements than I would need. On the lower part of the wall I actually seemed to benefit from wide, stiff boots that fit perfectly in many of the cracks. Higher, however, I stepped into the worst climbing situation of my career.

Far above protection in a 5.9 off-width crack, my foot jammed. When I tried to force it, the rigid sole kinked, slid down, and locked. I pulled, pounded with one free hand, and began to whimper shamelessly. I had a vision of my tibia remaining in the crack after I fell out.

Ten agonizing minutes passed. Layton told me to stop thrashing and hang on. Without a belay he nailed up to me and began hammering on my foot. It wouldn't budge. Finally he figured out that he could move it upward ⅛-inch at a time by hammering first under one side, then under the other. My arms began to feel like two feather pillows, and I doubted I could continue to wriggle up as my foot crept higher with each blow. Finally it came loose. I held on in desperation as Layton clipped me in, lowered me, then led the rest of the pitch.

I was able to continue my share of the leads and we made good time to our last bivouac just half a day below the top on our third night. A few raindrops hit us as we fought for territory on top of a desk-sized ledge. Layton grabbed me in a bear hug and jokingly said, "We're going to have a lot of fun tonight!"

We wriggled, couldn't get comfortable, and ended up sitting most of the night. Layton talked not of what he was going to do, but of what he wasn't going to do.

He wasn't going to do alpine climbing. He wasn't going to waste another year in Camp 4. The first inkling that I had that he might stop serious climbing altogether was an offhanded comment that the *Salathé* might be his last wall. His words drifted out of my mind as I watched him unwind at daybreak into slings and begin nailing a headwall with jerky, rapid motions like a locomotive getting underway.

In the early afternoon I photographed Layton coming over the top. He stayed there—body below the edge, head above—with a look of serenity I had never seen.

Layton Kor emerges onto the top of El Capitan after making the second ascent of the *Salathé Wall*.
Photograph Galen Rowell/Layton Kor Collection

10

THE BOOK OF KOR

Ed Webster

After the sixties, Layton Kor continued his spiritual quest and also began climbing again. In the eighties he made several first ascents with Ed Webster in the Black Canyon of the Gunnison. Ed recalls their adventures in this new chapter adapted from an article he originally wrote for *Climbing Magazine.*

. . .

"I could quit climbing after this one."

His tone of voice was half serious, yet firm.

"This might be my last climb ever in the Black Canyon," he continued. "It's too frightening a place to climb for a man of my age!"

At forty-nine, Layton Kor is a phenomenon. Strong as an ox, quick on the trail, and fast on rock, Kor still bursts with an impatient vertical restlessness. With little difficulty I can picture him over 2 decades ago—truly he must have been an unstoppable force. Backing off a climb just wasn't an option. Human failure (never his own), or failure because of the weather—those terms he could occasionally accept.

The *Gothic Pillar,* the 2,000-foot left skyline of the Hooker Buttress in Colorado's Black Canyon, had been in Kor's mind ("On my list," he declared) for almost 20 years.

"I first saw this climb when you were still a baby!" he would rave. "I can't believe it hasn't been done yet."

"Ed!" The same strong handshake that nearly lifted you off the ground, the friendly chuckle, the distinctive grin. It was great to see Kor again. I hadn't even noticed him standing there—all 6'5"—behind the counter in the back of the small climbing shop in Eldorado Springs. He always seemed to re-enter my life at periods of personal transition. During the past month or two I'd been feeling like I was shedding my old skin for a new one, but in what direction I was heading next, I wasn't yet sure.

Then out came Kor's long-dreamt-of secret:

"If I show you a picture of this climb, you've got to promise you won't go steal it," Kor said sternly, glaring down at me.

Everyone else gathered in the room laughed out loud.

"Don't show it to him, Kor! You can't trust him!" protested one.

In 1987 Layton Kor and Ed Webster pioneered the *Gothic Pillar*
up the center buttress in the Black Canyon of the Gunnison.
Photograph Ed Webster

Ed Webster at a belay stance on the
Gothic Pillar.

"He's the worst possible person you could show it to!" yelled another.

"Sure, okay, I promise," I agreed, pausing long enough in uncertainty just for the effect. Kor produced a color print of the Black Canyon.

A reverent silence gripped the room. The moment of creation, the unveiling. Several other climbers crowded round the photo. Silently, Kor's index finger traced the elegant profile of a prominent pillar from bottom to top. In my 11 years of Black Canyon rock climbing I'd never noticed any possibility of that route before; I doubted if others had seen the line either. It was an improbable-looking first ascent, right up the front edge of a 2,000-foot pillar. Add in a few roof bands, some wide, snaking dikes of brittle white pegmatite—all were dwarfed by a predominant verticality.

"Well, what do you think?" stammered Kor impatiently.

"You always had a good eye for a line," I replied.

"I'm trying to convince Justin we should leave this afternoon to do it," he said with a telling glance at his prospective, but youthful, partner. Justin looked sheepish at the prospects, like a lamb being led into the lion's den by the master gladiator himself.

As they prepared to depart, I wrote down my new phone number and handed it to Kor, just in case. They sped off in a cloud of dust, destination unknown.

A couple of evenings later, the phone rang.

"Ed? Kor. How ya been?" I sensed he and Justin hadn't gotten very far, and his semi-hushed tone of voice convinced me I was in for trouble.

"Fine, and you?"

"Well, do you want to do that new route in the Black Canyon this weekend?"

That customary Kor directness. In my subconscious, I'd known he would ask me to do the route with him. I already had plans for the coming weekend, but thought my climbing partner would let me out of them.

"Sure, I can go," I said.

"Great, great," he answered softly. More quiet words flowed over the phone lines, and I pictured Kor rubbing his hands together in glee. He'd successfully snared another lamb. We agreed to firm up more detailed plans in a couple of days.

In the excitement of the moment, it hadn't hit me. But after I hung up the phone it did—like a bullet between the eyes. My stomach tightened and I leaned against the wall, eyes closed. I'd been postponing this day for over 3 years.

In approaching Kor's new Black Canyon climb, we would hike down S.O.B. Gully, past the scene of my girlfriend's death—where Lauren had died, cradled in my lap after a terrible fall. Rarely a day elapsed when I didn't think of her, when the memories didn't come flooding back, of how I held her in my arms that one last time, how the sun mercilessly baked us during its slow passage across the azure sky. Of her eyes clearing to translucent, reaching a fathomless depth. Her breathing slowing to an eternal stillness. Of passing into a new life, without her. I nearly called Kor back, but didn't. Maybe this was meant to be.

Kor wanted to do the climb over 3 days, Friday through Sunday. Unfortunately, I couldn't leave Boulder until 10 p.m. Thursday night. The drive took 6 hours.

Next morning, amidst rustlings of wakefulness, the outside world intruded.

"Morning, partner. You look awful." It was Kor's stubbly face, peering into the back of my truck camper.

"Thanks. That's a hell of a drive," I croaked, feeling amorphous from lack of sleep, flowing outside the normal boundaries of self.

An hour later we'd packed enough gear for El Cap: three gallons of water, hammocks, pins, bolt kit, spare clothing, sleeping bags. In a soporific state, overburdened by baggage, we began the descent into a raging inferno. Peeling off excessive layers of clothing, I suddenly wondered why I hadn't mentioned to Kor that most sensible people postpone Black Canyon climbs until October. September can be hot as a blast furnace.

Ten minutes down the gully, various formations—a ridge, the final traverse ledge—took shape in my mind. My breath quickened as I paused to recall the sad events of June 17, 1984. Kor went on ahead. He knew full well the story, of what was happening to me, coming here again. He'd helped me then, only 2 months after Lauren's death, when he and I first met. And he would help me today.

Tears came. How could they not? I tried to locate the spot where Lauren had died. Here? Perhaps. . . . No, I don't think so. Maybe over there? I couldn't tell. Somehow the

Layton Kor sorts gear from the back of Ed Webster's truck before a Black Canyon climb.
Photograph Ed Webster

gully appeared to have changed; the hiking trail had eroded into the embankment. My mind reeled as the sobs and soul-destroying agony of loss began to replay in my mind and body. Three long years ago she had fallen. That afternoon in 1984 I'd become a different person, born from Lauren's death to see the world with tear-flooded eyes, and burdened by a wrenching, stabbing pain that seemed never to diminish.

"Ed! Ed! Are you okay?"

It was Kor, down below, waiting.

"Yes, I'm fine," I lied. "I'm coming."

I wiped away my new tears with my shirtsleeve, forcefully pushing the dark, bloodied memories back deep within me, set apart and shielded from everyday living. Beneath the mind-numbing weight of my load, I followed Kor's well-spaced footprints down the dusty, loose trail.

After water and a snack and a brief rest beside the Gunnison River, we scrambled up broken ledges at the base of the Hooker Buttress, trending left, toward the start of Kor's proposed *Gothic Pillar,* his name, a moniker that I agreed possessed just the right dose of foreboding. To our dismay, the gallon milk jugs I'd brought were both leaking water at a constant drip. Like sand slipping through an hourglass, it was only a matter of time before our attempt became futile. Stubbornly, we persisted.

The heat was silent, pervasive, oppressive, and finally, overpowering. I tried my best to keep up with Kor, who led the way, always looking up expectantly at the route. But too little sleep and too much heat combined to undo me. Keeping up with Kor was like trying to run a race with a locomotive.

The ledge system we'd been tracing finally ended. Without roping up, we could go no higher. We sat atop a small ridge of rock below the main pillar, and immediately to the right of a huge drainage gully running all the way back up to the canyon rim, a shadowy black defile that also separated us from the next immense buttress to the west.

"You really don't look so good, partner," said Kor.

The heat had consumed me. After removing the pack, my arms and fingers tingled from loss of circulation. I cradled my head in my hands, trying not to pass out from the nausea swirling through my head and brain. I tried, weakly, to pull myself together. Already, in half a day, we'd drunk over a gallon of water between us. Once on the wall, such consumption wouldn't be possible.

"We'll never make it, partner," Kor said, "but we might as well go have a look."

We rappelled into the drainage gully and hiked up unburdened toward the route's start. The climb was there: steep thin cracks, some tough-looking direct aid on the second pitch, then roofs and pegmatite above, with the hint of enough cracks to link the whole fantasy together. Higher still, the incredibly steep final pillar rose up to touch the sky.

Kor nodded appreciatively. "Just as I thought it would be."

After a short jumar back out of the gully, we left behind a gallon of water, re-packed our gear, and began retracing our steps. Our uphill retreat to regain to the canyon's north rim back up S.O.B. Gully became a foot-by-foot suffering, a seemingly endless penitence. The brutal heat was our crown of thorns, our monstrous packs, the crosses we bore. Even Kor began to slow down, and I relished this glimpse of his humanness. Refreshed, marginally, by our reconnaissance of the pillar, I actually now found myself beginning to enjoy the ordeal of our fight, and flight, back to the rim. If anything, the

grueling struggle was preparing me to walk past the scene of Lauren's death for the second time in the same day.

My pace oddly quickened as I approached the location. Even with my huge pack, I nearly jogged uphill, charged with adrenaline. This time, I was determined to find the exact spot. But I couldn't. It was there, somewhere, right in front of me, this unforgiving place where Lauren had died, but my eyes could not see it. Where, where, where had she died? Anger and sadness intermingled. Some of the tragic events of that June afternoon were evidently buried so deeply that they would never resurface.

I cried. I let my tears loose, again. Tears to join the millions I'd already shed in the last 3 years, many of them having fallen as I rolled, sobbing, clutching, and clawing at my own body, tossing like a madman first in one direction and then the other, on the rug of the small apartment in Boulder that for several months before she died, Lauren and I had shared.

I yearned for Lauren to smile. To be alive again.

I would have done anything to change, to correct . . . no, *to eliminate,* TO DESTROY, the error in judgment that killed her.

I was unashamed of having opened my stream of tears. Kor stepped slowly up the trail to join me, and we crouched like hunchbacks beneath our packs.

"It's okay, partner, really," Kor said. "I know how you feel."

"It was years before I could even think about climbing, with a smile, after John Harlin died on the Eiger Direct," he continued. "I used to sob like a baby, too, just like you are now. So don't feel bad."

"We were right up there!" I shouted, pointing. "Moving across those horizontal ledges; see where they narrow? The rock was loose. My mind never registered the danger. We were both tired. And dehydrated. The sun had been hot that day, too."

"'Do you want to rope up?' I asked her."

"'No, I'll be fine,' she said."

"The day before, finishing another climb on the south side of the canyon, I'd insisted Lauren rope up. I even told her, quite pointedly, 'This is harder than it looks.' And then I tied her into the climbing rope. But the next day I gave in. I relaxed my guard with her for the very first time. 'Okay,' I told myself, 'she can decide for herself what she wants to do.' To use the rope, or not to use it."

"Don't you see I had to let her make her own decisions? I had to give her that respect, for growing abilities as a climber.

"Up there, at the right-hand end of the horizontal ledge system, I was 20 feet away from her when she fell. I'd turned toward her moments before; I was watching her. I asked her how she was doing. She yelled back that she was coming. . . . Then I saw her reach up with her right hand. The handhold she'd grabbed broke. She hadn't tested it."

After a silence, Kor spoke. "The death of a close friend is impossible to relate to, unless you've experienced the same loss yourself," he said. "When I'm climbing with another man, if something were to happen, well, that's just part of the game, a part of climbing. Everyone who climbs knows the risks. If you don't realize them, you're just deceiving yourself. But climbing with your girlfriend, or wife. . . ."

He stopped. He was shaking his head. "I don't know about that. If anything ever. . . ." Kor contemplated the words, but couldn't finish. His calm tone and the deep look of sympathy in his eyes revealed the hurt Kor had known. He took a measured breath, then continued:

"Harlin and I, well, we had a lot of plans. Many people criticized John for his publicity seeking, his way of selling his own climbs. Finally it caused him and Royal Robbins to part. After their climb on the Dru, they couldn't even speak to one another, which I always thought was too bad.

"John was a mover, though. A man who loved to get things done and head on to the next project. The more I got to know him, the more I found we had things in common. Harlin was a man of action," Kor said firmly, "and when he was killed, life just wasn't the same. For me, and for several others, his spirit was irreplaceable."

Kor glanced up at the fading sunlight on the canyon rim.

"Come on, partner," he said, his voice returning to normal. "We'd better get going."

Exhausted by our quasi-military maneuver, we stumbled wearily back into the North Rim campground at 6 p.m. Over dinner, I convinced Kor to accompany me on a new free climb on the canyon's cooler, shady south side the following day. It was a route I'd begun with Lauren the day before she died; we'd been rained off the first pitch. To climb it now with Kor seemed fitting. During the darkest days of the summer of 1984, our conversations helped me more than he knew.

After registering for our climb at the South Rim Ranger Station, we headed down old Headquarters Draw the following morning. Kor had been the first to descend this gully in the sixties.

"And here I am still doing the same darn, stupid thing—climbing," he muttered.

"I just want you to know that you're the only person I'd do this for," moaned Kor sometime later as we crashed down the loose gully through dirt, mud, leaves, and prickly bushes.

"But why did you have to pick me to come along today?" he continued. "Is this some kind of special torture for elderly people?"

And so it went. Kor the Oppressed. Kor the Elder. Kor the Magnificent.

Layton Kor leads an A2 pitch on the *Gothic Pillar*.
Photograph Ed Webster

My rusted carabiner and wired nut were still in place near the top of the first pitch. The free climbing was sustained and spectacular, up the center of a steep blank slab. I hand-drilled a few bolts on the lead to protect the crux sections. Kor was able to follow a short 5.11 section first try, his second 5.11 ever, he told me delightedly.

"What's 5.12 like?" he added. I told him I'd arrange a climb for him with Christian Griffith, back in Boulder.

We savored our sideways view of North Chasm View Wall on the opposite bank of the Gunnison River's foaming rapids. It was an imposing, some might even say terrifyingly steep, face—now perfectly framed by two other walls on the canyon we were slowly but surely escaping from.

"You know, I'd love a photograph of that for my living room. You can see three of my routes!" Kor chortled. Hours of scrambling and two island-tops later, the *Wheel of Life* had been climbed . . . and the *Gothic Pillar* remained.

"You'd think with all these hot young climbers about," Kor continued, "someone would have done that route by now."

The next weekend it was still hot. Colorado was in the grip of some of the warmest Indian summer weather I could remember, several weeks of brilliant, uninterrupted sunshine. How about the next weekend, Kor asked? Then, putting up a new route in Eldorado Canyon, I strained a finger. And Kor hurt his back at a new job, laying stone, then weathered the 24-hour flu.

"At least we'll have plenty of excuses," he chirped over the phone. The next, and promised, weekend drew closer.

"Let's do it, partner," Kor commanded. "We won't get better weather than this. And, you know, neither of us, particularly me, is getting any younger," he added to seal the deal. "Boy, am I looking forward to this one. That upper part of the pillar is going to be wild!"

We re-convened at the Silver Dollar Restaurant on Friday evening for another home-cooked dinner with the cowboys of Crawford, Colorado.

"Better enjoy that last beer," advised Kor.

By midnight neither of us had slept, then Kor said his stomach felt bad. Minutes later, he was outside, crouching over some nearby bushes.

"At least those bushes will be well fed," he quipped.

Oh boy, what a start to the climb, I thought.

At 6 a.m., two alarms sounded in the stilled darkness. I peeked outside. A full sky of stars overhead, and no wind. We switched on the headlamps, and the packs, for a change, were reasonable.

"My back, I have to protect it," Kor said. "You get the big load. Anyway, I know you need to train for that next big expedition of yours."

S.O.B. Gully looked entirely different in the dark, illuminated by the bobbing lights of our headlamps. We made our steps carefully, in no hurry to injure an ankle, or worse. When I hiked by Lauren's spirit's resting place I made a silent cross over my chest and thought of the good times we'd shared during our single year together. A faint, brief smile broke to the surface. Then the sun rose.

The rock-hard reality of the 2,000-foot vertical and overhanging pillar stood before us. Kor had, by now, fully woken up and seemed to harbor no ill effects from his early morning gastrointestinal purge. We rappelled into the side gully with our loads, then soloed up some frightening 5.4, still carting our packs, to a ledge below the first pitch.

Kor gave me the lead, a thin crack system in the back of a slight groove. It began vertical, and didn't let up. Kor wanted the steep aid on the second pitch, which appeared to be one of the route's cruxes. My modern rack was soon put to work.

"What are these little guys, anyway?" Kor marveled, examining a TCU. "I can't believe all these little goodies you have on your rack! If we'd only had these things when I was younger."

Near the groove's top, I branched right up a parallel corner. Kor had to move the belay up 30 feet, then I placed a bolt, the only one on the climb, to anchor us to some questionable, fractured rock.

Kor had been baking, standing and belaying in the growing heat, and was eager to come to grips with the next lead. At my belay stance, he didn't bother to sort any of the gear, or re-stack the ropes.

"Okay, you can put me back on belay," he said, grabbing two fistfuls of jumbled hardware and slings.

"We've got to get going, partner. That was a 2-hour pitch you led. It's noon already," he barked. Although at first Kor's speed-is-of-the-essence style rankled me a little, I soon realized that moving quickly up any type of terrain was simply, and purposefully, his all-out method of climbing.

Kor traversed left, placed a knifeblade, clipped in a sling, stepped in it—and the pin immediately popped. Our rack was diminished by one pin, a biner, and a runner. Almost instantly, Kor was in a frenzy:

"These cracks are all blind!" he raged. With his massive forearms, he quickly solved that problem, obliterating several more knifeblades into the rock, crack or not! Later, Kor told me the story of how Yvon Chouinard had once presented him with a newly forged piton, a Lost Arrow blade supposedly stronger than any of his others.

"Come on, have a go at it!" urged Yvon.

Kor later returned the piton to him . . . curved into a half-moon shape, ruined.

Several more of Chouinard's finest pitons appeared to be suffering the same fate as Kor nailed a ladder of chrome-moly up the thin cracks. Here at last was the legendary and undefeatable Kor, effortlessly finding passage up soaring impregnable rock. I took photographs of his masterly aid technique as he progressed upward, then disappeared around an outside corner to the left.

After lowering out the haul bag, I jugged up, cleaning. I prayed I'd be able to extract all his pitons, remembering too well how Pat Ament, suffering the agony of following a Kor lead in the Black Canyon 2 decades earlier, had felt Kor's wrath after he'd been unable to remove several pitons. Luckily, I was able to hammer out all the pitons save one, a recalcitrant angle.

Reaching Kor's belay stance, as casually as possible I told him, "I only had to leave one pin."

"You what?" Kor bellowed.

"I couldn't remove one piton, the angle," I repeated a bit louder.

"Oh," said Kor, relaxing—and apparently relieved.

"I thought you said you couldn't get out *any* of the pitons."

The next pitch, overhanging, brooded above. The light brown wall was plastered with randomly placed fragile flakes, pierced by occasional thin cracks, and crowned by a horizontal band of roofs. Above—the netherworld.

"I figure we have a 300 to 1 chance of getting to a bivy ledge for tonight," Kor declared. "I want you to climb like you never climbed before in your life, partner."

The routefinding was complex. After free climbing the side of a huge detached block directly above Kor—now cringing and anchored in the line of fire—I aided on marginal TCUs up a bottoming crack to better aid placements. At last I could inspect the ominous roof band at close quarters.

"You know," mused Kor, his voice rising up from below, "maybe we shouldn't name this route the *Gothic Pillar,* otherwise no one will ever repeat it."

As I hung in aiders amidst a fractured canvas of brittle flakes and meandering seams, contemplating the roofs jutting savagely out over my head, it struck me too as rather unlikely our line would ever attain trade-route status.

Hanging on tiny wired nuts, I finally swung out the roof's lip above 600 feet of exposure, and pulled over. Then, the rock changed abruptly, becoming black, solid, and surprisingly free-climbable. A left-hand dead end stymied me before I headed up right, discovering a sloping stance and (above) a hand crack behind a huge (secure) flake leading to a mini ledge. Heaven!

"We've got it!" I shouted down to Kor.

The bag swung free for another in-space ride, and Kor started up.

"I hate prusiking!" he yelled out.

"Please toss me the haul line and put me on belay!" he ordered politely.

When Kor reached my stance, we shook hands. "I'm impressed," he said, "that was really fast work." As I sorted the gear, Kor continued, "You don't know how much I hate to prusik. Ever since Harlin's accident, I just can't stomach it. I knew there was a reason why I didn't go on climbs like this anymore."

Then, the next command: "Okay, Big Daddy, go for it," he directed. "It's 6 p.m. You've got 1 hour of light."

I liebacked up another immense flake that fortuitously gave passage through a 40-foot pegmatite band. Cutting left, I manhandled up a second strenuous flake to jugs, and reached an obvious depression where we thought a ledge might lurk. Kor demanded a forecast. "Nothing!" I shouted. I hauled up some extra gear, plus my headlamp, just in case. Above, an approachable vertical crack beckoned.

Aid climbing like a fiend, I leapfrogged TCUs up the crack, rapidly gaining height. Then a small wired nut ripped through the parallel-sided crack, and suddenly I was airborne for 15 feet.

I went right back up—and hammered in a piton. I'm sure the sound of it ringing was music to Kor's ears. I imagined him thinking, "Now Ed's doing some real climbing!"

Higher, the dead-vertical stone at last relented as daylight dimmed. I discerned another indentation and two small bushes—a possible overnight harbor, rays of hope in this otherwise smooth precipice. I grabbed the edge of the ledge; it was flat and big enough for one person to sit on. I placed the anchors quickly. Kor jumared up, appearing out of the dusky murk, and said, simply and kindly, "You were the right person to invite on this climb."

Then he noticed the tiny, triangular-shaped, flat-rock seat at the bottom of the V-groove corner rising above us into the night.

"Oh, my back, you know, my back is really starting to act up. . . ."

"Layton, please, please," I said, motioning toward the small ledge. "This is for you."

We worked at getting comfortable. Kor sat down while I wriggled into loops of etriers. Eventually I hung beside him. Our single sleeping bag we draped over us as best we could. The night, fortunately, was calm and relatively warm. A three-quarter moon hung aloft above the velvet ramparts of the opposite south rim. Soon our earlier panicked movements were replaced by the slow acceptance of our oncoming nightlong vigil as Kor contently crunched away on his favorite food, a carrot.

"The best food comes straight from the ground," he said, between bites. He probably would have brought along his famed diet of lettuce, too, except that it didn't pack particularly well on big walls. Kor spoke of fasting for a month in Texas, which he insisted cured him of pleurisy and saved his life. He lost nearly fifty pounds, but was healthy upon returning home. Friends warned him otherwise, but Kor had not listened.

That night not once did we talk of retreat. There was only up and tomorrow's fair morning light. And now it was my turn to listen:

Kor regaled me with climbing stories that entertained and warmed us for the next several hours. His pantheon of partners from the Yosemite's Golden Era—Robbins, Chouinard, Pratt, Roper, Beckey—became real people in Kor's all-too-human anecdotes. He spoke of Robbins's ego and his unrelenting drive to become the world's best rock climber; of Chouinard's well-rounded attitudes and love of all types of climbing, even ice and mountaineering; of Pratt's free climbing excellence, which none of them could match; of Roper's speed as an aid climber and ability to go the distance; and Beckey's never-ending quest for new routes, plus his unmistakable wardrobe.

Then Dr. Kor dispensed one sleeping pill each. "The secret of my bivouac success," he quipped, and we feigned sleep. The moon arced across the night sky, and as bivouacs go, it wasn't too bad.

At breakfast, we sampled some water from the two one-gallon water jugs I'd brought. Each had originally been filled with Pace Picante sauce. But these plastic containers were almost indestructible, and they had solid handles, too. I was proud of my inventiveness; I'd washed them out with soap and boiling water to get rid of the aftertaste. I handled Kor the first bottle.

He took a big swig—then promptly spat it out.

"Taco juice!" he ranted. I guessed I hadn't rinsed out the bottles quite enough.

"Partner, everyone in the world is going to know that you brought taco juice on this climb!"

In the brisk air we sorted out the ragtag equipment chaos of the night before, and Kor announced: "I can do this next one. You save your strength."

He scampered left across a face up under the left end of a horizontal ceiling, then underclung back right nearly 50 feet. "I've never done a pitch like that before!" he enthused. Then he led a second pitch, up rounded, bottoming, but free-climbable cracks, finishing across a devastatingly exposed 5.9 traverse to a belay ledge on the left.

"I'm just going to hand-over-hand the haul bag," he shouted down. "This technique with the jumars is just too slow sometimes!" And up went our seventy-five pound sack, zip, zip, zip.

The next pitch headed up a moderate crack to a terrace where we could fully relax in the warming sunshine. I lost patience hauling the bag up a short stretch of lower-angled rock; swearing made me feel awkward, then repentant, in Kor's presence. He calmly helped me. Now only the upper pillar remained.

Another unexpected crack system laced the steep face immediately left of the main arête, beckoning us into another exceptionally airy proposition. But access to the pillar's final fissure was barred by a short, blank-looking, overhanging headwall.

"You're going up that?" Kor queried, surprised by my choice of route. "This is definitely your lead."

I launched up the barrier on good holds at first, rigging two wired nuts before the headwall bulged. Hidden edges appeared, square-cut and positive, but were separated by big reaches. I felt out the moves, up, then down, puzzled and unsure. Just when I was giving up hope, a perfect Friend placement in a shallow slot materialized, and with its security I was up and over the 5.10 crux.

As Kor reached my small stance positioned on the upper, air-washed arête, he declared, "Like any good Dolomite climb worth its salt, right on the edge."

The sunshine bore down on us; the temperature was rising. Kor led. Three successive chimney cracks took us to another terrace. One hundred feet more, and we'd be done. Then to our dismay we discovered we were on an island of rock, separated from the canyon rim by a notch, an unpleasant, time-consuming, typically frustrating Black Canyon phenomenon. I led a short pitch, then Kor hiked to the false summit.

We searched for a rappel anchor to get us the 70 feet back down into the notch keeping us from the rim. The midday heat now conspired against us, breaking our concentration. Sitting beside each other on two separate boulders, we were more tired than we realized.

"What about this rock for an anchor?" asked Kor, pointing.

We both reached for it simultaneously. It was a sizeable boulder. Perhaps we could get a sling over it? I wasn't sure. Impulsively, I grabbed its top edge and reefed on it, hard. Although appearing to be solid, a chunk of the boulder detached in my hands—and I catapulted backward, tumbling in an instant toward the island's edge and the 2,000-foot drop to the river.

"*Ed!*" screamed Kor.

I went head-over-heels out of control—and crashed to a halt on a single flat slab of rock a mere 10 feet from the void. I shook my head, woke up from a very bad dream, and meekly crawled back up to my partner, rubbing my new bruises and a few small cuts.

"*Don't ever do that again!*" ordered Kor.

"I thought you were a goner," he added, obviously distraught. "I really thought you were going over."

Shocked, and trying to relax, I sat down next to Kor. I'd been a split-second from oblivion. That had been way, way too close. With awful insight, I suddenly knew and felt the hopeless thoughts Lauren must have had in her final moments. The coincidence was too great that I'd had an almost identical experience, here, and now . . .

"Boy, and you're going to Everest next year," drawled Kor laconically. "Try to be a little more careful, huh? Gosh, with all the loose rock around here, this place is like the Eiger."

"You never can let down your guard, can you?" I whispered.

"No one's perfect," said Kor. "Death is a possibility every time you rope up. The point is, with every climb you do, you've got to keep on learning. And trying. You can't dwell on the danger—or the past."

We completed the climb subdued, dog-tired, and with the utmost care. I snapped a couple of shots of Kor coming over the final rim, grinning his grin. We'd made it. I wondered what he was thinking. He scrambled up to the top, a tree, and safety.

"My luck, I'll probably be gored by a deer," he joked.

It was near dusk again when we reached the North Rim campground, escaping from the clutches of the scrub oak jungle. Kor sped off down the dirt road toward Crawford and his long-awaited T-bone at the Silver Dollar. I joined him.

Kor said he was "tickled pink" that he'd finally completed his 2-decade dream of climbing a new Grade V in the Black Canyon. Me, I'd survived another close call, and roped up with one of my greatest heroes, someone I could call a friend. Kor declared he could go back home for the rest of the winter and be content—but next spring, maybe there'd be another climb? He'd have to see.

I woke up the next morning at Kor's house in Basalt, Colorado. His family had already gone off to work and to school. And Kor was back on the job, laying stone.

On a bookshelf I spotted some of his climbing books, in particular *Directissima,* the story of the first ascent of the 1966 Eiger Direct in winter. The dust jacket was tattered and torn, the book well thumbed over many years. I opened it carefully.

"To Layton," read a penned inscription, "a small token, Big Daddy, of the Great Days. Dougal."

Layton Kor finishes up the final pitch of the *Gothic Pillar* at the end of a long day of climbing.
Photograph Ed Webster

AFTERWORD

From early in my climbing career I had dreamed of the great classic routes of North America and the Alps. With the ascent of the *Salathé Wall* and the numerous other big climbs I had done during 10 years of high-standard climbing, the dream had come true, but I found that my appetite for extreme climbing was beginning to diminish. For 10 years I had been a driven man, with eyes mainly for new climbs, and particularly the thrill of first ascents. In the space of a decade I had chalked up more climbs than I could even have conceived of in those early days when I first pounded pitons into the clay embankment of a creek in Wichita Falls, Texas. I had been many places, seen many things.

On the positive side is the undeniable fact that in many ways my climbing experiences have contributed significantly to who I am today. It is impossible to imagine the kind of person I might have become had I not become involved in climbing, except to say that I probably would have been different. Climbing gave me a vehicle through which to expand my social horizons. I was able to travel and share intense experiences with a unique group of individuals.

On desert pinnacles I benefitted from my good friend Huntley Ingalls's scholarly knowledge. On a first ascent with Dave Dornan in Eldorado Canyon I shared the enthusiasm of virgin rock. In Fred Beckey I found a kindred spirit, a companion with as much wanderlust and energy as myself, with a philosopher's insight into life and mountains that I could not but appreciate and benefit from. Bob Culp's dry sense of humor and innate sense of decency was never less than inspirational. In George Hurley I found a reserved and gentlemanly manner that contrasted to my wilder actions and provided a good example. Tex Bossier's willingness to jump into the deep end on such epic adventures as the *Diagonal Direct* and Chasm View Wall, and come through smiling, was a lesson in fortitude and good spirits in the face of adversity. Likewise Steve Komito, always there with a smile and a quip when difficulties loomed. Larry Dalke was a shining example of the best qualities a person and climber can aspire to. With Pat Ament in the virgin territory of Eldorado, I shared climbing adventures and first ascents. Wayne Goss, with his constant enthusiasm, remains in memory as indefatigable in situations that would have stopped lesser mortals in their tracks. With Mike Covington I shared a rare level of communication and learned much from him as our personalities and interests dovetailed. On Proboscis, in the Gunks, and other walls, I profited from my relationship with a mentor whose name is forever etched in the history of American climbing—Jim McCarthy, a repository

Layton Kor makes a free rappel after the first ascent of
Kor's Kastle in Arizona's Black Mountains in 2009.
Photograph Stewart M. Green

of climbing and worldly wisdom, and generous with both. On the vertical walls of Yosemite, Steve Roper, Glen Denny, and Galen Rowell welcomed me as an outsider into the closed circles of Yosemite, showing both generosity of spirit and considerable tolerance toward a person such as I, invading their territory. In the Alps I benefitted from shared experiences with Chris Bonington, Don Whillans, and Rick Sylvester. There will always be a special place for Chuck Pratt as I mentally thumb through the list of memorable relationships—a friend whose climbing ability and personal qualities were peerless. Yvon Chouinard, the master technician, was a person who always impressed me with the depths that lay hidden beneath his exterior modesty. In contrast to my own extroversion, Royal Robbins's careful genius and unmatched depth of experience made him an unparalleled mentor. And, of course, John Harlin and Dougal Haston, two true spirits with whom I joined for a journey exploring the limits of extreme climbing, while at the same time learning much about ourselves. These and the many, many others with whom I shared countless climbing experiences were the blessings. I thank them all for the experiences we shared, and for their contributions to this book.

As positive as these experiences were, toward the end of the sixties the excitement I felt for climbing began to diminish. Though now questioning my purpose in life more consciously than before, I still continued to do such difficult climbs as the first winter ascent of The Diamond in Colorado and the *Salathé Wall* in Yosemite.

During my intense climbing in the sixties I had no religious interests whatsoever; in fact, if anything, the subject was always an uncomfortable one. This was true for the majority of people I associated with during this period. They were usually climbers and climbing was what we talked about, rarely matters of spiritual concern. That line of demarcation seemed consistent.

Shortly after returning from my last climbing trip to Europe, I embarked on a second fast at the same clinic as before in San Antonio, Texas, this time for general health reasons rather than because of a chronic problem. During my stay I shared a room with a quiet, but most interesting man, who was one of Jehovah's Witnesses. I also met two Canadians at the clinic who were also Witnesses. Some very interesting discussions between the four of us followed. I was very impressed with their sensible, nonemotional approach to the delicate subject of religion.

Returning to Colorado, my curiosity had been aroused, and I called up the local congregation of Jehovah's Witnesses to find out when their meetings were. I had reached a point where I was beginning to speculate about the nature of things, and wondering if there was some higher purpose behind the surface aspects of life. Does God really exist? The more I studied, the more my interest in extreme climbing cooled. During that same general period I embarked on two climbs with Larry Dalke, an unsuccessful attempt on the Painted Wall in the Black Canyon of the Gunnison, and a repeat of Spider Rock, both occasions prompting soul searching and discussion of matters of conscience. As I studied more it became clearer and clearer that spiritual activity provided a far more meaningful outlet for my energies than had 10 years of extreme climbing.

My studies gradually made it clear to me that there is indeed a source of life, a Creator, whose personal name is Jehovah; that the Bible does contain God's message; and that there is a purpose to man's existence. As I looked at the world around me and observed what a dangerous situation the human race was in, I was impressed to read the numerous passages in the Scriptures that shed light on contemporary social problems in the aftermath of World War I and to learn that God's Kingdom (a government of divine origin) will return peace and security to the earth, a problem that many

Layton Kor looks for new routes in the Black Mountains in western Arizona.
Photograph Stewart M. Green

different governments down through time have tried desperately to solve. I became satisfied that the Bible was divinely based and that Jehovah's Witnesses were practicing true Christianity.

From the perspective of this new context, and with aid from the Scriptures, I came to realize that many things in my earlier life were wrong. Consequently, a number of moral adjustments had to be made if I were to continue in this new way of life.

I became more and more involved in studying and more involved in spiritual matters; then, as the Scriptures say, "Your life is no longer your own." From that point on my Christian responsibilities, meetings, the ministry, and spiritual obligations all took precedence, allowing me neither the time nor freedom to travel to climbing areas throughout the country. In 1968 I was baptized as one of Jehovah's Witnesses. I married my wife Joy in 1969, and the responsibilities of marriage also meant a change in the vagabond lifestyle I had been leading. I had two children, Jamie and Julia, and it would be irresponsible of me to put my life on the line in pursuit of extreme climbing at their expense, as I can no longer justify it. I also find that I no longer drive recklessly.

Layton Kor edges up a steep slab near the top of *Wheel of Life* on the South Rim of the Black Canyon.

Photograph Ed Webster

There were climbs at this time that I had wanted to do for many years, including the Eiger Nordwand and the Walker Spur of the Grandes Jorasses. I had developed my abilities to the level where climbs of this standard were certainly within my reach, and for some time I had thought about them as being next on my agenda. It was not an easy decision to put them aside in my mind and commit myself to a life of spiritual priorities. My heart was still partially in climbing and after spending so many years of intense involvement, desire doesn't disappear overnight.

Since that time of change I have continued climbing, although it takes second place to my family and other priorities. I still enjoy easy to medium routes providing they can be safely protected. The fundamental difference for me today is that climbing is no longer a way of life, it is a recreation. Nevertheless, there are occasions when I cannot help but reminisce and reflect back to the earlier days when my climbing companions and I stood silently on the scene, shaded by the huge wall that loomed mightily above us while we carefully tied on the nylon rope, that bond of friendship and security that allowed us to climb upward into a world beyond the vertical.

A humorous look at the first ascent of *Kor's Kastle* in the Arizona desert in 2009. From left to right, Stewart Green, Ed Webster, Dennis Jump, and Layton the Great 'Un.
Drawing Dennis Jump